Luminos is the Open Access monograph publishing program
from UC Press. Luminos provides a framework for preserving and
reinvigorating monograph publishing for the future and increases
the reach and visibility of important scholarly work. Titles published
in the UC Press Luminos model are published with the same high
standards for selection, peer review, production, and marketing as
those in our traditional program. www.luminosoa.org

Violent Impacts

Violent Impacts

How Power and Inequality Shape the Concussion Crisis

Kathryn Henne and Matt Ventresca

UNIVERSITY OF CALIFORNIA PRESS

University of California Press
Oakland, California

© 2025 by Kathryn Henne and Matthew Ventresca

This work is licensed under a Creative Commons (CC BY-NC-ND) license.
To view a copy of the license, visit http://creativecommons.org/licenses.

All other rights reserved.

Suggested citation: Henne, K. and Ventresca, M. *Violent Impacts: How Power and Inequality Shape the Concussion Crisis*. Oakland: University of California Press, 2025. DOI: https://doi.org/10.1525/luminos.241

Cataloging-in-Publication Data is on file at the Library of Congress.

ISBN 978-0-520-42258-2 (cloth)
ISBN 978-0-520-39698-2 (pbk.)
ISBN 978-0-520-39699-9 (ebook)

GPSR Authorized Representative: Easy Access System Europe,
Mustamäe tee 50, 10621 Tallinn, Estonia, gpsr.requests@easproject.com

34   33   32   31   30   29   28   27   26   25
10   9   8   7   6   5   4   3   2   1

CONTENTS

This project began to take shape over ten years ago and became a collaborative endeavor back in 2016. As such, we have many people to acknowledge and thank—certainly more than a few pages allow.

The research for this book was made possible thanks to funding from an Australian Research Council Discovery Early Career Researcher Award (DE170100819), a Futures Scheme Award from the Australian National University, and postdoctoral fellowships at Georgia Institute of Technology, Queen's University, and the University of Calgary. This book also benefited from both of us receiving invitations to speak about this work at different stages of the project. Our sincere thanks to hosts based at Brock University, Georgia Institute of Technology, the University of Calgary, the University of Queensland, and the University of Waterloo. The feedback from those discussions strengthened our thinking and therefore this book.

Many thanks to Jude Blacklock, Aleks Deejay, Jenna Imad Harb, and Madeleine Pape for their research assistance and to Jasmine McNamara for her editorial advice. We are indebted to Neil Gunningham who was the first person to read Kate's grant application on this topic and provided the kind of critical, yet encouraging feedback only he can. We also thank Jude Blacklock (again!), William Bridel, Samantha King, and Mary McDonald for countless conversations about parts of this book. We really mean it when we say that all errors are our own. We owe a shout-out to colleagues who generously volunteered to discuss our ideas as they developed—Adam Ali, Kathleen Bachynski, Meredith Edelman, Estée Fresco, Blayne Haggart, Colin Klein, Tate Morgan, Dan Morrison, Emma Nyhan, Susan Sell, Rita Shah, Kate Starre, Nancy Theberge, Natasha Tusikov, and John Noel Viaña. Susan, we wish you were here to see it in print.

We are honored to have our book published with the University of California Press. Special thanks to Maura Roessner, who has provided insightful comments from the beginning. Sam Warren has been incredibly attentive through the production process, and Gabriel Bartlett has provided valuable reminders about writing for broader audiences. Three reviewers gave us precisely the kind of feedback we needed to make this a better book.

Kate is fortunate to have family who have supported her throughout this project. David Henneberger and Lesley Nelson listened patiently to many rambling thoughts about various chapters. When they were with us, George Henneberger provided comic relief, and Scooter was ready for pets and long runs when needed. Kent Weyand was—as always—there through thick and thin.

Matt is extremely grateful to his all-star team of family and friends who have supported him through the writing of this book. Special thanks to Scott Carey and Christian Ventresca, who epitomize what it means to have someone's back. He also wants to express the deepest gratitude to his parents, Dominic and Mary Ann, for their endless generosity and love. Matt's partner, Katie Hemsworth, is simply the best.

We appreciate the permissions to reprint portions of previously published articles. Selections of chapter 5 are in Kathryn Henne, "Brain Politics: Gendered Difference and Traumatic Brain Injury in Sport," in *Sociocultural Examinations of Sports Concussions*, ed. Matt Ventresca and Mary G. McDonald (London: Routledge, 2019), 151–69, and portions of chapter 7 were published as Kathryn Henne and Matt Ventresca, "A Criminal Mind? A Damaged Brain? Narratives of Criminality and Culpability in the Celebrated Case of Aaron Hernandez," *Crime, Media, Culture* 16, no. 3 (2020): 392–413.

We could not have written this book without the participants and interlocutors who made this study possible. We hope this book contributes to new critical conversations about brain injury that mobilize action, prioritize prevention, and seek justice for those affected by violence.

Introduction

Over a decade ago, two tragic deaths became intertwined with the growing recognition of a concussion crisis in sports. On December 1, 2012, twenty-two-year-old Kasandra Perkins was murdered by her boyfriend, Jovan Belcher. Belcher played linebacker for the Kansas City Chiefs of the National Football League (NFL), and, after killing Perkins in their home, he drove to the team stadium. Following an emotional conversation with then-general manager Scott Pioli and then-head coach Romeo Crennel, Belcher died by suicide in the stadium parking lot. He was twenty-five years old. Belcher and Perkins had a three-month-old daughter named Zoey.[1] It was not immediately apparent how concerns about brain trauma would figure into explanations of Perkins's and Belcher's deaths, yet their story reveals a complex range of forces that constitute the concussion crisis.

Media coverage of Perkins's and Belcher's deaths generated three main narratives: football, violence, and brain injury. Regarding football, they died the day before a full slate of Sunday NFL games was scheduled to kick off. Belcher's team released a statement shortly after his death, announcing that their game against the Carolina Panthers would be played as scheduled.[2] The Chiefs defeated the Panthers, with coverage highlighting the team's perseverance in the aftermath of tragedy. It was reported as an "uplifting victory," with Crennel affirming his team's commitment to their sport by saying, "As far as playing the game, I thought that was the best for us to do, because that's what we do. We're football players and football coaches, and that's what we do, we play on Sunday."

The second narrative revolved around Belcher's acts of violence that led to Perkins's murder. Some reports provided chilling details of the events, suggesting that Belcher's impulsive actions were fueled by anger and, ultimately, by guilt.[3] Coverage considered Belcher's contradictory character traits, problems in his relationship with Perkins, and his psychological state in the final hours of his life. Stories linked Perkins's murder to the broader issue of violence against women, with journalists reporting that Belcher's team held a moment of silence for "all victims of domestic violence" at their game against the Panthers.[4] Perkins's killing also became part of commentaries concerned with domestic violence committed by NFL players and the broader normalization of violence against women.[5]

The third narrative was different: it raised the possibility that brain injuries sustained throughout Belcher's football career contributed to his acts of violence. In the immediate aftermath of the murder-suicide, some reports cited Belcher's concussion history and linked his behaviors to symptoms of chronic traumatic encephalopathy (CTE), a neurodegenerative disease associated with repetitive brain trauma that was becoming increasingly connected to football.[6] Media referred to Belcher's story in their coverage of a Boston University study published two days after his death, which found evidence of CTE in the brains of twenty-eight deceased football players.[7] Journalists compared his demise to the story of Hall of Fame linebacker Junior Seau, who died by suicide in May 2012 and who was diagnosed posthumously with CTE.[8] In December 2013, Belcher's mother, Cheryl Shepherd, launched a wrongful death lawsuit against the Kansas City Chiefs. She claimed Chiefs management was negligent in not adequately warning him about the risks of repetitive brain trauma associated with football.[9]

Analysis of Belcher's brain found neurodegeneration characteristic of CTE.[10] Subsequent media reports speculated about whether this finding meant that violence against others was an outcome of CTE. Many of these stories repeated statements from neurosurgeon Julian Bailes, who compared Belcher's death to the 2007 murder-suicide involving World Wrestling Entertainment (WWE) wrestler Chris Benoit, who had also been diagnosed with CTE.[11] Other articles focused squarely on the relationship between football brain injuries and violence against women. A *Time* magazine article asked, "Are NFL head injuries causing domestic violence?"[12] Sam Mellinger of the *Kansas City Star* called Belcher's diagnosis "a potentially game-changing development at the intersection of two of the NFL's biggest threats—head injuries and domestic violence."[13]

This third narrative introduces elements that have become central to the concussion crisis in sports: scientific evidence detailing the neurological and psychological consequences of repeated traumatic brain injury (TBI), legal proceedings, accusations of corporate negligence, and concerns about the relationship between sports and violence, both on and off the field. Yet this narrative offers only a limited account of these factors and leaves important questions unanswered about how Perkins's killing and Belcher's suicide became intertwined with understandings of TBI. How are TBI and sports violence linked by cultural influences and societal circumstances? Are there broader connections between TBI and violence that extend beyond sports? What makes brain injuries seemingly plausible explanations for violent crime? How do social, political, and economic forces contribute to how TBI is experienced, studied, and reported on? This book reflects on these questions by considering how TBI has emerged not simply as a neurological problem but as a burgeoning health crisis.

THE RISE OF THE CONCUSSION CRISIS

The deaths of Perkins and Belcher provoked a resurgence of media narratives sounding the alarm about the dangers of concussions and the long-term neurological consequences of collision sports. The media increasingly reported on male athletes of all ages struggling with prolonged neurological and psychological symptoms postconcussion. CTE was already established as the focal point of scientific investigations into the long-term consequences of repetitive TBI.[14] Findings from postmortem CTE studies, alongside athletes reporting severe cognitive and psychological decline, fueled documentary films and media stories.[15] In 2011, a class action lawsuit alleged the NFL had intentionally misled its players about the dangers of brain injury. These developments informed calls for sports to take concussions more seriously.

Subsequent developments cemented the notion that a concussion crisis was occurring in sports. According to a widely cited figure from the Centers for Disease Control and Prevention (CDC), there may be as many as 3.8 million concussions per year during sport and recreation activities in the United States.[16] Research indicates youth under the age of eighteen experience up to 1.9 million of these injuries.[17] Two studies from Boston University caused further alarm about the potential prevalence of CTE among collision sport athletes: a 2015 study found CTE in the brains of eighty-seven of ninety-one deceased NFL players, and a 2017 study diagnosed 110 of 111 dead NFL players with CTE.[18] These findings generated a surge of media coverage and became statistical touchstones in public understandings of TBI risks.

Collision sports—such as boxing, football, ice hockey, rugby, and Australian rules football—have been at the center of this crisis. CTE has been mostly diagnosed in deceased athletes from these hard-hitting sports. Studies also suggest concussions might not be the primary source of CTE; instead, CTE likely develops from the cumulative damage of repeated non-concussive impacts[19]—that is, brain trauma that does not result in a concussion diagnosis or immediately produce obvious symptoms. These impacts are ubiquitous in collision sports in which countless, seemingly inconsequential hits to the head are an inherent part of the game.

Concern for the neurological health of young athletes has also intensified, with some research indicating that even one season of collision sports participation may induce structural changes to a child's brain.[20] These and similar findings have sparked debate about the future of collision sports. Calls for rule changes and improved protective equipment, too, have emerged alongside evidence of declining participation rates.[21] Meanwhile, sports organizations have funded marketing campaigns and scientific research to persuade the public that these sports remain safe activities.[22]

Public understandings of the concussion crisis typically revolve around men's sports. TBI among women athletes has only recently become a focus of media coverage and scientific research. The dominance of sports across concussion crisis narratives has meant that other groups affected by TBI tend to be overlooked. TBI among military service members has received some public attention after being referred to as the "signature injury" of post-9/11 combat. Since 2000, more than 310,000 US active-duty service members have been diagnosed with TBI, a far greater incidence than detected in previous conflicts.[23] Approximately 80 percent of these injuries are classified as concussions or "mild" TBI, with many diagnoses following blast injuries. Researchers continue to investigate how these injuries affect current and former military personnel as they age, examining links between TBI and CTE, dementia, post-traumatic stress disorder (PTSD), and other conditions. They have also drawn parallels with TBI in sports. For example, a 2018 study of military veterans with histories of TBI found similar neurological irregularities to those observed in retired football players with suspected CTE.[24]

Popular narratives about concussions rarely acknowledge that most people affected by TBI are not athletes or military veterans. They are more often children, the elderly, and people who have experienced interpersonal violence. Sports TBI is estimated to comprise only 20 percent of mild TBI, yet it dominates news coverage.[25] TBI among victim-survivors of domestic and family violence receives comparatively little public attention. The same can be said for TBI among people who are criminalized, incarcerated, precariously housed, or who use drugs—even though many of them experience multiple forms of violence that contribute to high rates of TBI. Global estimates suggest that over sixty-nine million people are diagnosed with TBI per year and that rates are increasing across lower-income countries. Athletes thus represent the tip of the iceberg in terms of worldwide prevalence.[26] How, then, has the concussion crisis come to be represented in such narrow terms?

Advocates emphasize that dominant conceptions of the concussion crisis only represent part of a larger epidemic of TBI. The CDC acknowledges that approximately 2.5 million people per year visit US emergency departments with TBI, but countless more go unreported and untreated. This problem is intensified among people facing systemic discrimination. Even in sports environments with established concussion protocols, studies suggest that large numbers of TBI cases (between 32 percent and 62 percent) are not reported to coaches or trainers.[27] It is estimated that over five million Americans currently live with a TBI-related disability, but many do so without adequate resources.[28] Visible scars or bruises do not always accompany TBI. It cannot be treated using casts or braces. TBI is an "invisible injury" that can be easily overlooked in terms of its severity.

Despite characterizations of TBI being an epidemic of invisible injuries, there are distinct ways that TBI *is made visible* and afforded public attention—often through experiences of men in collision sports and (to a lesser extent) the military. Importantly, collision sports and military environments have notable similarities. Both valorize individuals, particularly men, for their bravery and heroics. They are domains in which violence and injury are expected and celebrated. Sports and the military are often portrayed as providing economic opportunities for working-class men if they work hard and play by the rules. Both are sites of immense private and public investment, with billions spent annually on operations, marketing, and technology development. This visibility provides both institutions with significant influence in shaping responses to TBI—though, as we discuss in later chapters, such efforts can conflict with their vested interests in preserving the social acceptability of bodily risk in sports and the military.

It is perhaps not surprising, then, that sports and military organizations have funded scientific research on TBI. However, potential financial and ideological conflicts of interest have clouded these scientific collaborations.[29] They are poignant reminders of how scientific knowledge is not value-neutral; it is situated within social structures and power relationships. In addition, the rush to fund scientific research around TBI reinforces how the brain has become a key site for making sense of social problems.[30] As neuroscience enables the linking of mental states and cognitive processes to activity within the brain, it has become influential in understandings of personhood and behavior. The rise of TBI and CTE as popularly recognized health concerns is, in part, propelled by neuroscientific innovations, as well as broader awareness of the brain sciences in society.

There have been consequences to this neuroscientific turn, particularly when trying to understand and explain social problems. Sociologist Victoria Pitts-Taylor cautions that reliance on neuroscientific evaluations can marginalize humanistic and qualitative fields of study, undermining nuanced accounts addressing the influence of social inequities. Forms of reductionism can take hold, incorrectly suggesting that inequalities can be explained by inherent differences in brain structure. As Pitts-Taylor states, such practices can "pathologize women and racial minorities" as seemingly neurologically deficient, which has "the potential to dominate the understanding of health, wellness, and personal identity in everyday life."[31] Sociologist Oliver Rollins elaborates on these points in relation to neuroscientific research on violence, explaining that certain "neuro-knowledges" can uphold social hierarchies through their failure to directly challenge processes of marginalization, particularly those shaped by racism.[32] In other words, advances in neuroscientific knowledge might not provide a full picture of brain afflictions because they negate societal influences and inequities. There is thus an urgent need to explore how social relations shape experiences and conceptions of TBI across specific contexts.

Violent Impacts considers these critical insights to analyze how notions of a concussion crisis have taken shape and influenced constructions of TBI as a health problem. We acknowledge the prominence of concussion crisis narratives in the United States as well as how they have circulated transnationally, especially in relation to collision sports. As fully tracing these global connections is beyond the scope of a single book, we ground our analysis within three countries where we have conducted research for more than a decade: Australia, Canada, and the United States. In each, we have observed the rise of concussion crisis narratives, first in the United States and Canada, then in Australia. Across these sites, scientific knowledge has informed understandings of TBI. This trend, however, cannot be disentangled from interlocking systems of domination and oppression, which crosscut class, disability, ethnicity, race, sexuality, and other social markers of difference. They inform the inequities we see—and do not see—in popular representations.

This book illustrates such dynamics through examples drawn from public discourse and in-depth fieldwork. We draw out similarities and distinctions in what becomes visible within—as well as what becomes forced to the margins of—the concussion crisis. In addition to an analysis of legal cases, media, and scientific findings that comprise concussion crisis narratives in Australia, Canada, and the United States, we draw on participant observation at professional and scientific conferences, and forty targeted interviews with athletes, brain injury advocates, journalists, legal experts, military veterans, and scientists. Given the breadth and depth of our data, we do not aim to provide clear-cut comparisons of these national jurisdictions, especially as examples from the United States remain central to concussion crisis narratives. Instead, we seek to convey a deeper understanding of underlying dynamics shaping articulations of TBI as a social problem.

Violence emerges as the dominant theme across these sites—and not just through physical acts and injuries. Violence also transpires through cultural forces and societal structures. The visibility of bodies that engage in sports or military violence makes masculinity a clear marker of the concussion crisis. Masculinity alone, however, does not explain the range of societal inequities that contribute to TBI-related violence. The emphasis on masculine forms of physical violence in concussion crisis discourses, in fact, masks social inequities and disregards other forms of violence associated with TBI. We therefore pay critical attention to the role of structural violence—that is, how "social structures or institutions cause harm to people" in ways that "constrain them from achieving the quality of life that would have otherwise been possible."[33] We employ an intersectional lens that is attentive to how interlocking systems of inequality and oppression shape TBI experiences. This approach broadens understandings of the relationship between brain trauma and violence by considering the symbolic and structural dimensions of TBI diagnoses, recoveries, and life histories.

TRACING TBI AS A HEALTH PROBLEM

In this book, we examine how certain bodies and brains have become central to the construction of TBI as a health problem. Our research fits within a longer tradition of work in medical sociology and social problems research. Social constructivism is often traced to sociologists Peter L. Berger and Thomas Luckmann's observations about how social processes become institutionalized over time through collective agreement on how things are done. There are, however, many ways to analyze how social worlds take shape and are maintained.[34] Definitions of social constructionism vary and reflect different influences, including poststructuralism and science and technology studies (STS).[35] In *Violent Impacts*, we embrace the latter. We heed the advice of STS scholars who have criticized some constructivist approaches for presenting social problems as stable, thus missing opportunities to investigate how social processes shift and evolve across different contexts.[36] Rather than repeating narratives that represent TBI as neurological events affecting groups at epidemic levels, we examine how these narratives are created and become dominant. Like anthropologist S. Lochlann Jain's study of cancer, we interrogate the processes that have brought the crisis of TBI into being—to bring them "out of the closet."[37]

Instead of conceptualizing TBI as a static "thing" or isolated affliction, we acknowledge it is constituted by *assemblages* with social, cultural, economic, historical, and material dimensions. Assemblages comprise complex connections between bodies, ideas, processes, and things that come together to generate new conditions and possibilities.[38] The recognition of a singular concept, such as TBI, only occurs through the merging of diverse factors that make brain injuries possible while shaping how they occur, how they are experienced, and how they are understood. In short, our approach recognizes that the concussion crisis extends beyond the brain to include heterogenous components and processes. Despite this complexity, the narration of TBI as a problem retains important structural elements.[39] As queer theorist Jasbir Puar elaborates, assemblages facilitate inquiry into shifting forces, such as geopolitics and institutions, as well as configurations of class, disability, ethnicity, gender, nation, race, and sexuality.[40] This approach enables capturing the dynamic modes through which structural violence materializes in forms of harm and injury.

Violent Impacts reflects our commitment to "thinking with assemblages."[41] Although the concussion crisis may seemingly result from an increasing number of injured human brains, its emergence as a matter of cultural concern reflects more complex interactions between bodies, ideas, objects, people, and places as well as commercial interests, legal decisions, media narratives, medical and scientific practices, technologies, and power struggles. As many such concerns are often erased in appeals for more straightforward forms of evidence, we seek to uncover these nuances rather than minimize them. Approaching the concussion crisis as an assemblage helps shed light on the messiness of patterns and variations that emerge *across* Australian, Canadian, and US contexts, something a comparative study of TBI in different countries would not capture.

This approach extends earlier analyses that acknowledge TBI-related issues are not limited to the counting of physical injuries. Sociologists Daniel Morrison and Monica Casper define CTE as more than a disease, but something involving "masculinity and money, bodies and brutality, spectacle and showmanship, health and self-image"—all factors demonstrating how men's bodies acquire value within and beyond sports.[42] As we discuss further in chapter 2, CTE is not exclusively located in the brain but materializes through societal processes. CTE happens because of specific social conditions that make repetitive brain trauma possible and recognizable, yet its characteristics are contested by scientists, debated by media, and tested in the courts. The fluctuating conceptions of *what* CTE is and *why* it matters are thus shaped by factors beyond the brain. They include social conditions that support certain types of scientific inquiry, inform media discourses, and impact legal proceedings. Neuropathological features and clinical symptoms of CTE cannot be disentangled from the societal processes in which they emerge.

We focus our analysis around four institutional forces: law, media discourse, scientific knowledge, and regulatory practice. Since each domain comes with distinct genres of documentation and information sharing (e.g., court dockets, scientific journal articles, news stories, rule books), we appreciate how documents constitute these institutions by giving them material presence in the world.[43] Consider, for instance, how scientific knowledge is not simply produced in the laboratory or through clinical experiments. It is fashioned for public consumption through news releases and press conferences; it is reported on by journalists; and it is scrutinized in legal proceedings. Comments from scientists are heavily featured in media coverage about TBI, while commentaries evaluating the accuracy of this media coverage have been published in scientific journals. Lawsuits and criminal cases involving people with histories of concussion have required scientists to serve as expert witnesses, with some proceedings becoming major media stories. In short, law, science, media, and regulatory practice are constitutive parts of the concussion crisis. They coalesce to inform how and when TBI does—and does not—become an issue of concern. In addressing these connections, we examine how they contribute to constructing TBI as a health problem, focusing on how forms of knowledge are generated and shaped across sources.

Exploring how intersecting inequalities affect experiences and understandings of TBI is essential to making sense of the concussion crisis. Feminist scholarship provides valuable insights into how social forces manifest themselves in and through violence. Philosopher Iris Marion Young outlines how oppression persists through institutional modes of exclusion, describing its five "faces" as exploitation, marginalization, powerlessness, cultural imperialism, and violence.[44] For Young, violence is systemic: its influence is not limited to direct or individual instances of victimization. Sociologist Patricia Hill Collins elaborates, explaining how interlocking forms of oppression become salient across class, gender, race, and other social categories of difference.[45]

We draw on feminist scholarship throughout this book to help make sense of which bodies and brains become disproportionately prone to the violence that contributes to TBI. Attending to these social inequities, our approach also acknowledges important observations about racism, which, according to geographer Ruth Wilson Gilmore, is "the state-sanctioned or extralegal production and exploitation of group-differentiated vulnerability to premature death."[46] As such, we go beyond the recognition of TBI among individuals with different identities. We instead demonstrate how inequalities are institutionalized through *infrastructures of harm*—the societal arrangements of practices, systems, and values that appear normal and routine but contribute to the uneven distribution of TBI risks.[47] We question these taken-for-granted configurations, looking at how power relationships sustain hierarchies that scientific accounts of TBI cannot explain.[48]

UNVEILING THE INVISIBLE INJURIES
OF THE CONCUSSION CRISIS

Violent Impacts explores how power and inequality not only contribute to understandings of the concussion crisis but also how institutions have sought to address this problem. Academic and media investigations have focused on corporate influences that shape TBI-related legal outcomes, medical protocols, and scientific results—particularly strategies used by professional sports leagues, including the NFL and the National Hockey League (NHL), to minimize concern about the long-term consequences of TBI among players.[49] These tactics manufacture doubt about the causal links between TBI and severe health problems, with sports organizations and aligned scientists often asserting that more conclusive research is required before taking action to reduce the occurrence of TBI. This sense of uncertainty regarding the relationship between TBI and collision sports enables corporations to deflect responsibility for the neurological ailments of their employees. Government committees and independent researchers have uncovered conflicts of interest across TBI research partnerships involving sports organizations that can benefit from favorable study results.[50] Such conflicts of interest have gained public notoriety through investigative journalism and films such as the 2012 documentary *League of Denial* and the 2015 movie *Concussion*, which portray the NFL as an unethical and deceitful organization.

Although explorations of corporate power offer valuable insights into sports TBI, they draw limited attention to how intersecting forms of oppression contribute to understandings of the concussion crisis. While some research has examined exploitative labor conditions, gender norms, and racial inequities related to TBI, few studies have systematically explored them together.[51] In one such example, Brendan Hokowhitu, S. John Sullivan, and Les R. Tumoana Williams situate concussion-reporting behaviors among Māori men in Aotearoa/New Zealand within a context shaped by limited economic opportunities, masculine ideals of toughness, racial stratification, and rugby's colonial history.[52] Their analysis reveals how experiences of TBI cannot be captured or explained by isolated variables. *Violent Impacts* retains a similarly critical focus on intersectionality, drawing connections across social categories and different causes of TBI within and beyond elite sports.

We also acknowledge that some social categories of difference, including gender and race, are increasingly visible within the concussion crisis. Indeed, gender was a focus in media coverage of the Perkins/Belcher story, both in constructions of domestic violence and in characterizing the NFL's masculine spectacle of physical brutality. Yet, despite Perkins and Belcher both being Black, race did not feature in news regarding their deaths. There was no mention of how a majority Black workforce in the NFL means that the players at risk of TBI are more likely to be Black.[53] There was similarly no discussion of how Black women disproportionately experience physical violence in intimate relationships compared to white women.[54]

A key aspect of the book's argument focuses on how the bodies and brains rendered visible in the concussion crisis reflect gendered and racialized power relations. As feminist STS scholar Donna Haraway argued over thirty years ago, vision "is *always* a question of the power to see—and perhaps of the violence implicit in our visualizing practices."[55] Acknowledging larger debates about visuality and what becomes seen or hidden, we are concerned with what is at stake when certain bodies and brains become synonymous with the concussion crisis while others are pushed to the margins.[56] We draw on techniques from visual criminology and sociology to illuminate how social forces make some features of TBI visible while masking others, selectively incorporating images to assist in illustrating these elements of our analysis.[57] Following cultural theorist Mieke Bal's call to think critically and reflexively about visuality, we hope this book destabilizes accepted narratives about TBI "so that alternative narratives can become visible."[58]

Of course, the concussion crisis is not simply seen or viewed; it is embodied and felt. STS guides how we studied how TBI becomes a thing in the world. We follow Steven Woolgar and Javier Lezaun's recommendation to investigate how the actors and objects that animate the concussion crisis "are brought into being."[59] By employing what they refer to as a situated approach, we draw on interviews, news stories, media, and participant observation to illuminate relations that inform who and what becomes recognized as part of the concussion crisis. Our approach extends multisited ethnography, a practice that enables the analysis of how "people, objects, ideas, symbols, and commodities circulate and become interconnected within transnational processes."[60] Our work tracing how TBI materializes across national sites recognizes how globalized relations contribute to the formation of distinct, yet interrelated, concussion crisis narratives in the United States, Canada, and Australia.[61] Throughout *Violent Impacts*, we draw on various vantage points gleaned through close observations to shed light on the power dynamics informing both the visible and underappreciated dimensions of TBI as a social problem.

OUTLINE OF THIS BOOK

We present our analysis in two phases. The book's initial chapters examine the contexts commonly associated with TBI and its impacts—men's and youth sports, as well as the military. After exploring these dominant sites, we then consider experiences that are not central to concussion crisis discourses. Throughout *Violent Impacts*, we illustrate how connections between elite sports and TBI science anchor concussion crisis narratives but extend into other contexts. We also draw attention to how concerns of economic and social marginalization, as well as considerations of structural violence, remain peripheral within popular narratives. Recognizing these dynamics as networked relationships, we do not present a linear story of how the concussion crisis came to be. Instead, we offer a structured narrative that captures the diversity of actors that are highlighted or negated in concussion crisis narratives.

Chapter 1 examines the consequences of conceptualizing TBI as an injury associated with male athletes, a group that makes up a comparatively small percentage of the population experiencing TBI. After illustrating how TBI is visualized in sports media, we consider concussion as part of the political economy of men's collision sports. We trace how the sports that profit most from selling spectacles of violence, including American football, boxing, and ice hockey, have been at the forefront of public debates about TBI. Their proposed responses to the concussion crisis, such as better equipment, medical protocols, and rule changes, reflect their interests in preserving these violent spectacles. We analyze two influential narratives that help maintain the social acceptability of violent sports: athletes' alleged consent to violence and sports organizations' presumed capacity to regulate themselves. We underscore how these narratives shift responsibility for the consequences of TBI away from organizations and onto individuals.

Chapter 2 documents how CTE emerged as a dominant signifier of TBI's long-term consequences across multiple national contexts. We unpack how scientific research, legal proceedings, and media have contributed to the framing of this neurodegenerative disease and expanded public perceptions of the cumulative health risks of TBI. We argue that the focus on finding definitive neuroscientific proof of what causes CTE limits the conceivable range of possibilities for addressing TBI as a social problem. Scientific research remains a valuable source of knowledge about CTE, but the centrality of neurobiological causality within these debates stifles examination of the economic, political, and social forces that enable violence and make CTE—and other sport-related harms—possible.

Chapter 3 marks a shift away from TBI in men's professional and elite sports institutions to look at how concussion crisis discourses have impacted youth sports and prompted legislation to protect children from TBI. Cultural narratives of childhood are powerful modes of promoting regulation, particularly in spaces of legal reform. Here, we consider how notions of childhood innocence and vulnerability inform ideas about TBI risk in youth sports. We reflect on how prominent concussion laws appeal to norms of whiteness in honoring specific victims of TBI, as well as how advocates downplay TBI risks by promoting the inherent value of organized sports for children and by depicting TBI as less risky than other stigmatized health conditions such as childhood obesity. We conclude by showing how the defense of youth collision sports is strongly influenced by cultural values and commercial interests.

Chapter 4 examines shared interests between sports and military institutions as evinced through TBI research partnerships. It investigates three interrelated forces that inform the production of knowledge about TBI among athletes and military members: (1) cultural synergies across sports and military enterprises; (2) research partnerships involving military bodies, sports organizations, and academic institutions; and (3) a shared desire to ensure people's bodies are not incapacitated by injury so they can remain productive laborers in spaces of violence. After considering gendered and racialized inequities that affect patterns of military TBI, we question the selective recognition of TBI resulting from military conflict, which often excludes injured residents of places targeted by US military operations. We query dominant forms of knowledge around military TBI that have remained focused on understandings internal to the body and brain rather than the geopolitical underpinnings of military violence.

Chapter 5 highlights gendered dimensions of the concussion crisis and its limited consideration of women's TBI. We introduce this section with an examination of efforts aimed at raising awareness of brain trauma among women. The tendency to champion female bodies within TBI science positions the scientific study of female brains as the most viable mechanism for addressing women's TBI. Here, we examine how this approach can privilege explanations of sex difference in ways that negate gendered disparities in favor of seeing sex as an inherent attribute.

Using high-profile examples of women in professional soccer who have pledged to donate their brains for TBI research, as well as grounded examples from our fieldwork with scientists, we examine how narratives around women's TBI often unintentionally frame female bodies as naturally more susceptible to injury. As these accounts minimize other social categories of difference and contextual factors, advocates often find themselves negotiating—and renegotiating—the limitations of sex-oriented framings.

Chapter 6 extends our analysis of gendered concerns, looking at TBI in the context of domestic and family violence, a social problem that has been described by the United Nations as a shadow epidemic. We examine advocacy around partner-inflicted TBI. These efforts, like those of other feminist coalitions, reflect a concerted attempt to raise awareness of violence endured by women at home. The efforts to increase visibility of TBI among victim-survivors, however, become entangled with institutional and legal logics that shape responses to domestic and family violence, which have disproportionately harmed Black, Brown, and First Nations communities in the three countries studied over the course of our research. We document how well-intended efforts to support women who have experienced multiple forms of trauma often draw on unrealistic imaginings of how state-provided resources support victim-survivors with TBI. In doing so, such efforts often fail to adequately attend to how multiple forms of inequality and marginalization inform who might benefit from—or be further punished by—proposed reforms.

Chapter 7 scrutinizes relationships between TBI, crime, and violence. It explores claims that long-term consequences of brain trauma may include emotional instability and aggression, and it focuses on the ways that CTE and crime are often constructed as matters of individual culpability and psychology. This logic underpins accounts of athletes with histories of concussion who have been accused of criminal acts, perhaps most visibly through the murder trial of former NFL player Aaron Hernandez. The Hernandez case shines light on certain forms of violence, while masking others: individual spectacles of violence receive ample attention, but state violence remains overlooked. This chapter attends to broader patterns of TBI and violence among criminalized people, particularly as inflicted by state actors, such as the police, highlighting how racism contributes to the recognition of both TBI and state violence. We end this chapter by addressing the need to bring questions about culpability and injury into dialogue with calls for criminal legal system reform and stronger accountability for state violence.

We conclude *Violent Impacts* with a reflection on key insights described in the chapters, emphasizing how structural violence not only contributes to brain injury but also influences which bodies are captured in—and absent from—concussion crisis narratives. While biomedicine provides important knowledge about TBI, its dominance supersedes calls for health equity and social welfare reform. Rather than suggest these are mutually exclusive projects, we argue that a greater focus on social marginalization and structural violence is essential to understanding TBI as social problem. Doing this can support research that helps a wider range of people who experience TBI and inform strategies that address forms of violence sustained by sports, military, and criminal legal institutions. This focus promises new ways of understanding the concussion crisis and appreciating the impacts of normalized violence in society.

1

Spectacles of Violence in Sports

Understanding the concussion crisis requires examining how impacts to the head are given meaning within sports cultures. Consider, for example, this photograph taken during a 1963 heavyweight boxing match at Madison Square Garden in New York City between established contender Doug Jones and young star and Olympic gold medalist Cassius Clay (fig. 1). The camera captures Clay (soon to be Muhammad Ali) appearing powerful, with a fierce expression noticeably different from that on Jones's contorted face. Jones's head is on the receiving end of Clay's right hook. The twist of Jones's neck and his compressed facial features are testament to the violent force of Clay's punch.

This photograph tells two intertwined, yet competing, stories. The first is about power and violence: it is a story celebrating boxing's culture of masculine aggressiveness and toughness. The image shows Clay dominating his opponent, personifying the strength and fortitude central to narratives of boxing greatness. The young Clay's display of power in this picture foreshadows the fame he would achieve as Muhammad Ali. The second story revolves around Doug Jones. Since the image shows his body absorbing the force of Clay's punch, Jones is vital to the narrative celebrating Clay's athletic aggression. Boxing photography can freeze a split-second impact in time to showcase the often-grotesque disfigurement of the fighter's head.[1] The picture thus provides an opportunity to acknowledge that the blow to Jones's head is an embodied experience of physical damage. As philosopher Susan Sontag suggests, still photographs of violent confrontations invite the spectator to "pay attention, to reflect, to learn" about the extent of others' pain.[2]

Such photographs are snapshots of how sports function as cultural sites for learning about pain and violence—and the value of persevering through injury.

FIGURE 1. Cassius Clay and Doug Jones at Madison Square Garden in New York City (Bettman via Getty Images).

By the time Clay and Jones squared off at Madison Square Garden, cultural and scientific accounts of the cumulative neurological damage incurred by boxers were becoming more common.[3] Any public concern for Jones's well-being, however, took a back seat to the photograph's portrayal of Clay's remarkable power and the allure of sports violence. This photograph—and countless others like it—are part of a larger visual economy of images, broadcasts, and films through which the physicality and brutality of violent sports are commodified and packaged for audiences. Much of this visual economy revolves around men's collision and combat sports such as boxing, American football, ice hockey, mixed martial arts (MMA), and rugby, where media coverage and marketing often dramatize violent acts as exciting performances of masculine aggression. As such, these sports become public spectacles that normalize violent acts, often making them profitable forms of mass entertainment.[4]

Growing concerns about the concussion crisis have unsettled the visual economy of violent sports. Images and video footage of violent sports, once uncritically celebrated, are now consumed in a cultural moment increasingly defined by unease about the consequences of brain trauma. Some of the most enduring images of the concussion crisis in sports depict intense scenes of physical violence: collisions of bodies that leave one or more competitors injured and incapacitated.

Like the Clay/Jones photograph, many such images display the *moment of impact* when an athlete's head is struck by another body or crashes into part of the playing surface. Others show the bleak aftermath of these impacts, often an athlete lying motionless with their body splayed out on the ground.

These pictures appear across numerous media contexts—from online news stories to social media posts, to experts' PowerPoint presentations. While these images are sometimes used to visually supplement descriptions of specific concussion experiences, they are also frequently used to represent the broader problem of traumatic brain injury (TBI). These pictures operate as a visual shorthand for the concussion crisis in sports. They offer striking visual representations of the dangers of sports violence and can evoke concern and sympathy for the athletes who experience them. They align with Sontag's claim that photographs are opportunities to reflect on the magnitude of others' pain. Moreover, by showcasing the most severe and visually shocking examples of TBI, these images convey scenes that capture what brain trauma can look like: a violent impact followed by a devastating outcome. The images held up as evidence of the concussion crisis help viewers build a narrative of cause and effect in which a violent action produces an identifiable health consequence.

Despite capturing glimpses of the violence contributing to brain injury, these images do not provide a complete picture of TBI. As filmmaker and anthropologist John Jackson explains, "there is far too much that the camera (like 'the naked eye') doesn't or can't capture—that lies just beyond its rectangular frame or what transpired before the camera was turned on."[5] These photographs cannot capture the actions, people, histories, values, and storylines that shape these scenes. They nonetheless reflect and convey dominant ideas of how TBI happens and to whom, conditioning and constraining how we might see the problem and what can be done about it.

In this chapter, we examine the emphasis on sports violence within debates about the concussion crisis. Despite headlines that ask, "Is football too violent for our youth?" or assert that "NHL concussions reignite debate about hockey violence," many debates about TBI and sports violence are limited by narrow conceptions of what counts as violence in sports.[6] Heeding sociologist Kevin Young's call for a definition of sports violence that moves past the "isolated snapshot" of specific types of violent behavior, we focus on the cultural conditions and systems through which TBI and sports violence converge.[7] In particular, we consider how the cultural and economic power of men's collision sports influences approaches to TBI, which limit some violent actions while justifying others. Like images associated with concussion, they tend to make certain bodies and types of violence visible while pushing others out of view. We explore how the unseen dimensions of sports violence—that is, those that are hidden or invisible—are instructive for understanding power relations at work.[8] Calls to manage violent acts in sports do not necessarily challenge cultures of sports violence, nor do they necessarily disrupt the social acceptance of broader forms of violence that extend beyond sports.

CONCUSSION AND VISUAL ECONOMIES OF SPORTS VIOLENCE

Concerns about the link between sports violence and brain injury are by no means new. Scientists have studied neurological injuries in boxing for over one hundred years. By the 1950s, the brutality of boxing and the consequences of repeated hits to the head fueled calls to abolish the sport.[9] Debates about the dangers of football have similarly taken place since the 1890s.[10] Incidents of ice hockey players suffering severe and sometimes fatal brain injuries in the early 1900s also provoked disputes about the sport's embrace of violent behavior.[11] Proposed safety measures or outright bans of violent play have typically been resisted as threats to the nature of each sport. Without these violent elements, proponents have argued, sports would lose much of their appeal, as well as their capacity to instill masculine values of aggression and toughness in boys and young men.[12]

These historical flashpoints illustrate how cultural apprehensions about TBI have long been linked to debates about violence in men's collision and combat sports. They also demonstrate how sports institutions have withstood pressure to modify violent styles of play. The social acceptability of sports violence has been historically intertwined with the promotion of aggression and toughness as idealized masculine traits.[13] Thus, despite concerns about TBI and early calls to regulate violence in sports, the last century has been characterized by popular and profitable sports spectacles that celebrate violence: from boxing's heavyweight title fights to the billion-dollar industries surrounding professional and college football. The contemporary concussion crisis, however, has revived longstanding debates about the ethics of sports violence since new scientific research showed elevated TBI risk for collision and combat sports athletes.[14] Investigative journalism, government hearings, and lawsuits have also questioned how sports organizations profit from the promotion of violence while not adequately safeguarding athletes' neurological health.[15]

Narratives linking violence, science, and corporate corruption have contributed to TBI becoming a newsworthy topic. Yet some of this public interest can be attributed to the already extensive media focus on professional men's collision sports. The overrepresentation of men's collision sports in media discourse means that athletes from these sports are often recognizable public figures and their struggles with TBI make for compelling stories. For example, when ice hockey player Sidney Crosby missed substantial parts of two NHL seasons due to prolonged concussion symptoms, his celebrity status elevated the story's significance for media audiences.[16] Other NHL athletes Wade Belak and Derek Boogaard and NFL players Aaron Hernandez and Junior Seau were well-known when they died and were subsequently diagnosed with CTE.[17] In this way, these popular male athletes have become symbols of the concussion crisis and their stories reinforce the notion that frequent, high-impact hits are the primary cause of life-limiting TBI.

The visibility of men's collision and combat sports makes them appear representative of what sports TBI look like. Unlike other scenarios that carry concussion risks such as heading a soccer ball or falling from an apparatus in gymnastics, the spectacle of the "big hit" in American football, ice hockey, or rugby powerfully depicts the dangers of TBI, as do images showing the unsettling aftermath of these moments of impact. The athlete's motionless body, lying helplessly on the ground, attests to the severity of a collision. Sometimes, as in the picture of Nathan Horton from the 2011 NHL playoffs (fig. 2), the athlete is being attended to by medical personnel, another visual cue establishing the athlete's vulnerability. A side-by-side comparison of figures 2 and 3 demonstrates an eerie resemblance between concussion images and the iconic "blood on the pavement" aesthetic of 1920s and 1930s crime scene photography that was front-page material for tabloid newspapers of the day.[18] In each case, the lifeless figure of the athlete or gangster represents unnerving evidence that violence had taken place—communicating the sobering consequences of violent acts.

Yet the capacity for images of concussion to communicate such lessons, or even evoke sympathies, is diminished by the routine frequency of intense portrayals of injury within violent sporting spectacles. These visuals are often accompanied by brief expressions of concern from commentators and onlookers, after which the action typically resumes without much disruption. These representations allow fans to momentarily confront the dangers underlying their enjoyment of violent sports, but the familiarity and fleeting nature of these images limits their power. As such, sports spectacles make the consequences of violence seem normal and acceptable, particularly when athletes returning from injury are celebrated for their heroics.[19] These values fortify the economies of violent sports.

These trademark representations of the concussion crisis may make it visible, but they only capture select aspects of TBI. The images show an injured body, but the damaged brain cannot be seen. Neither can a full range of TBI symptoms or the rigors of an athlete's recovery. These visuals attach TBI to moments of seemingly extreme violence and injury. They thus push more routine hits or nonconcussive impacts outside the scope of the crisis. These portrayals make TBI in violent men's sports far more visible than the similarly harmful injuries in women's sports and sports not known for violent play—for example, baseball, basketball, cheerleading, gymnastics, soccer, and softball.

The frame of these sports photographs, by design, isolate individuals in ways that do not show the networks of actors and institutions that inform the management of TBI. Except for the occasional presence of a team doctor or trainer, TBI-related medical personnel and scientific infrastructures remain behind the

FIGURE 2. National Hockey League player Nathan Horton being attended to by a team trainer after sustaining a concussion in 2011 (Damian Strohmeyer/*Sports Illustrated* via Getty Images).

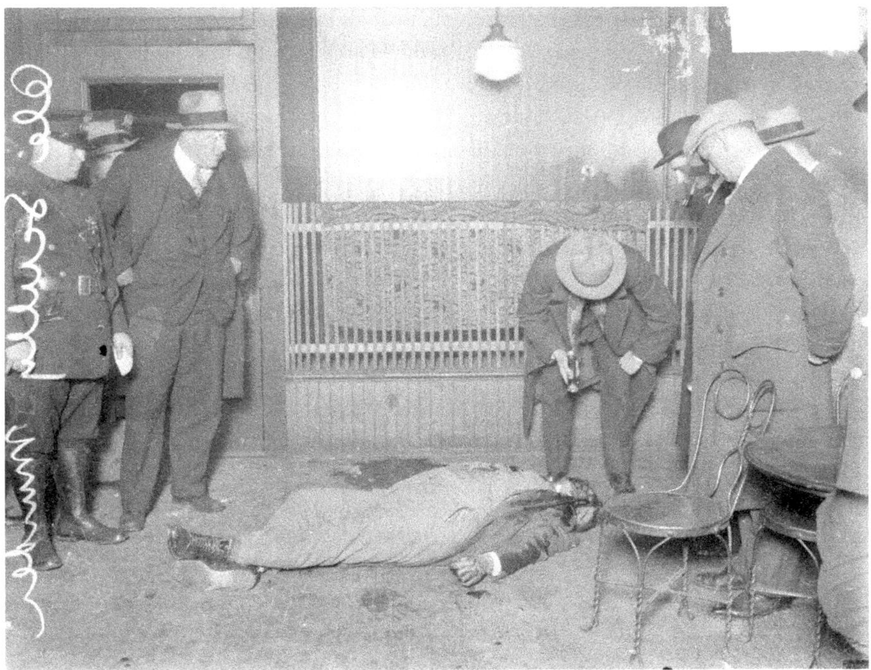

FIGURE 3. Murder victim Ole Scully, a key witness in the Ranieri kidnapping trial, surrounded by police in Chicago in 1928 (*Chicago Sun-Times*/*Chicago Daily News*/Chicago History Museum via Getty Images).

scenes. The commentators, corporations, executives, and lawyers whose work may condone, regulate, or oppose sports violence are also not captured. Sports media are an absent presence in the symbolic system of concussion crisis imagery. The workings of sports media stay mostly hidden behind the camera, even though their technological platforms and storytelling capabilities convey contradictory messages of injury as both normal and devastating. The concussion crisis reflects entanglements of ideology, media, and sports, which carry over into debates about TBI risk.

FRAMINGS OF CONSENT, SPORTS VIOLENCE, AND TBI RISK

The media has shed light on debates about the extent to which athletes can freely accept the risks that come with violent sports. Some athletes have asserted they were not adequately educated about the risks of brain trauma associated with their sport and were unaware of how their careers might impact their neurological health. Retired NFL player Leonard Marshall conveys this sentiment clearly:

"I knew when I signed up for the National Football League that I would get beaten, battered and bruised, but what I didn't know was that traumatic brain injury will become so prevalent."[20] Mirroring Marshall's comments, a main complaint in class action lawsuits against the NFL and NHL is that the leagues withheld information about TBI risks, which prevented athletes from making informed choices to protect their brains.[21]

Contrasting narratives have emerged in which athletes publicly declare their consent to participate in violent sports despite the greater awareness of TBI risks. For example, NFL cornerback Richard Sherman wrote a column for *Sports Illustrated*, stating, simply, "we chose this profession."[22] Sherman expresses frustration with league rule changes designed to protect receivers from hits to the head. He argues that these more stringent rules are unnecessary since players understand the health risks of football and continue their careers despite these risks. Sherman writes, "We understand this is a dangerous game with consequences not just in the short term, but for the rest of our lives." He asserts that, unlike past players who were not made fully aware of the potential short- and long-term risks of brain trauma, current NFL players are better informed: "Today, we're fully educating guys on the risks and we're still playing. We have not been hidden from the facts." Similarly, a former captain of the New Zealand All Blacks rugby team, Sam Cane, has confirmed that, although he is concerned about the long-term health effects of his career, "concussions are a risk that [players] accept."[23]

Such comments construct TBI risks as acceptable and necessary aspects of playing violent sports. They also illustrate how notions of consent have become central to many framings of TBI risks. Scholars have demonstrated that athletes' consent to participate in violent sports is what separates ritualized, controlled sports violence from criminal acts of violence that intentionally violate a person's physical safety.[24] Violent sports can be viewed as socially acceptable forms of aggression because they operate under the assumption that the athletes involved understand and have accepted the injury risks associated with participation. However, understandings of consent in relation to violence are not universal; they maintain distinct cultural contours.[25] They are also informed by social hierarchies and values that can be contextually specific. These dynamics come to the fore when scrutinizing expressions of consent to TBI risks.

While often constructed around notions of individual choice, narratives of consent within the concussion crisis cannot be separated from their gendered underpinnings. The embrace of violence is a core tenet within the masculine value systems of many combat and collision sports. As violence contributes to the maintenance of hegemonic masculinity, violent sports are a primary cultural sphere for the celebration of ideals and behaviors that normalize patriarchal values.[26] In fact, critics have framed the introduction of TBI-related protocols and safety regulations as threatening the supposedly natural connections between violence and masculine power. Former world middleweight champion Bernard Hopkins, for example, voiced his displeasure about potential changes to boxing's safety protocols in 2018, saying the sport is "dangerous but it's also something that the majority of us love. The thrill, love the challenge, love the daring part of it. That's what makes us who we are."[27] Hopkins's comments illustrate how many boxers' identities are inextricable from the sport's unapologetic celebration of danger, physical violence, and masculine aggressiveness.[28] This embrace of competitive violence is a valued expression of masculinity, incentivizing not only consent to the bodily risks it presents but also the preservation of boxing's violent features.

Others have framed injury risks within broader expectations about the personal and health sacrifices that professional athletes should make to earn their salaries. Former NHL tough guy Krys Barch condemned the league's attempts to reduce head impacts in 2012, explaining that TBI risks are "part of the sport," with players "paid huge money to [play,] and most of the time [when] you get paid big money it comes with a lot of risks involved and we're compensated."[29] Barch compares hockey players to soldiers "going over to Iraq and Afghanistan" who are "doing it for their country and not getting compensated near as much," concluding that if "we're going to sit here and cry because one guy's making $5 million and he's out with a concussion then shame on us." Here, he points to the financial benefits of a professional sports career as warranting any exposure to TBI and its health consequences. In other instances, athletes justify TBI risks by appealing to ideas about work and loyalty. NFL Pro Bowl wide receiver Calvin Johnson has characterized playing through concussions as "part of life" in the NFL, explaining:

> Guys get concussions, they don't tell the coaches. It happens. I don't tell the coach sometimes 'cause I know I got a job to do. The team needs me out there on the field. And sometimes you allow that to jeopardize yourself, but that's just the nature of the world.[30]

While it is well-documented that some athletes may refuse to report concussion symptoms because they internalize norms of masculine toughness and want to avoid disappointing their teammates and coaches, Johnson's comments demonstrate how professional athletes can view TBI risks as simply part of the job.[31] The perspectives from Barch, Hopkins, and Johnson embrace cultural values of masculine aggressiveness and risk-taking, economic success, and dedication to work.

Across these narratives of consent, athletes emerge as active agents who accept TBI risks on their own terms. At the same time, these depictions make it seem like professional leagues are absolved from responsibility for the consequences of TBI because the athletes knew what they signed up for when they chose a dangerous career.[32] News stories about athletes who have retired from their sport to limit their exposure to repetitive brain trauma amplify these logics of agency and consent. An ever-expanding number of star players—including NFL linebacker Luke Kuechly, NHL player Rick Nash, and rugby league players Stevie Ward and Boyd Cordner—have retired, citing lingering effects of multiple concussions.[33] Perhaps the most provocative illustration of this trend involves NFL player Chris Borland, who retired in 2015 at the age of twenty-four following a promising rookie season. Despite not having a significant history of diagnosed concussions, Borland cited football's connection to brain trauma and neurodegenerative disease as prompting his decision, and he was widely supported for preemptively prioritizing his health over an NFL career.[34]

The retirement decisions of players like Borland nonetheless reinforce narratives of consent built primarily around the idea that individual players can simply move on from their sports careers if they are no longer willing to accept TBI risks. Such narratives reinforce perceptions that athletes are in positions where they can assess and take responsibility for risk on their own terms. This way of thinking, however, takes pressure off organizations and institutions to improve athlete working conditions or to shift the social values underpinning violent sports.[35] This framing conveys professional athletes as being free to make choices about TBI risks even though they are a diverse group of workers, many of whom are not as independent, financially or otherwise, as popular depictions suggest. As such, these narratives mask the complexities that contribute to the acceptance of TBI risk.

NARRATIVES RECONSIDERING CONSENT, POWER, AND TBI RISK

Some media coverage unsettles simplified narratives of consent by showing how athletes' capacity to make informed choices about TBI risks can be limited by power imbalances within sports systems. The most common manifestation of this trend has come through in reports highlighting tensions faced by professional athletes in balancing health decisions with threats to their job security. Consider, for instance, how NFL running back Tyler Varga describes the "depth-player" mentality, which is when lesser-known or less talented players feel pressure to persevere through injuries to maintain their tenuous status on a team. Specifically, he explains:

> I didn't want to go through the concussion protocol and maybe lose my job. That's the pressure. I can't miss anything. There's no wiggle room. I hardly get any reps in practice as it is, and I'm missing days, I'm getting even fewer. I don't get to show the coaches I know my stuff. And if I don't get to play in the game, I get replaced.[36]

Varga's comments underscore how sustaining a concussion does not make you exempt from the "next-man-up" philosophy of professional football, in which a substitute can overtake their injured teammate's position to become a permanent replacement.[37] This phenomenon is also well-documented among ice hockey enforcers—that is, players primarily employed for their skill as fighters. Despite the mythology of these fighters as essential members of hockey teams, they often face threats of reduced playing time or demotion to the minor leagues if their willingness to fight wanes.[38] Retired Colorado Avalanche enforcer Scott Parker lamented the precarity that came with the enforcer role, "If you're hurt, it doesn't matter. You're made to think 'I have to fight, or I'll lose my job.'"[39] Being successful does not necessarily ensure job security, prompting athletes to make risk calculations that can jeopardize health and safety.

The concussion crisis has magnified how the commodification of violent sports revolves around an athletic workforce seen as dispensable.[40] A growing number of athletes who were employed in North American professional leagues have become outspoken about the unequal power relationships that allow team owners to maximize profits at the expense of players' well-being. Richard Sherman has described how NFL players navigate a labor environment characterized by threats of injury and mistreatment. He asserts:

> as dedicated as we players are to this game, it's getting more and more difficult to ignore the fact that we don't have a league that shows the same kind of dedication when it comes to taking care of the players who are laying their bodies on the line every Sunday. [The NFL is a] bottom line business. If you can increase their bottom line, then they'll love you . . . If you're not making them money, then at the end of the day, they're going to find somebody else.

Sherman also emphasizes that most NFL players "don't come from affluent backgrounds" and the potential financial gains offered by even short professional football careers can provide unmatched opportunities to "chang[e] their family's lives" for the better.[41] In other words, the potential social and economic benefits of a professional career for players can outweigh the inherent injury risks of violent sports.

These dynamics are intensified for Black players, who comprise the majority of NFL rosters. Although Black sports sociologists, such as Harry Edwards and Billy Hawkins, have described the slim chances of Black men reaping the rewards of playing professional sports at the highest level, research shows higher rates of Black football participation at the youth and high school levels in the United States.[42] Journalist Alana Semuels similarly describes a trend of "white flight" from football, with white families, conscious of the sport's TBI risks, steering their children and teenagers toward less violent sports.[43] Semuels's work emphasizes how a greater proportion of Black families continue to embrace football as a source of opportunity for education and social mobility, suggesting that racial disparities in football participation rates "paint a troubling picture of how economic opportunity—or a lack thereof—governs which boys are incentivized to put their body and brain at risk to play."[44]

Similar trends have been mapped among men from American Sāmoa who embark on university or professional football careers with hopes of socio-economic advancement through migration to the mainland United States.[45] The growing prominence of Māori and Pasifika players in rugby union and rugby league has also reinforced the visibility of these collision sports as professional pathways that can provide support for players' families and communities.[46] Many such athletes accept the prospect of bodily risks when pursuing a sport as a pathway to socioeconomic mobility.[47] Reflecting on rugby in Aotearoa/ New Zealand, Brendan Hokowhitu has described how the sport emerges as a powerful form of "positive racism" that reinforces masculine stereotypes of Māori men (tāne).[48] He discusses how depictions of Māori aggression and physicality frame them as naturally violent, with sports being a positive and productive outlet for them. These framings, however, normalize the acceptance of risks associated with pursuing sports-related goals. Moreover, many athletes sustain multiple TBIs throughout their careers but never reach the levels of athletic success that provide social mobility.

For many male athletes pursuing careers in these sports, managing TBI risks is but one part of a more complicated path shaped by economic inequities, gendered ideologies, racism, and colonial hierarchies. As anthropologist Lisa Uperesa explains, in relation to Sāmoan men drawn to American football, the sport presents not only a "viable avenue for accumulating economic capital" but something much more:

> Pride of accomplishment and representing one's family and community . . . [and] other forms of cultural capital in the form of prestige, adulation, and connection to people invested in their performance on the field. In Sāmoan communities and beyond, the opportunity to "give back" once successful and established—fulfilling the obligation and privilege of performing *tautua* (service, in this case expanded and transnationalized), has been important for many.[49]

While the socioeconomic footprint of collision sports may afford some athletes pathways to education, migration, social mobility, and community connection, the potential benefits incentivize taking bodily risks. Concussion crisis narratives of consent grounded in representations of individual choice fail to capture the interlocking systems contributing to who participates in violent sports, who becomes exposed to greater TBI risk, and who is positioned to step away from these risks. The ways in which TBI in sports is intertwined with social inequities has been, until very recently, relatively absent from conceptions of the concussion crisis, even with growing athlete activism around related issues. By contrast, media and sports organizations pay much more attention to the possible reduction of TBI through the management of violent play and incremental rule changes designed to improve athlete safety. In the next section, we consider their focus as a set of strategic regulatory maneuvers.

TBI REGULATION AS TARGETING
AND ENABLING SPORTS VIOLENCE

Many sports organizations have responded to public concerns about TBI by implementing new rules for reducing the amount and severity of head impacts. Over the past two decades, the NFL has implemented new rules that penalize hits on "defenseless" players unable to protect themselves from contact and helmet-to-helmet hits.[50] The National Collegiate Athletic Association (NCAA) has created rules penalizing "targeting" players with helmet-to-helmet hits in collegiate football.[51] The NHL went from only penalizing blindside hits to the head to punishing any collision in which the head is the "primary point of contact."[52] This means that collisions can still result in head impacts, but the league will penalize a player when they strike their opponent's head first before another part of the body. World Rugby has similarly enacted rules to prohibit high tackles, defined as an illegal hit that involves clear head contact or that reaches a height to cause the head of an opposing player to forcibly move in a backward direction.[53]

Many rule changes have been met with backlash. When Richard Sherman, Krys Barch, and Bernard Hopkins made comments about athletes accepting TBI risk, their statements were fueled by disapproval of regulatory interventions within their respective sports. Their discontent reflects broader trends in which athletes, coaches, and fans perceive TBI-related rule changes as watering down celebrated aspects of violent sports.[54] A notorious example of a sport being framed as "going soft" comes from US President Donald Trump, who derisively condemned NFL rules penalizing hits to the head as "ruining the game" during a Florida campaign stop in 2016.[55] These and similar complaints mark clear instances of how efforts to curtail the effects of violence clash with dominant values of aggressive masculinity in sports.

Faith in the effectiveness of rule changes to prevent TBI is often grounded in biomechanics, as well as epidemiological research that has sought to identify types of impacts that most commonly result in concussion diagnoses.[56] Following this logic, the creation of rules supported by empirical findings should reduce the frequency of these impacts. Yet studies of the effectiveness of high-profile rule changes have produced mixed results; new rules do not always result in substantial drops in the number of concussion diagnoses.[57] Despite inconclusive outcomes, the optics of these interventions appear to make sports safer because they aim to remove the most visibly jarring head impacts from view. Banning the most egregious hits from collision sports reconfigures, but does not entirely disrupt, the economies of sports violence.

Contrary to the backlash about new rules spoiling the enjoyment of collision sports, recent amendments designed to protect athletes in fact work to preserve cultures of sports violence. Many rule changes approach sports violence as something that can be managed effectively through incremental adjustments. This focus narrows debates about sports violence to technical or scientific questions rather than social or ethical ones. Instead of confronting what TBI reveals about the problems with sports violence, these strategies implement marginal modifications that do not require transforming the broader cultures of violent sports. They do not pressure sports institutions to reconsider their promotion of (and profiting from) violent play. Instead, they put the onus on athletes, coaches, and officials to abide by and enforce new rules.[58]

This process of shifting accountability has important legal and symbolic functions. Rules aid in making distinctions between socially acceptable physical aggression and objectionable violence in sports. Rules inform a process of social decriminalization: that is, violent acts often considered malicious or unlawful outside of sports are permitted because sports have policies in place to manage them. Rules serve this social function by providing assurance that sports violence takes place in a regulated space where athletes are seemingly held accountable for unsafe or unacceptable actions.[59] The implementation of new rules to improve player health and safety is therefore as much about maintaining the social acceptability of violent sports as about addressing injury risks.

As social decriminalization involves a transfer of authority from the state to sports organizations, much of the process hinges on the perceived capacity of sports organizations to regulate violence with limited government or legal intervention. The concussion crisis, however, has disrupted trust in the self-regulation practices of sports leagues. A 2021 report from the United Kingdom Parliamentary Digital, Culture, Media, and Sports (DCMS) Committee expresses dismay at the failure of national sports organizations to adequately address TBI, emphasizing the need for external oversight over athlete health and safety practices. The DCMS chair, Julian Knight, commented on the committee's findings, stating, "What is astounding is that when it comes to reducing the risks of brain injury, sport has been allowed to mark its own homework."[60] The NFL has similarly been the target of criticism for its practices around TBI, including accusations of manipulating scientific data to downplay TBI risks and stacking regulatory committees with league-friendly experts.[61] These conflicts of interest have been the subject of US congressional hearings that reprimanded the league for its negligence in relation to TBI. Even so, the proceedings have minimally affected the league's ability to regulate its approach to player health.[62]

Leaving sports organizations largely responsible for regulating violence allows them to address TBI according to interests beyond the health and safety of athletes. How these organizations conceptualize feasible solutions to the problem of TBI is also influenced by issues beyond health, including branding and marketing campaigns, broadcast rights and advertising, legal liabilities and insurance policies, and public relations practices.[63] When the NFL launched its concussion prevention strategy *Play Smart, Play Safe* in 2016, the league communicated its commitment to brain health by publicizing its $100 million donation to TBI research initiatives. The league also outlined four pillars of its concussion strategy: changes to game rules and tackling techniques to protect players; advanced technologies; medical research; and TBI knowledge sharing.[64] In doing so, the NFL created a template for addressing TBI without measures that could threaten its business model. Similar strategies are evident in debates about fighting in professional hockey, which we discuss next.

FIGHTING IN THE NHL, WHERE SELF-REGULATING VIOLENCE THRIVES BUT STILL FAILS

While fighting in men's professional ice hockey has long been a controversial topic, the concussion crisis has intensified these debates.[65] Fights represent the sport's most extreme spectacle of violence: they involve outbursts of bare-knuckle boxing, including direct punches to the head that can leave participants bloodied and bruised. In their most severe form, fights can lead to loss of consciousness either from a knockout punch or when a player's head hits the ice. Images of these startling moments of injury are recognizable as depicting a concussion's devastating aftermath.

The incidence and effects of TBI among enforcers have received much attention, especially following the unanticipated deaths of NHL enforcers Derek Boogaard, Rick Rypien, and Wade Belak in the summer of 2011, all of whom were found to have CTE pathology in their brains. Other deceased players known as prolific fighters in life, such as Todd Ewen and Steve Montador, have also been diagnosed with CTE post-mortem.[66] While living with chronic cognitive or psychological difficulties is not an inevitable outcome for players in the enforcer role, a growing number of accounts show that retired enforcers have indeed suffered such ignominious fates.[67] Their stories make for captivating media coverage: men once revered for their toughness and fearlessness are shown struggling with the emotional and physiological aftereffects of careers built on violent combat. The NHL, however, has repeatedly denied that there is an established link between a career as an enforcer and long-term neurological damage.[68]

The number of fights in the NHL has dropped dramatically in recent years, falling from 734 fights in the 2008–9 season to 224 in the 2018–19 season.[69] While the number of NHL fights has risen slightly in the 2020s, they have not returned to pre-2010 levels.[70] This decrease is commonly attributed to a gradual decline of the enforcer role following a league-wide trend toward rostering versatile multi-skilled players instead of one-dimensional fighters. The NHL has, however, also implemented rules to manage how and when fights happen. From 2013 on, for

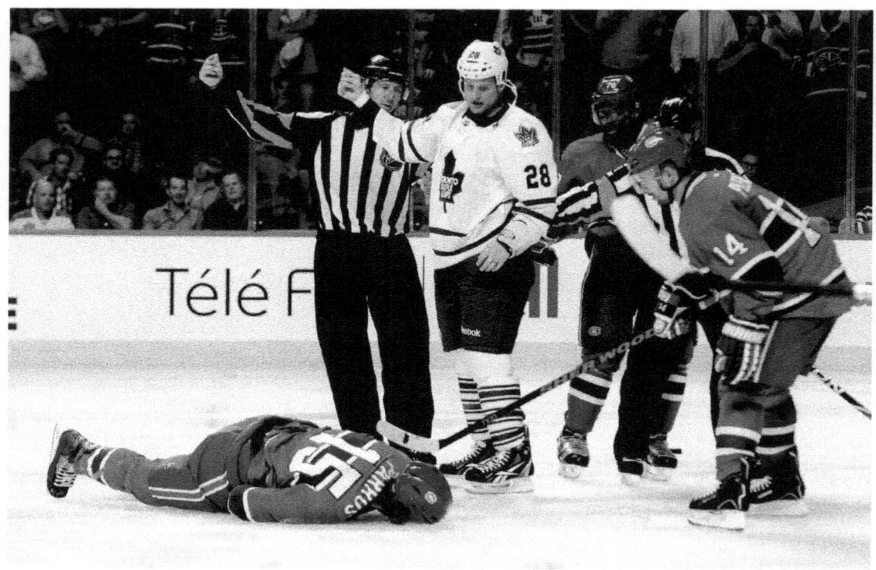

FIGURE 4. National Hockey League player George Parros of the Montreal Canadiens lying motionless on the ice after a 2013 fight with Colton Orr of the Toronto Maple Leafs (Richard Wolowicz via Getty Images).

example, established penalties for purposefully removing helmets before a fight begins. This rule is designed to reduce the risk of severe injuries during fights, such as skull fractures, and discourage preplanned or "staged" fights when players agree to fight in advance of any genuine on-ice tension between combatants.[71] Yet despite calls for the NHL to ban fighting completely to protect players from brain injury, the league has refused to do so or to impose harsher punishments to deter fighting.[72] Fighting overall remains coded into the NHL's rulebook as an acceptable infraction warranting a five-minute major penalty, after which players can typically return to finish the game.

The league's inaction is supported by arguments about the supposedly essential place of fighting in ice hockey culture. In the face of public pressure to reduce TBI risks, many athletes, commentators, and fans have defended fighting by reasserting its role in upholding the sport's informal code (often simply referred to as "The Code") through which players police themselves.[73] The logic of The Code is that the threat of violent retribution deters unacceptable actions, such as blindside bodychecks, hits from behind, and assaults with sticks or skates.[74] The NHL's embrace of fighting conveys support for this form of self-policing and boosts the league's promotion of its players as rugged and masculine. In short, the spectacle of violence remains central to the most celebrated elements of men's ice hockey.

The NHL's response to the concussion crisis also draws on evidential claims to justify fighting's place in professional ice hockey. A 2013 study indicated that fights led to far fewer concussions than legal actions such as bodychecks.[75] This finding has since been reflected in media discourse and official league statements. For example, in a 2016 *Globe and Mail* op-ed, former NHL player and Quebec Major Junior Hockey League team owner Bobby Smith cites these 2013 findings while drawing on narratives of consent, writing, "a player has a choice whether or not he wants to accept an invitation to fight. Nobody is asked his permission before being blindsided or hit from behind." Veteran enforcer Shawn Thornton has also rejected what he sees as a misconception about the relationship between fighting and concussions: "How many guys get [concussions] from fighting? It's few and far between. It actually kind of pisses me off a little bit that the fighting thing is the first thing that's thrown out there when they talk about concussions."[76] League commissioner Gary Bettman has reiterated that players use fighting "to minimize other forms of dangerous plays," repeating this argument when testifying before a Canadian parliamentary subcommittee in 2019.[77]

These public conversations about fighting in ice hockey shed light on specific ways of seeing TBI, which foreclose other ways of framing the problem. Current debates reinforce sports leagues' self-regulation of violent play as a central response. The NHL remains steadfast in its resistance to outside interference on the grounds that the league (and its players) can understand and manage the risks of their sport better than anyone else. The league presents the issue as if it can be mitigated through small strategic regulatory tweaks that leave the overarching violent culture of men's ice hockey undisturbed. The presumed specificity and precision of these rule changes make calls for a drastically less violent version of the sport seem extreme or unnecessary.

Writer and NHL Hall of Fame goaltender Ken Dryden explains how changes to NHL rules are intertwined with the league's promotion of violence, writing:

> You have to allow some hits to the head because you have to allow fighting—because fighting has always been part of hockey, hockey fans love fights, and fights symbolize the commitment of a hockey player that is different from the commitment of a player in all other sports. A hockey player, literally, is willing to fight for his team.[78]

Dryden highlights how narratives of consent to TBI risks are supported by, and contribute to, ice hockey's mythology of masculine violence. Yet this symbolism—and the NHL's capacity to profit from it—exacts a toll on the bodies and brains of players. If, as Dryden argues, the symbolic importance of fighting is what justifies resistance to the complete elimination of hits to the head, then fights can be indirectly responsible for other vicious bodychecks and collisions that lead to TBI.

The league's persistence around fighting has also made one type of player—the enforcer—the focal point of hockey's TBI debates, minimizing how other players experience repeated high-speed collisions. The focus on fighting also perpetuates the disproportionate attention given to men's ice hockey and the NHL at the expense of women's ice hockey, a version of the sport typically played without sanctioned bodychecking or fighting.[79] The centering of fighting, which is only one form of violence in the sport, and the NHL, which is only one organization in the wider ice hockey landscape, pushes other acts of violence—as well as other bodies—to the periphery of the concussion crisis.

SEEING SPORTS VIOLENCE
THROUGH THE LENS OF TBI

The growing body of scientific research regarding the neurological impacts of high-speed collisions has informed efforts to diminish violent play in many sports. This research, as well as widespread media coverage, has supported government hearings and lawsuits that seek accountability from sports stakeholders who promote violence. Although these developments are important, they cannot be separated from how cultural narratives of sports violence condition popular understandings of—and, in turn, responses to—concussion. The tendency to present individualized acts of violence and their cumulation as the focal point of the concussion crisis pervades the images and stories that comprise popular depictions of TBI. In doing so, this discourse, which shifts the burdens of choice and responsibility onto athletes, emerges in tension with demands for a widespread reckoning with the dangers of sports violence.

Exploring the politics of visibility around sports TBI aids in understanding this complex landscape. Although certain violent sports—American football, boxing, ice hockey, MMA, and increasingly Australian rules football and the major rugby codes—have become associated with the concussion crisis, they retain cultural popularity, economic benefits, and media attention. The centrality of violence in these sports may raise awareness of elevated TBI risks, but the investments in these sports afford stakeholders public platforms to downplay these risks. As this chapter illustrates, many responses to the TBI problem in sports often deflect or soften concerns about the neurological consequences of sports violence. Responses frequently involve incremental rule changes, evoking assumptions of athletes' willingness to expose themselves to TBI risks and engrained beliefs that bodily sacrifice is an inevitable aspect of athletic labor. Such narratives and practices work in the service of upholding the acceptance of violence as a source of mass entertainment.

In contrast to popular narratives, the materialization of widespread TBI in sports is not a series of isolated events. Rather, it is the outgrowth of a more complicated set of entanglements made up of corporate and economic relationships, cultural values, gendered norms, law and regulation, media narratives, scientific and medical infrastructures, and racialized hierarchies. Systems and structures—not simply individuals—make violent collisions possible and permissible in sports. These forces enable stakeholders to frame TBI as a necessary and manageable risk rather than as an indicator of the inherent problems with sports violence. In the next chapter, we explore how CTE has come to play a prominent role within narratives about the concussion crisis, discussing how diagnoses and scientific explanations of CTE aid in making some elements of TBI visible while masking other important considerations.

2

CTE and the Brains behind the Concussion Crisis

After retired National Hockey League (NHL) enforcer Todd Ewen died by suicide in 2015, media coverage speculated that he had chronic traumatic encephalopathy (CTE). The neurodegenerative disease had been identified in the brains of other hockey fighters and collision sports athletes, including some who had died by suicide. Yet when neuropathologist Lili Naz-Hazrati examined Ewen's brain in 2016, she did not diagnose him with CTE. Ewen had exhibited many symptoms associated with CTE, and reports stated he was "terrified by the thought of a future living with [the disease]." A lesson from Ewen's death, Naz-Hazrati told reporters, was that researchers were "still in the very early stages of understanding the disease" and that she hoped "people who have concussions won't kill themselves because they think they have CTE."[1]

That same year, NHL commissioner Gary Bettman cited Ewen's nondiagnosis when refuting connections between hockey and CTE. Echoing Naz-Hazrati and referencing lawsuits against the league, Bettman described Ewen's suicide as "the type of tragedy that can result when plaintiffs' lawyers and their media consultants jump ahead of the medical community and assert, without reliable scientific support, that there is a causal link between concussions and CTE."[2] A month after his statement, a group of US researchers published an editorial suggesting that sensationalized media coverage about CTE was responsible for Ewen believing he had an "an untreatable condition" and "commit[ing] suicide."[3]

In 2018, Boston University neuropathologist Ann McKee, the world's foremost scientific authority on CTE, reexamined Ewen's brain. In contrast to Naz-Hazrati, she confirmed a CTE diagnosis.[4] Ewen's wife, Kelli, responded publicly to the findings, saying, "People need to know that Todd killed himself because he had CTE." In March 2019, over sixty scientists published a letter calling for better "balance" in reporting about CTE, suggesting more media attention was needed on the uncertainties around the relationship between CTE pathology and lived symptoms. Rebuttals followed from scholars criticizing the letter's overemphasis on uncertainties around CTE causation and inattention to conflicts of interest within CTE research.[5] In April, Kelli Ewen filed a wrongful death lawsuit against the NHL. The lawsuit culminated in a 2021 settlement but did not put an end to overarching CTE debates.[6]

Controversies around CTE highlight a friction between constructions of science as a cautious, slow-moving institution and the tragic immediacy of athletes' deaths. Such controversies can be divisive and involve contested findings, competing claims of scientific authority, and conflict-of-interest accusations. Questions about causation emerge at the heart of this tension: Do concussions or nonconcussive impacts cause CTE? Is CTE pathology responsible for the cognitive and psychological decline of athletes with histories of brain trauma? The answers to these questions engage foundational scientific distinctions between correlations and causes of disease. In this chapter, we explore how the representations of athletes and their brains are central to constructions of CTE and the concussion crisis more broadly. We then consider controversies around the science and scientists contributing to the CTE knowledge base and how the resulting tensions inform contemporary responses to the concussion crisis.

THE SCIENCE BEHIND CTE IN SPORTS

CTE is defined scientifically as a "neurodegenerative disorder associated with exposure to head trauma."[7] The neurodegeneration characteristic of CTE is produced by the abnormal accumulation of a microscopic protein called *tau* in specific parts of brain cells (neurons and astrocytes) located in cortical folds deep inside the brain. In a healthy brain, tau protein supports fragile parts of cells to promote brain function. If brain cells become damaged by trauma, tau can detach from one cell and become entangled with other cells. These irregular tangles impair brain activity and induce cell degeneration.[8] Research indicates that the development of abnormal tau is likely not a result of isolated incidents of concussion but is associated with cumulative exposure to frequent head impacts (concussive and nonconcussive) over time.[9]

Individuals diagnosed with CTE have experienced symptoms that include cognitive impairments and dementia, but also psychological issues, including emotional dysregulation and depression.[10] Scientists stress the difference, however, between CTE neuropathology (sometimes called CTE-Neuropathologic Change) and the clinical symptoms associated with the disease.[11] This distinction reflects how CTE diagnoses are exclusively conducted through postmortem examinations of brain tissue. Currently, symptoms alone are deemed insufficient to confirm a CTE diagnosis, with no reliable scientific methods to detect CTE pathology in the brains of living people.[12] Thus, athletes experiencing relevant symptoms cannot verify the presence of CTE pathology in their brains while they are alive.

CTE is sometimes misunderstood as a scientific discovery made in response to sports' contemporary concussion crisis. Yet research into the long-term consequences of repeated brain injury among athletes dates back over one hundred years, with landmark findings published throughout the twentieth century.[13] This longer history foreshadowed the more recent rise in scientific interest in CTE. Between 1998 and 2008, fifty-one scientific articles on CTE were published. By 2019, there were 913 more—an over 1,600 percent increase in just over ten years.[14] This immense growth was largely sparked by the work of forensic pathologist Bennet Omalu, who documented the first cases of CTE in American football players. Omalu initially detected CTE in the brain of retired NFL offensive lineman "Iron" Mike Webster. Webster had died of heart failure in 2002, having experienced severe cognitive problems in his final years. As depicted in the film *Concussion*, Omalu soon identified CTE in the brains of other retired players who had died after experiencing psychological problems.[15] These cases garnered widespread media interest and reignited debates about the neurological risks of playing football.[16]

These cases also prompted the expansion of the scientific infrastructure around CTE, with new research centers established to study the disease. Most notably, the Boston University (BU) CTE Center was founded in 2008, along with its own bank of donated brains. Formed out of a partnership with the United States Department of Veterans Affairs (VA) and the nonprofit advocacy group the Concussion Legacy Foundation (CLF), the VA-BU-CLF Brain Bank (now called UNITE) has become the largest repository of athletes' brains in the world. It is the source of most CTE diagnoses, which are based on examinations performed by McKee. Approximately two-thirds of published studies on CTE in brain tissue have come from BU, including two sets of benchmark findings that have become significant touchpoints in the concussion crisis: a 2015 study identifying CTE in the brains of eighty-seven of ninety-one deceased NFL players and a 2017 study diagnosing CTE in 110 out of 111 NFL players.[17]

CTE research has since grown internationally, showing how concerns about the disease have transcended the US. Research centers and brain banks have been established in Canada (2010), Australia (2018), Scotland (2018), and New Zealand (2019). The Canadian Concussion Center (CCC) in Toronto has become the second-largest lab devoted to the study of sports TBI. The Australian research center has examined athletes from the country's various football codes, identifying CTE in dozens of brains from donors.[18] In Scotland, the Glasgow Brain Injury Research Group has launched the Football's Influence on Lifelong

Health and Dementia (FIELD) study using tissue from the Glasgow Traumatic Brain Injury Archive. The FIELD study has shown that neurodegenerative diseases, including CTE and Alzheimer's, are more likely to be found in the brains of deceased professional soccer players and international rugby players than in nonplayers.[19]

CTE's ascendence as a globalized concern comes with questions about the severity of the threat that sports pose to athletes' brains. Importantly, not everyone who experiences repetitive brain trauma develops CTE. Accordingly, most athletes, especially those without noticeable symptoms, do not have their brains donated and are not included in CTE studies. As such, high rates of CTE often emerge because of selection biases: most of the brains in these research samples are from athletes who have experienced symptoms, which makes a CTE diagnosis more likely. These circumstances make estimating CTE prevalence among athletes a difficult task. Statistical analyses accounting for selection biases have estimated the lowest possible prevalence of CTE among NFL players to be somewhere between 9 and 15 percent, which many experts consider an unacceptably high level of probability.[20] It is challenging, though, to extend these estimates to other levels of American football (collegiate, high school, or youth) or other sports.

Scientists still seek answers for why some individuals with histories of brain trauma develop CTE and others do not. Some studies point to career duration as a major factor in determining CTE risk; athletes with longer sports careers expose themselves to more impacts over more years.[21] Other research has investigated genetic characteristics that may predispose individuals to CTE onset and more severe outcomes, but conclusive evidence is lacking.[22] As we explain in chapter 5, CTE has almost exclusively been diagnosed in men. In fact, 2023 marked the first CTE diagnosis in a female athlete: Heather Anderson, a former Australian Football League Women's (AFLW) player and medic with the Australian Army who died by suicide at twenty-eight years of age.[23] Accordingly, women athletes have been encouraged to donate their brains to diversify CTE research.

The inability to diagnose CTE in living people is an obstacle for growing the evidence base. Such a breakthrough would enable more reliable connections between lived symptoms and underlying pathology. It would also support efforts to better track disease progression, provide opportunities to more definitively identify risk factors, develop methods for early detection, and explore treatments to slow disease progression.[24] Scientists are, however, making strides toward developing such a test using advanced neuroimaging techniques or detecting biomarkers in blood, saliva, or cerebrospinal fluid.[25] In the meantime, the development of CTE pathology remains largely hidden from scientific scrutiny until a person dies and their brain can be examined under a microscope.

Athletes' brains are thus central to scientific investigations into the disease and media coverage about such findings.

REPRESENTATIONS OF CTE WITHIN CONCUSSION CRISIS NARRATIVES

Media coverage of postmortem CTE diagnoses has made the disease a focal point of concussion crisis narratives. These accounts have also provided the disease with a distinct visual profile.[26] The reliance on postmortem examination means that visual depictions of CTE are largely limited to photographs of dissected brain tissue (fig. 5). Cross-sectional images that display the degeneration induced by CTE are often contrasted side by side with images of a "normal" brain. Other common representations of CTE involve microscopic photographs in which the tangles of tau protein appear as dark blotches made visible through chemical staining. Both types of images are sometimes accompanied by labels and arrows directing viewers' focus to regions of the brain where damage is most severe or areas of the microscope slide where tau is most dense. These scientific mappings are given meaning through explanations linking degeneration in specified brain regions to cognitive impairment, emotional disorders, and deviant behaviors. The images do not speak for themselves but are instead made persuasive through expert narratives that tell audiences what CTE looks like.[27] The repetition of such imagery across media discourses helps make the disease recognizable to nonexperts. The ubiquity of these images also cements neuroscience as the dominant site of knowledge production within concussion crisis narratives: concerns about TBI are most legitimate when the source of athletes' decline is revealed inside the brain.

Yet CTE's emergence as a defining component of the concussion crisis has been facilitated by more than neuroscientific knowledge. Media stories narrating the deaths of high-profile athletes diagnosed with CTE have also shaped public understandings of the disease. While Mike Webster's CTE diagnosis in 2005 prompted concern about the disease in the United States, it was the 2012 suicide of Hall of Fame NFL linebacker Junior Seau that intensified fears about the neurological aftereffects of American football. Seau was diagnosed with CTE in 2013 and became the most famous football player diagnosed with the disease. Seau's death was a focus of renewed media coverage calling the NFL's inaction on TBI into question.[28] As we discussed in chapter 1, the 2011 deaths of popular hockey enforcers Derek Boogaard, Rick Rypien, and Wade Belak—all of whom were subsequently diagnosed with CTE—inspired reflection about fighting's place in Canada's national game. CTE diagnoses in Graham "Polly" Farmer and Shane Tuck generated a wider recognition of CTE in Australia—including a 2023 Senate inquiry into sports-related brain trauma.[29] Farmer, who died in his eighties, was the first Australian rules football player diagnosed with CTE in 2020, followed

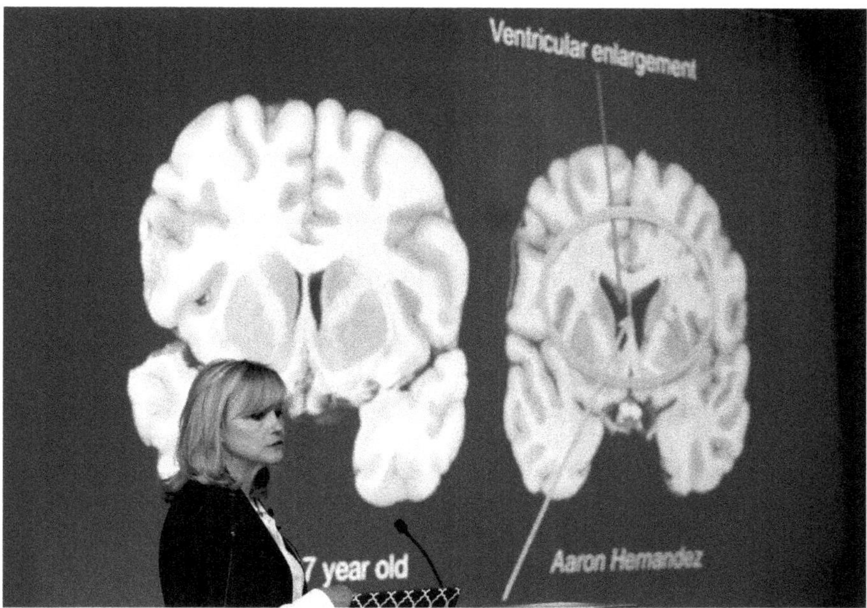

FIGURE 5. Ann McKee of Boston University describing the degenerative brain disease identified in the brain of former NFL star Aaron Hernandez following his death (Steven Senne via
Getty Images).

by Tuck, a retired Australian Football League (AFL) player who died by suicide
that same year, when he was only thirty-eight years old.[30]

Whereas scientific knowledge is often produced without acknowledging the
identities of research subjects and specimens,[31] "putting a face to the brain"
contributes affective dimensions to CTE. CTE diagnoses are publicized in the
aftermath of athletes' deaths that typically come with outpourings of rever-
ence for the deceased. The deaths of celebrity athletes are indeed already cultural events involving media tributes, memorial ceremonies, and other forms of
public mourning.[32] CTE diagnoses expand the emotional narratives of athletes'
afterlives; they emerge as sad stories of sports figures who became victims of an
unforgiving disease.[33]

Popular narratives around Seau's death depicted his legacy as transcend-
ing his athletic achievements and as representing broader social ideals. For
example, sportswriter Ryan Phillips remembered Seau as "gregarious, charm-
ing, fun-loving, dedicated and, above all, kind. He was the perfect example of
all that could be good in the American experience."[34] Such characterizations
noticeably clash with reports of Seau's CTE diagnosis, in which family members
described a process of psychological decline leading up to his death. These portrayals not only point to the purchase of CTE as a neuroscientific explanation

for behavioral changes but they also provoke emotional responses to an admired athlete's demise.

Tributes similarly followed the deaths of Boogaard, Rypien, and Belak, which highlighted how each player's reputation as hard-hitting tough guys was not representative of their demeanor off the ice. For example, Rypien was called "a good kid with a huge heart" whereas Belak was labeled "the sweetest, most gentle guy ever."[35] Comparable characterizations were made after the death of Ewen, whom reporters described as a compassionate person who wrote children's books after he retired. Like representations of Seau, media stories following a CTE diagnosis contrasted these admirable traits with alarming depictions of behavioral changes. One report disclosed that the usually sociable Belak became increasingly introverted and irritable over time, also showing signs of memory loss. Ewen was susceptible to bouts of confusion while developing aggressive and antisocial tendencies in the years leading up to his death.[36] These representations supported a burgeoning storyline showing many enforcers to be willing yet conflicted participants in the spectacle of hockey violence. As Belak's wife, Jennifer Belak Liang, asserted, Wade "didn't love [fighting], but he was fine with it [because] he wanted to stay within the NHL and have his career." CTE diagnoses in these cases provided unsettling evidence of the toll exacted on men whose dangerous work sustains the NHL's brand of violent entertainment. These layers of meaning demonstrate how the brains behind the concussion crisis do not speak for themselves but are most persuasive in their biographical and cultural contexts.

Many media narratives place neuroscientific explanations of CTE within profiles about athletes living with dementia and other psychological difficulties. For example, a news story about fifty-nine-year-old former AFL player Greg "Diesel" Williams describes him as "one of the toughest and most uncompromising centres to ever play the game." Yet Williams acknowledges he "can't remember much of his life," including his wedding, the births of his children, and major events in his football career. He attributes these issues to CTE; the article supports his claim with quotations from medical experts.[37] These stories about dementia in athletes invite feelings of disbelief and sadness from media audiences because they disrupt memories of sports heroes as embodiments of health and strength. This emotional framing intensifies when stories show athletes experiencing cognitive decline in their forties or fifties—often not far removed from their playing days. Such portrayals stand in stark contrast with more familiar representations of dementia in much older people.[38] As such, neuroscientific conceptions of CTE and cultural understandings of dementia come together in the way media audiences witness the struggles of former players.

Scientists and other commentators have criticized media for exaggerating scientific findings and failing to sufficiently account for uncertainties around CTE.[39] Some critics also contend that emotional representations of athletes' lived experiences detract from balanced assessments of CTE risk.[40] They worry media have perpetuated "an agenda of one-sided headline news and [a] sensationalized state of fear" around CTE, which can negatively impact athletes' mental health or discourage sports participation.[41] However, such critiques do not sufficiently situate CTE narratives within broader sports media landscapes. CTE coverage is consumed in the context of sports media's default portrayal of sports violence as normal and acceptable. By encouraging audiences to critically reflect on their enjoyment of sports violence, CTE stories can serve as important counternarratives within a sports media industrial complex typically intertwined with the interests of sports organizations. A journalist we interviewed reflected on this tension in connection with the NFL, saying "The league's [public relations] edifice is enormous, and they always have a bigger megaphone or a bigger platform for whatever they want to say . . . so the degree to which there is any sort of agenda on the part of [reporters] who might cover [CTE], it's in reaction to that."[42] Tracing the corporate and economic connections underlying media narratives and scientific research is indeed essential for understanding the framings of CTE.[43]

QUESTIONS OF ETHICS AND THE MANUFACTURING OF DOUBT

Prominent concussion crisis narratives revolve around the negligent and sometimes deceitful practices of professional sports leagues. Mistrust of these organizations largely grew out of investigative reports about the NFL, including the noted 2012 documentary, *League of Denial*, which exposed how the league's refusal to acknowledge a link between football and CTE was clouded by their active concealing and manipulation of scientific evidence. These revelations contributed to the NFL's reputation as a large institution profiting from the damaged bodies—and brains—of its players. The movie *Concussion*, player lawsuits, and US congressional hearings into football-related brain trauma have solidified this image of the league.[44] The NHL, AFL, and major rugby organizations have also been accused of intentionally downplaying the long-term TBI risks associated with their respective sports.

The notion of denial looms large within these narratives. During court proceedings that culminated in a 2018 concussion settlement by a group of retired professional hockey players, the players' lawyer referred to the NHL as "the new league of denial."[45] In Australia, a 2022 news article profiled former AFL players with severe memory loss, who chided the league for doing "everything it can to deny, deny, deny" that its brand of football has a TBI problem.[46] Within these claims, scientists skeptical of CTE's relationship to sports TBI are sometimes labeled "CTE deniers," presumed to be receiving compensation from sports organizations tainting their research. In contrast, experts endorsing the link between CTE and sports-related brain trauma are celebrated as defending scientific truth and fighting corporate corruption.[47] One review of *Concussion* describes the movie as documenting "the heroic struggle of Dr. Omalu to force the corporate goliath that is the NFL to 'tell the truth.'"[48]

These polarizing depictions of denial and truth-seeking fail to capture more subtle tactics sports organizations use to downplay the dangers of CTE. Leagues have generally moved beyond straightforward rejections of CTE risks, instead attempting to "manufacture doubt" about the magnitude and probability of these risks.[49] This manufacturing of doubt involves leagues and aligned experts strategically emphasizing scientific uncertainty, particularly what is *not yet known* about a sport's relationship to CTE. This tactic helps leagues deflect criticism and defend themselves in concussion lawsuits; they can ward off calls for accountability by characterizing existing evidence as inconclusive and asserting the need for more research before such measures can be pursued. Doing so effectively requires the mobilization of like-minded scientists to support these claims. Accordingly, many statements casting doubt on the relationship between CTE and TBI have been made by scientists funded by or affiliated with sports organizations.[50]

Such direct ties between scientists and sports organizations raise important concerns regarding conflicts of interest. Sports organizations engaged in these practices are most commonly compared to tobacco companies that funded studies disputing the link between smoking and lung cancer in the 1950s and 1960s.[51] While the NFL is most frequently likened to "Big Tobacco" for sponsoring research disputing the connection between American football and CTE, this label has also been applied to the AFL and NHL to convey distrust of their stances on TBI issues.[52] Accordingly, critics have expressed alarm over sports industry pledges to sponsor scientific research on CTE in response to legal and public pressure.[53]

These issues also surround perhaps the most influential scientific body in sports TBI: the International Concussion in Sports Group (CISG). The CISG is an international collective of TBI experts that has been widely criticized for its ties to major sports organizations.[54] The group hosts a conference every four years to assess the state of research on sports TBI and produce the Consensus Statement on Concussion in Sport. The Consensus Statement, first published in 2002, is an overview of scientific and medical knowledge that informs concussion guidelines for sports organizations and clinicians.[55] In addition to receiving funding from sports associations such as the International Olympic Committee (IOC) and soccer's Fédération Internationale de Football Association (FIFA),[56] thirty-two of the thirty-six members of the CISG expert panel had formal connections to sports leagues and governing bodies affected by the TBI issue, including the NFL, NCAA, NHL, and AFL.

Public scrutiny of the CISG intensified in 2022 when its cochair, Paul McCrory, was accused of at least ten counts of plagiarism in academic publications about sports TBI. McCrory was lead author of four consensus statements and had written several commentaries minimizing the dangers of CTE in contact sports.[57] The misconduct allegations led to nine of McCrory's articles being retracted and forced him to resign from the CISG.[58] McCrory's resignation sparked international media coverage, raising further questions "about the quality of evidence behind some concussion policies."[59] In Australia, these concerns had direct resonance given McCrory's close ties to the AFL, which some have framed as compromising the league's concussion protocols while stifling CTE research involving former players.[60]

The CISG has a history of producing sport-friendly viewpoints on CTE. The 2012 Consensus Statement, the first CISG report to mention CTE, emphasizes that the disease has an "unknown incidence in athletic populations" and that "a cause-and-effect relationship has not yet been demonstrated between CTE and concussions or exposure to contact sports."[61] The updated 2017 Consensus Statement repeats this conclusion. These assertions support the broader manufacture of doubt around CTE and have provided sports organizations with an authoritative source to draw on when downplaying CTE risk. Consider, for example, NHL commissioner Gary Bettman's proclamation of no "causal link between concussions and CTE" following Todd Ewen's 2015 death. He has repeated this assertion in response to subsequent criticisms of the NHL's handling of TBI.[62] Similarly, the NFL had long claimed that the connection between TBI and CTE was "unproven"—a link that the league later acknowledged in 2016.[63] By the time the NFL conceded a connection between American football and CTE, officials involved in the AFL, NHL, and professional rugby had publicly questioned the cause-and-effect relationship between CTE and TBI.[64]

The CISG's stance has prompted criticism. In 2021, an interdisciplinary group of seventeen scholars—including one of the authors of this book—called the CISG's process "narrow, compromised, and flawed" and advocated for more "complete, candid, and unbiased" consensus statements.[65] The group proposed a more thorough vetting process and disclosure of members' conflicts of interest, the inclusion of experts from critical social sciences and humanities disciplines, and additional assessment of consensus documents by independent reviewers. These recommendations have since been echoed in commentaries questioning the CISG's biased selection of experts, exclusion of more critical academic disciplines, and overall lack of transparency.[66]

These findings of overlapping corporate and scientific networks have supported demands for greater integrity and accountability in TBI research. While there are troubling connections between sports organizations and some researchers, the commitment to eliminating conflicts of interest still constrains the range of social responses to CTE. The emphasis on ensuring scientific integrity, while necessary, can risk reinforcing neuroscience as the dominant source of evidence about CTE. Doing so suggests that restoring scientific objectivity provides clear pathways to uncovering definitive neuroscientific proof of CTE causation. This assumption, however, overlooks two key insights. First, there are multiple, competing scientific standards for determining causation. CTE skeptics can strategically cite established scientific principles to undermine reasonable claims of disease causality and thus delay action to reduce the occurrence of sports TBI. Second, while neuroscience supplies important concrete representations of the embodied consequences of TBI, an overemphasis on neurobiological causation can sideline crucial public health and social science evidence that can improve sports safety. A closer look at debates surrounding CTE causation illustrates these shortcomings.

PURSUING AND DEBATING CTE CAUSATION

Until recently, CTE's connection to sports TBI was typically described in the scientific literature as an association rather than causation.[67] This foundational scientific distinction represents the difference between (1) recognizing that many athletes exposed to repetitive head impacts through sports have had CTE develop in their brains; and (2) determining that there is strong enough evidence to conclude that such exposure *is what causes* the development of CTE. Environmental health expert Adam Finkel and neuroscientist Kevin Bieniek outline how debates about CTE causation tend to revolve around three primary questions: is it possible to definitively rule out other possible causes of CTE beyond brain trauma? What is the likelihood that exposure to head impacts will result in CTE? Is there conclusive evidence that CTE pathology is responsible for athletes' experiences of cognitive and psychological decline?[68] The answers to these questions have high stakes. Proving that CTE is caused by exposure to brain trauma through sports could strengthen arguments for public health interventions, government regulation, and legal action against sports organizations.

Like media representations of CTE, a perception of polarization pervades scientific debates. Many experts have expressed growing confidence of a causal link between sports-related TBI and CTE. They argue that current evidence, while imperfect, is sufficient to justify drastic action to reduce the occurrence of brain trauma in collision sports.[69] Other commentators reject this perspective by referencing factors that they maintain demonstrate substantial uncertainty around CTE causality. For instance, skeptics often criticize the quality of scientific evidence behind causal arguments, citing biases in the selection of brains used in landmark CTE studies.[70] Some studies claim to have found CTE postmortem in people with no histories of brain trauma.[71] Some researchers propose factors other than TBI as leading to CTE onset, such as genetic predispositions, normal aging, and the use of alcohol, performance-enhancing drugs, or opioid painkillers.[72] Beyond questioning the source of CTE pathology, critics contend it is unclear how much CTE contributes to cognitive or psychological problems since the disease sometimes co-occurs with other neuropathologies associated with similar symptoms.[73] While these arguments have been refuted in subsequent research, they remain influential in casting doubt on assertions of certainty around CTE causation.[74]

These seemingly polarized positions emerge in part from applications of established scientific principles. The CISG, for example, has highlighted that its refusal to endorse CTE causation is informed by the Oxford Levels of Evidence criteria. The Oxford criteria rate randomized controlled trials (RCTs) and longitudinal cohort studies as producing the highest levels of research evidence because they involve experimental comparisons with a control group or measure outcomes in large groups of people over long periods of time.[75] As such, the Oxford criteria would stipulate that most CTE findings come from "lower-quality" methods such as case series reports and retrospective case-control studies, which lack a control group or longitudinal designs. The CISG thus insists that claims about CTE causation should not be made without definitive results from higher quality studies. This logic, however, sets an unrealistic standard of evidence for a disease as complex and dangerous as CTE. It is unreasonable to rely on knowledge gained through RCTs given their reliance on comparisons between experimental and control groups. Such an experiment could entail unethically subjecting individuals to repetitive TBI for the purposes of systematic comparison to an unexposed group.[76] Even other experimental designs favored by the Oxford Levels of Evidence, such as longitudinal cohort studies, can be inadequate for addressing many public health issues because they demand long-term research during which an urgent health problem remains unresolved.

A public health approach to CTE follows an alternative understanding of causation. Finkel and Bieniek point out that RCTs and other longitudinal studies generate knowledge that helps clinicians establish causation at an *individual* level—that is, to gain a better understanding of the development of CTE in a specific athlete's brain or how much CTE influenced that specific athlete's behavior. In contrast, public health experts are concerned with risk at a *population* level: a substantial rate of CTE among collision sports athletes warrants intervention even if causation cannot be conclusively established in every case.[77] Such an approach does not mean public health burdens of proof are lower or less rigorous than other standards of evidence. Rather, a public health understanding of causation serves different purposes: to mitigate health risks across a population by decreasing exposure to *the most probable cause* of a health problem.

The logic follows that the consequences of leaving a health issue unaddressed are far worse than the perceived costs of intervening too quickly. Advocates for a public health approach to CTE tend to apply the precautionary principle, which requires undertaking reasonable measures to reduce the occurrence of TBI even without absolute certainty of the mechanisms or thresholds that initiate CTE onset.[78] The precautionary principle has informed calls for stronger regulation to reduce the number of head impacts in elite sports, placing limits on collision sports participation for children, and eliminating headers from youth soccer.[79]

The conflicting standards of evidence within CTE debates illustrate how causation is not a monolithic concept.[80] Recognizing varying understandings helps explain how overly narrow conceptions of causation maintain influence in undermining recommendations for protecting athletes' well-being. Arguments that manufacture doubt still draw on scientific values. Calls for more conclusive evidence from longitudinal studies or RCTs typically draw from the tenets of evidence-based medicine (EBM), a school of thought advocating for medical practice to be informed by systematic application of the best available scientific or clinical research. The Oxford Levels of Evidence used by the CISG, for example, are a foundational document in the EBM paradigm.

Evidence-based medicine is often celebrated as a gold standard. Yet EBM represents a form of "epistemological imperialism" through which proponents exercise control over what counts as acceptable evidence.[81] The CISG is largely comprised of scientists who follow the tenets of EBM, the rigid application of which negates other research approaches that might be valuable to CTE debates. The types of studies favored by EBM can also encourage the involvement of sports organizations in the research process. Large-scale longitudinal studies of sports TBI are expensive, sophisticated endeavors that are difficult to execute without substantial funding and access to athlete data supplied by major sports organizations. It is perhaps not surprising that some of the most heralded long-term studies of athletes' neurological health, including NFL-LONG[82] and the NCAA-Department of Defense Grand Alliance CARE Consortium, have been developed through partnerships between CISG members and sports organizations.

Importantly, the institutional dominance of EBM means that experts working within this framework are likely to perpetuate its principles when evaluating knowledge about CTE, irrespective of whether they have formal ties to sports organizations or are advocates for sports participation. Indeed, we spoke with an injury epidemiologist who emphasized that he has little personal investment in sports culture but is still skeptical about CTE's relationship to collision sports. He asserted that his views on CTE stem from following methods for determining the best available evidence.[83] Adherence to a specific scientific paradigm, not simply loyalty to an organization or affinity for sports, can thus guide conclusions about CTE causation.

Debates about CTE causation therefore remain at a crossroads. In 2022, an interdisciplinary group of researchers published a report asserting that they "have the highest confidence in the conclusion that [repetitive head impacts] *cause* CTE."[84] The authors make this conclusion after applying the Bradford Hill criteria for disease causation, an alternative to the Oxford criteria used by the CISG. They contend the Bradford Hill criteria are better suited for understanding CTE causation since they were specifically developed to assess the relationships between disease and environmental or occupational risks. Their adherence to the Bradford Hill criteria thus follows a conception of repetitive brain trauma as an environmental or occupational hazard, meaning that exposure comes from "external" societal, lifestyle, or work-related factors (e.g., participation in a sport or being a professional athlete) rather than "internal" factors or genetic predispositions. The authors affirm that "the Oxford criteria were developed for clinical decision making, not for determining causation for environmental exposure." In other words, the principles of EBM are best suited for creating guidance on how to treat individual patients, not for managing the threat of health hazards to a given population. The report was published only a few months after the US National Institutes of Health (NIH) updated their official guidance on CTE to acknowledge a causal link between the disease and repeated blows to the head.[85]

Concussion crisis narratives have indeed shifted to reflect an appreciation of a causal connection. In the 2023 Australian Senate hearings on TBI in contact sports, for example, AFL general counsel Stephen Meade stated that his organization acknowledges that "there is an association between head trauma and neurodegenerative disease, including CTE."[86] Meade then asserted that the AFL "supports and adopts" the conclusions of causation established by the NIH. This statement represented a major change in the AFL's position, which had previously, with McCrory's guidance, questioned the causal link. This shift in thinking prompted AFL rule changes to limit brain trauma, such as reducing the number of tackles in training sessions.[87]

Yet influential stakeholders continue to question scientific findings on the grounds of remaining uncertainties. Earlier in the same 2023 Australian hearings, Sharron Flahive, the chief medical officer for the National Rugby League (NRL), stated, "There is an association with repeated head trauma, but we won't know how strong this association is, and we don't know what type of head trauma this involves—the medical evidence is not clear." Representatives from Sports Medicine Australia similarly explained that their position on CTE would evolve with updated guidance from the CISG, which has since published a revised 2023 Consensus Statement.[88] In that statement, despite stronger statements on CTE by the NIH and other experts, the new CISG only tentatively conceded that it is "reasonable to consider" that exposure to repetitive head impacts is "potentially associated" with the onset of CTE. The group again criticized the quality of evidence produced by existing studies, stating that establishing a causal connection would require "well-designed case-control and cohort studies" that account for potential confounding variables.

As the CISG Consensus Statement will likely remain an influential document informing TBI guidelines and policy, uncertainty appears to persist as a resource for CTE skeptics. Given the centrality of neuroscience in conceptualizing CTE, it makes sense that uncovering neuroscientific proof of causation would present a breakthrough for justifying improvements to athlete safety. This narrow definition of causation, however, has a twofold effect: (1) it enables a prolonged pursuit of scientific certainty that can delay meaningful public health action; and (2) it overlooks valuable insights into the sociological origins of CTE.

CTE BEYOND NARROW CONSTRUCTIONS OF CAUSATION

Having public health action hinge solely on neuroscientific conceptions of causation is an imperfect solution that limits possibilities for confronting TBI-related harms. This emphasis, although providing important scientific knowledge, can obscure how athletes experience repetitive TBI in contexts that shape the manner and aftermath of their exposure. A focus on social conditions reveals how CTE is not only caused by repetitive brain trauma but is also an outcome of the sports cultures that permit and celebrate violent collisions. Such a focus shows how TBI and CTE are not isolated outcomes but are intertwined with other sports-related harms.

Consider, for example, how painkilling drugs are cited as an alternative source of CTE pathology. The idea that drugs could contribute to neurodegeneration among athletes first surfaced in public discourse through the NFL's official response to Webster's diagnosis in 2005.[89] Opioid painkillers have subsequently been cited as potentially complicating CTE's link to TBI given their common use among athletes and capacity to induce neurodegeneration among heavy users.[90] Some athletes diagnosed with CTE have indeed struggled with the use of prescription painkillers.[91] Yet this framing of drug use as an alternative source of CTE disregards how the disease is extremely rare in individuals without histories of TBI and overlooks that CTE pathology can be distinguished from neurodegeneration associated with opiate use.[92]

The conceptualization of TBI and opioid use as isolated or conflicting variables in determining CTE causation negates what their coexistence suggests about collision sports: that the normalization of sports violence results in athletes' bodies being routinely and severely damaged. A growing number of players describe suffering from overlapping effects of chronic pain, extensive opioid use, and repetitive TBI throughout their careers.[93] While a possible link between painkiller use and CTE is often suggested to exonerate sports organizations from responsibility for athletes' neurological decline, such arguments in fact further implicate sports organizations because they reveal how sports violence impacts athletes' bodies and lives in multiple debilitating ways.

A reoriented focus on the collective embodied consequences of sports violence would help address these overlapping harms and not depend on scientific certainty about CTE causation. These sociological insights offer important reminders of how cultural norms and social structures should be targets of intervention alongside biomedical approaches. But how are these debates shaping public health and regulatory responses to TBI? Chapter 3 examines areas where TBI regulations have been developed in an influential cultural context: youth sports.

3

Protecting the Children

In their 2011 book, *The Concussion Crisis*, health journalists Linda Carroll and David Rosner declared that TBI in children represented "a silent epidemic that had been exploding right under our noses."[1] Pointing to emerging science, the authors argued that hits typically dismissed as little "dings" or "bumps on the head" needed to be taken more seriously to protect children from neurological problems.[2] Neurosurgeon Robert Cantu's book *Concussion and Our Kids* was published the next year and explained "why children are vulnerable" to TBI by highlighting their underdeveloped brain structures.[3] This neuroscientific foundation would connect concussion crisis narratives to scientific theories of childhood brain development, but also ideas about children's inherent vulnerability.

This conception of a concussion crisis in youth sports created a larger cultural dilemma: it challenged the assumption that sports are healthy activities for kids. Sports are celebrated as promoting positive character development alongside health and social benefits for children.[4] Public concern about TBI unsettled these beliefs by casting doubt on the seemingly intrinsic good of sports participation. Youth sports organizations began addressing these concerns by implementing concussion protocols and rule changes. The cultural impact of the concussion crisis intensified, however, when scientists and advocates began recommending that youth limit their participation in popular collision sports, such as American football, hockey, rugby, and Australian rules football, or seek noncontact alternatives. Other scientists and commentators rushed to defend the safety of these activities, offering more conservative assessments of TBI risk and emphasizing the presumed benefits of youth sports. They argued that restricting children's sports participation could result in health and psychosocial problems more serious than TBI, such as obesity or depression.

This chapter explores how competing conceptions of children's vulnerability to TBI pervade concussion crisis discourses. Theories of child development underpin these claims: children—and their brains—are constructed as sites of *vulnerability and possibility* that must be carefully managed.[5] Across these debates, commentators often invoke a figure of "the child" that is most valued for what it might become.[6] These narratives construct "the child" as a symbol of vulnerability in need of protection to preserve its future potential. "The child" as a signifier, however, is not static or universal: it can carry multiple, often conflicting, meanings.[7]

Debates about TBI risk in youth sports revolve around contrasting claims about what is best for children's development, health, and future selves. Concussion crisis narratives tend to present simplistic portrayals of "the child," glossing over distinctions across youth experiences shaped by systems of class, gender, and racism. As such, the symbol of "the child" in concussion crisis discourses occupies an unacknowledged social position that normalizes whiteness and socioeconomic privilege as default attributes.[8] Closer attention to social differences overlooked in concussion crisis discourses reveals how intersecting inequalities are important for understanding notions of TBI risk and vulnerability in youth sports.

YOUTH SPORTS AND RESPONSES TO TBI RISK

Sports can be a source of regular exercise for kids, provide spaces for cultivating physical skills, and instill self-confidence and the value of hard work.[9] They are commonly promoted as ways to address social problems. Sports programs are frequently conceived as providing positive social development for low-income and so-called "at-risk" youth by curbing antisocial and delinquent behavior among young people.[10] Youth sports can also, however, reinforce harmful gender ideologies, encourage violence, and reproduce social inequalities while being sites of abuse and injury risk.[11]

Approximately 1.1 to 1.9 million sports concussions occur annually among youth under the age of eighteen in the United States. This estimate likely underrepresents the total incidence of TBI, since many concussions go unreported or undiagnosed.[12] Neuroscientific research has specified a combination of anatomical and neurophysiological factors that make children especially vulnerable to TBI.[13] Compared to adults, children have larger, heavier heads relative to the rest of their body and weaker neck muscles that make them less capable of withstanding the biomechanical forces that cause concussion.[14] Young people's developing brains are likely prone to damage from impact and less suited for repair than mature brain structures.[15] These attributes can make TBI outcomes more severe among young athletes and can mean that young people take longer to recover from concussion than adults.[16]

It is widely documented that young people experiencing subsequent impacts following concussion are susceptible to exacerbated symptoms, increased recovery times, and in rare instances long-term neurological impairment or death—a condition known as Second Impact Syndrome.[17] Concussion management strategies for youth athletes therefore emphasize immediate removal from play, reduction in physical and cognitive activity during the initial stage of recovery, then a gradual, monitored return to school and sport as symptoms subside.[18] Guidelines typically indicate that most youth athletes recover from concussion within two to four weeks, though some individuals experience symptoms for several months or longer.[19]

Some scientists are concerned that exposure to head impacts at younger ages might disturb brain development even when concussion symptoms do not occur.[20] Neuroimaging suggests that exposure to head impacts through sports, even over a relatively short time period, can alter children's neurophysiology and may negatively impact long-term sensory or cognitive function.[21] For example, studies have shown that changes to brain microstructures can materialize after only one season of youth tackle football.[22] Chronic traumatic encephalopathy (CTE) has been diagnosed in the brains of athletes who died before the age of thirty—findings that align with research demonstrating a link between CTE and younger first exposure to head impacts.[23] Yet—and this is similar to divisions among CTE researchers that we outlined in chapter 2—some studies have challenged these results, not observing similar age-related effects.[24]

The emphasis on biological features of children's brains informs a "pediatric concussion discourse" that merges broad and specific notions of childhood vulnerability.[25] The more specific construction of vulnerability is unique to TBI and built on precise neuroscientific conceptions of children's developing brains. At the same time, the pediatric concussion discourse invokes broader understandings of childhood innocence that position youth as inherently vulnerable to a vast assortment of societal threats to their well-being.[26] This "double vulnerability" manifests through clinical practice, public health campaigns, and government legislation that stress not only children's vulnerability to TBI, but also adults' responsibility for protecting young people.[27] Echoing this pediatric concussion discourse, responses to TBI risk in youth sports leverage cultural, medical, and scientific norms to make claims about children's vulnerability. While these influences can align to inform interventions that improve sports safety, experts and advocates sometimes pit these norms against each other in competing arguments. As such, these debates often involve clashing conceptions of vulnerability and contrasting justifications for protecting children. These contradictions manifest themselves across institutional approaches to addressing youth vulnerability to TBI and how much they seek to transform sports.

The most conservative responses to the concussion crisis in youth sports have involved the promotion of protective equipment. Helmets for collision sports, including American football and hockey, are a focus of many prevention efforts. There are over thirty certified models of youth football helmets available in the United States that are subject to laboratory testing and ranked annually for their ability to "provide a reduction in concussion risk."[28] The tangible benefits of wearing the highest-ranking—and often most expensive—helmets remain matters of debate. It is well-established that helmets offer strong protection against the *linear* forces of impact to the head that cause skull fractures and severe TBI.[29] Current helmet models, however, cannot fully prevent concussions because they do not adequately mitigate the *rotational* strain of brain tissue inside the skull. This crucial limitation means that helmets are similarly not well-suited to protect athletes from concussion or repetitive nonconcussive trauma.[30] While researchers and manufacturers continue to work on designs that address this flaw,[31] parents, guardians, and coaches must navigate a competitive marketplace of imperfect products all promoted as improving children's safety. Even if improved models consistently reduce TBI risk, socioeconomic inequalities will influence who can access increasingly expensive helmets.[32] Perhaps most importantly, though, helmets do not involve drastic changes to how collision sports are played.

Helmets are intermediary measures; they allow a sport's rules to remain unchanged and do not require taking the collisions out of collision sports. Better helmets also help preserve a sport's culture of violence. As discussed in chapter 1, organizational responses to the concussion crisis have largely focused on managing the consequences of violent acts in sports rather than confronting the systemic promotion of sports violence as acceptable. Helmets are another example of this trend. The NFL has been a strong advocate for helmets as a TBI prevention strategy, which allows the league to uphold its violent brand of football.[33] Equipment manufacturers similarly benefit from the preservation of these masculine values. Perceptions that football is violent and risky help position their products as providing necessary protection from these dangers.[34] Adopting helmets as a mode of concussion prevention may acknowledge children's vulnerability to TBI exposure through collision sports but it also constructs this vulnerability as manageable.[35]

Sports organizations have also proposed changes to athlete training techniques and game rules to make physical contact safer. The most notable example of such a strategy comes again from American football. Heads Up Football, a partnership between the NFL and USA Football, is a program that teaches young players to tackle without using their heads to create impact.[36] Designed to eliminate dangerous helmet-to-helmet collisions, this approach reflects long-standing practices in other collision sports, such as rugby, where shoulder-first tackling is a standard technique. Some studies, including those commissioned by USA Football, have suggested that Heads Up Football training can reduce concussion rates. Other investigations dispute the program's effectiveness, though, with commentators also questioning the conflicts of interest reflected in the NFL/USA Football partnership.[37]

In 2023, World Rugby lowered the allowable tackle height from the shoulder to below the sternum.[38] The logic for this rule change is straightforward: dropping the point of impact between tackler and ball carrier would reduce the number of direct hits to the head and decrease concussion rates. Like Heads Up Football, World Rugby's recommendation relies on athlete education and compliance in executing the "safer" tackles in fast-moving game situations. Like better helmets, these sports-led initiatives aim to address vulnerability to TBI through relatively minor adjustments that possibly mitigate—but do not eliminate—the dangers of repetitive collisions. These efforts not only concede that tackling is the primary source of TBI risk, but they also frame tackling as essential to each sport. TBI management is thus conceived as a matter of youth behavior modification while the sport itself remains largely unchanged.

In addition to engaging in industry-sponsored proposals for technological improvements and technical adjustments, governments have enacted legislation designed to protect children from the most catastrophic outcomes of TBI. Provincial governments in Canada and their state equivalents in the United States have passed laws mandating strict return-to-play protocols and facilitating concussion education for athletes, their parents, and coaches. A primary feature of such legislation is to require youth athletes to receive medical clearance following TBI to ensure full recovery before resuming play. This measure aims to reduce the risk of longer-term complications, neurological damage, or death from Second Impact Syndrome. The first of these laws, the Lystedt Law, was ratified in 2009 by the State of Washington, and by 2014 all fifty US states and Washington, DC had passed similar legislation.[39] In Canada, the province of Ontario implemented Rowan's Law in 2019, with rules requiring those involved in youth sports—for example, athletes, coaches, and parents—to review standardized concussion awareness resources. The province introduced removal-from-sport and return-to-sport protocols in 2022.[40]

These laws are built around neuroscientific understandings of the fragility of underdeveloped young brains and ideas about children needing adult protection. Indeed, concussion legislation typically tasks adult observers, including coaches, referees, and sideline medical staff, with identifying and responding to potential incidents of TBI. The focus on adult responsibility assumes young athletes might be unable to recognize TBI symptoms, be unwilling to remove themselves from play, or lack knowledge about the potential severity of brain injury.[41] These laws also symbolically enshrine specific conceptions of innocence when they are named after young athletes who experienced severe brain injury or died playing a collision sport. Zackery Lystedt was thirteen years old in 2006, when he sustained a concussion during a football game but was allowed to return to play. He collapsed at the end of the game, underwent emergency brain surgery, and lives with permanent neurological disabilities.[42] Rowan Stringer was a seventeen-year-old rugby player when she died mid-game from Second

Impact Syndrome in 2013.[43] In explaining her support for Rowan's Law, Ontario member of provincial parliament Lisa McLeod invoked notions of childhood innocence when she emphasized the tragedy of Springer's death, calling her a "beautiful little girl" who had a "bright future."[44] Stringer's femininity intensifies her story, as young girls are typically understood to be more vulnerable than boys, especially when participating in sport. These and stories from other jurisdictions humanized calls for concussion legislation by depicting heartbreaking scenes when the innocence of youth sports was shattered by a catastrophic—and preventable—injury.[45]

Such appeals are not uncommon: many laws and policies promoted as protecting innocent children and people from violence contain direct references to individual victims.[46] Such references construct an idealized victim whose specific circumstances and identities come to represent a broader, more complex issue.[47] These kinds of namesake laws, according to communications scholar Kate Wood, can misrepresent the range of children who experience violence. They tend to honor white, middle-class youth as idealized innocent victims but do not afford Black, Brown, and First Nations youth the same status.[48] Black children, especially Black boys and young men, are often excluded from societal presumptions of innocence and victimhood because they are understood as potential threats and perpetually "at risk" of pursuing criminal activities.[49] For Black children, supposedly universal childlike behaviors, including play, are subject to surveillance and policing. These norms are epitomized by the 2014 death of Tamir Rice, a twelve-year-old African American boy who was shot and killed by Cleveland police officers in 2014 while playing with a toy gun in a park. In contrast, the visibility of Lystedt and Stringer associates the concussion laws with a childhood innocence primarily ascribed to white children.

Whiteness masks how intersecting inequities affect patterns of youth injury. As discussed in chapter 1, adult athletes of color often accept TBI risks to pursue opportunities associated with a career in collision sports. This apparent self-selection into dangerous sports occurs at increasingly younger ages and is often a response to racial discrimination and socioeconomic disadvantage. However, social forces that may contribute to a child's exposure to TBI rarely emerge in narratives about the concussion crisis in youth sports. These discourses instead remain grounded in idealized notions of play as inherently innocent, pleasurable, and outside the influence of structural violence. As games studies scholar Aaron Trammell asserts, to understand "play as mere pleasure is a privilege, a privilege afforded to white people."[50] There is indeed a glaring need for more complex conceptions of how TBI risk is intertwined with social constructions of vulnerability and wider patterns of violence in society. Interventions should thus account for how social inequities influence young people's experiences of TBI and aim to address structural conditions that increase the likelihood of brain injury.

While concussion laws represent important strides for preventing severe outcomes of TBI in youth sports, they are largely reactive in nature and do not confront the institutionalization of violent play. These interventions align with training guidelines and helmet technologies in how they shift responsibility for children's safety onto coaches, officials, parents, and even young athletes themselves. In doing so, concussion laws shift responsibility away from the sports organizations promoting and profiting from youth sports.[51] It is perhaps unsurprising, then, that the NFL has publicly supported the Lystedt Law in the United States.[52] The legislation supports noticeable changes in how concussions are managed on football fields and encourages athletes to rethink playing through injury. However, the impression that these laws and other league-approved interventions make football "safer than ever" allows the sport's larger culture of violence to go mostly unchallenged.[53] More radical positions on eliminating TBI from youth sports have questioned this logic but have not yet been uniformly embraced.

THE CHALLENGES OF REFORMING SPORTS TO COUNTERACT TBI RISK

Some sports organizations have addressed TBI risk at youth levels by eliminating or drastically reducing behaviors likely to cause head impacts. In 2015, US Soccer banned headers for children under ten and implemented restrictions on headers in practices for youth between eleven and thirteen years of age. The new rules were announced as part of a "sweeping youth soccer initiative designed to improve concussion awareness and education" that resolved a pending lawsuit against the organization.[54] Football Australia, in contrast, has yet to implement a similar ban, with some national experts in sports medicine depicting such restrictions as unnecessary and detracting from young players' skill development. Opponents of a proposed heading ban have questioned the evidence linking headers to neurocognitive problems and have argued that learning heading skills at young ages is required to promote safe headers in older age groups.[55]

In Canada, similar debates exist around bodychecking in hockey. Hockey Canada raised the minimum age for bodychecking for boys from eleven to thirteen years of age in 2013.[56] Subsequent research demonstrated that this change resulted in a substantial (up to 64 percent) reduction in diagnosed concussions within the under-twelve age group.[57] These findings align with research showing that bodychecks are the primary mechanism of concussion in boys' hockey. This trend is not observed in girls' and women's hockey owing to bans on bodychecking—which are informed by enduring stereotypes about the inherent fragility of female bodies.[58] The suggestion that female bodies need extra protection reflects a harmful gender norm, but the change resulting from it can have practical health benefits. Studies indicate that girls in nonbodychecking leagues incur significantly fewer head impacts than boys of the same age playing in leagues with bodychecking.[59] A 2023 review has since concluded that the direct connection between bodychecking and TBI rates necessitates raising the minimum age again for boys from thirteen to fifteen.[60] Another study recommended that bodychecking should not be permitted until the age of eighteen, which the authors argue could reduce the total number of concussions in Canadian youth hockey by 88 percent.[61]

Whereas heading in soccer and bodychecking in hockey are traditional but arguably not essential elements of their respective sports, there have been attempts to reduce head impacts in sports in which collisions are understood as "fundamental" parts of the game.[62] A group of British academics and health professionals has called for tackling to be removed from rugby played in schools.[63] Their recommendation highlights that many schools in the United Kingdom include contact rugby in physical education classes starting at the age of eleven.[64] Recognizing that most rugby TBI occurs during tackles,[65] these experts contend that such a dangerous activity should not be part of school curriculums and advocate for a noncontact alternative. As their message focuses specifically on rugby in educational contexts, they have not suggested the removal of tackling in extracurricular rugby, as it assumes minors have chosen to participate, with their parents consenting to associated injury risks.[66]

Advocacy groups and lawmakers have similarly called for a delayed introduction of tackle football in the United States, where children can begin tackling at the age of five. A growing number of state representatives have introduced legislation that would ban tackle football for children under the age of twelve.[67] Although failing to gain significant traction, the proposed laws align with the Concussion Legacy Foundation's (CLF's) recommendation that children play noncontact flag football until the age of fourteen. The CLF's "Flag Football Under 14" campaign asserts that "a child's body is not designed for tackle football," citing young people's developing brains, weak necks, and head size as factors that make youth especially vulnerable to brain trauma.[68]

While drawing on observations about children's physical development, justifications for these rule changes also encourage shifts in cultural understandings of TBI risks. The most prominent adoption of this tactic is a campaign called "Tackle Can Wait." Its public service announcement (PSA) portrays young football players during a game, casually smoking cigarettes given to them by their coaches and parents.[69] As the boys smoke, a young voice declares, "Tackle football is like smoking. The younger I start, the longer I'm exposed to danger." The voiceover is followed by text stating, "Kids who start tackle at age 5 vs. 14 are 10 times more likely to get the brain disease CTE"—a claim based on research showing that a longer football career is associated with a greater likelihood of CTE diagnosis.[70] The PSA garnered much attention for comparing football to an unhealthy behavior.[71] The comparison reinforces a contradiction of the

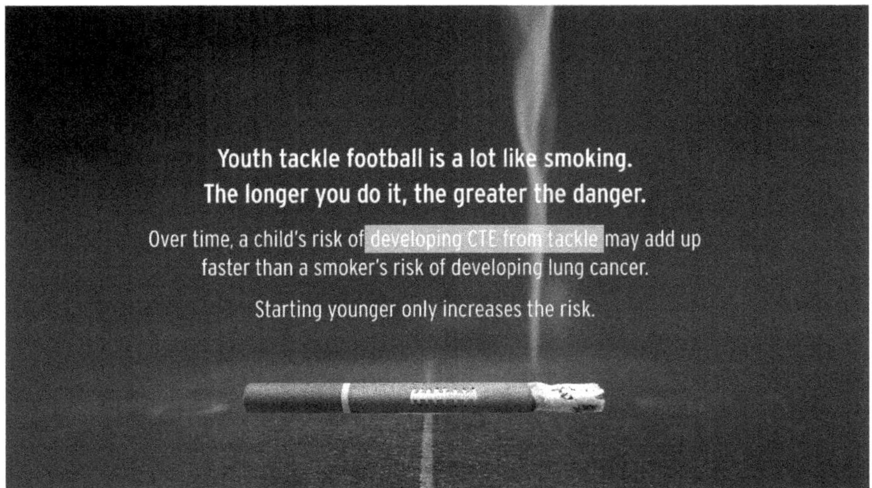

FIGURE 6. The Tackle Can Wait PSA paralleling tackle football risks to the risks of cigarette smoking (screen capture by author).

concussion crisis: that sports perceived to be healthy can in fact be detrimental to health (fig. 6).

Despite its powerful message, the PSA reproduces the dominant pediatric concussion discourse by positioning parents, rather than social or sports institutions, as primarily responsible for children's safety. A final question from the PSA's young narrator explicitly targets parents: "You wouldn't let me smoke, so why should I start tackling?" The Flag Football Under 14 website confirms, "As parents, you deserve to make an informed decision about your child's future health." There is no mention within the PSA of possible interventions beyond parental decision-making to hold youth football organizations more accountable for the negative effects of violent play.

The Tackle Can Wait PSA drew most of its criticism for equating an addictive, widely stigmatized behavior with a sport strongly associated with health and fitness. Neurologist Steven Broglio, for example, asserted that while "it would be imprudent to suggest football participation carries no risk for concussions or other injuries, the PSA falls short by drawing a parallel to smoking, which carries no known health benefits."[72] Broglio's statement is one example of how experts and stakeholders refute calls to reduce or prohibit youth participation in collision sports by affirming that the health benefits of participation offset potential TBI risks. Their arguments are largely grounded in scientific conceptions of risk that construct children as subject to multiple vulnerabilities that can be measured and assessed. Yet such evaluations also draw on conflicting cultural assumptions about health and its relationship to youth sports. Concussion and obesity emerge through these debates as competing health crises threatening young people.

YOUTH HEALTH CRISES AND THE FLATTENING
OF RISK IN SPORTS

Defenders of youth tackle rugby and football commonly justify their stance by citing multiple ways that young people benefit from sports participation. Such benefits include regular exercise, strength-building, and increased physical awareness; improved mental health and self-confidence; development of self-discipline and the ability to overcome adversity; and the cultivation of teamwork and leadership skills.[73] Most prominent among these justifications is the documented connection between physical activity and the prevention of poor health outcomes such as high blood pressure, diabetes, cardiovascular disease, and osteoporosis.[74] The presented risks emerge firmly situated within stated concerns about child obesity, accompanied by warnings that a decline in youth sports participation will only further encourage physical inactivity and sedentary lifestyles.

Such logics construct hierarchies of risk that position obesity and physical inactivity as an urgent health concern, with concussion as a lesser risk accompanying sport. A 2018 editorial written by a group of neuroscientists offers one such example. The authors warn against policies restricting participation in risky sports, describing such proposals as problematic given that "our society is perhaps the most sedentary ever, with obesity rates exceeding one-third of the young population."[75] Pediatric sports medicine physicians James MacDonald and Gregory Myer similarly write, "for many kids, sports are the only thing that will get them away from smartphones and off the couch."[76] MacDonald and Myer continue, "it is generally more dangerous for youth to be sedentary than to risk injury playing sports."[77] In 2016, neurosurgeon and NFL advisor Robert Harbaugh lamented the decline in youth sports participation, concluding, "The crisis of childhood obesity—unlike the mythical concussion crisis—is real and of great magnitude." These statements tend to characterize TBI risks in youth sports as significant but largely overblown. Many of these arguments mirror CTE discourses explored in chapter 2 that emphasize how scientific bias, ideological motives, and sensationalized media coverage promote misleading perceptions of the dangers of collision sports.[78]

While advocates for youth collision sports cite research and media bias as reasons to dispute the existence of a concussion crisis, they do not apply the same levels of scrutiny when describing the crisis of childhood obesity. Indeed, the certainty with which some advocates identify obesity as the greatest danger to children's health conflicts with critical scholarship that has questioned the cultural and scientific assumptions underlying this so-called epidemic. Assessments that foreground physical activity as the ultimate method to prevent child obesity discount the many intersecting factors that influence health: food and housing insecurity, geographic environments, poverty, racism, and other systemic inequalities.[79] Moreover, moralizing calls for kids to get "off the couch" and into sports frame good health as a product of personal choices without acknowledging the cultural and socioeconomic barriers that make physical activity inaccessible for many youth.[80] Although some supporters of youth collision sports highlight disparities in access to physical activity opportunities, they do not extend this analysis to consider how such inequalities impact health in other ways. In doing so, they ignore extensive research revealing how obesity crisis narratives stigmatize fatness and are informed by classist, gendered, and racialized stereotypes about what counts as a healthy body.[81] In short, a simplified conception of childhood obesity pervades many assessments of TBI risks.

Many narratives about the benefits of youth collision sports also emphasize how participation promotes young people's psychological and social development—for example, the cultivation of self-confidence, emotional intelligence, improved mental health, leadership skills, and perseverance.[82] Many of these sports-related benefits are framed as future-oriented; that is, they relate to what children might or might not become in terms of their health, social status, and even career success. For example, a survey of US surgery department chairs found that respondents (almost all of whom were men) played tackle football at higher rates than the general population.[83] The authors interpret these findings as indicating that exposure to TBI through sports *does not necessarily prevent* players from achieving prestigious jobs requiring high levels of cognitive performance. The analysis, however, has significant limitations: it does not consider other socioeconomic factors influencing career achievement; it reflects a selection bias in its pool of survey respondents; and it offers an ambiguous and largely speculative conclusion using professional success as a health indicator. Commentaries have since cited these findings as evidence of an even bigger claim: that collision sports participation *promotes* future professional achievement and socioeconomic success.[84]

Some advocates also muddle differences between lower and higher risk activities to defend youth collision sports from criticism. A *Nature Reviews Neurology* editorial compares concussion rates across twenty-five sports to show that TBI occurs in many noncollision and noncontact sports. The authors use this data to demonstrate how concussion risk is not exclusive to collision sports, decrying calls for "a selective ban on American football" as politically motivated.[85] They justify a focus on concussion rates by dismissing concerns about repetitive head impacts that are unavoidable in collision sports such as football. By overlooking a danger specific to collision sports, this narrow analysis flattens disparities in TBI risk. The editorial again downplays differences between sports when it asserts that "all athletic activities carry risks, including the risk of concussion, but they also confer substantial benefits."[86]

A similar logic runs through a comparison of the benefits of youth team sports and the risks of CTE.[87] The commentary affirms that the "unequivocally positive impact" of team sports on youth should outweigh concerns about neurological risks that come with participation. Despite their central focus on CTE and their stated disappointment with movements to restrict participation in collision sports, the authors do not make clear distinctions between sports with varying levels of exposure to repetitive head impacts. Instead, they emphasize general benefits of participation *in any team sport* without addressing how differing levels of TBI risk might shift a risk/benefit analysis. Physician Alec Lerner and bioethicist Norman Fost noticed similar tendencies in a 2015 statement from the American Academy of Pediatrics that supports youth participation in tackle football. Lerner and Fost highlight how the statement describes the health and social benefits of youth sports but offers "no evidence that football is uniquely associated with these benefits" or that these benefits are "sufficient to outweigh the disproportionate risks of harm" that come with the sport.[88]

Even as they blur important distinctions between levels of TBI risk, the commentaries we have examined carry substantial weight because they are grounded in discourses of health and science. While these studies are usually authored by scientists and doctors citing quantitative or statistical data, their cultural dimensions are masked by the authority of seemingly objective analysis. For other supporters, however, the benefits of youth collision sports lie definitively in the cultivation of values specific to aggressive, hard-hitting play. These claims reveal the cultural and political basis for the defense of collision sports, which we discuss in more depth next.

THE CULTURAL POLITICS OF DEFENDING YOUTH COLLISION SPORTS IN THE FACE OF CRISIS

When supporters cite benefits specific to youth collision sports, these assertions typically revolve around how the experience of forceful physical contact builds character and inner strength. For example, the NFL's Play Football website lists seven benefits of tackle football, but only one is framed as a specific benefit of the sport's collisions. Tackling, the site affirms, helps children build resilience and teaches them how to "independently pick themselves up when things get challenging"—implying that recovering after being tackled is a metaphor for responding to other life challenges.[89] A blog post on the USA Football website is more direct in its assertion that "tackle football teaches toughness and aggressiveness" and "is not a soft sport." The blog explains that "there is a literal and figurative lesson being taught [through tackling]: When you get knocked down, you must get back up."[90] This type of support for youth collision sports blurs the promotion of positive sports values with the defense of sports violence. Through this blending of ideals, youth development becomes intertwined with fostering masculine strength and power.

Historical research has traced over a century of narratives celebrating collision sports as cultivating traits that promote boys' development into men: aggression, physical dominance, and masculine toughness.[91] These philosophies continue to shape support for youth collision sports in debates about TBI risk. Studies demonstrate how supporters of youth tackle football tend to identify with traditional ideas about gender, including a belief in binary gender differences, male superiority in sports, and the association of femininity and male homosexuality with weakness or deviance.[92] Narratives conveying resistance to rules designed to reduce head impacts in youth hockey often describe children who do not participate in collision sports as vulnerable to becoming emotionally fragile and physically weak—that is, feminized in ways that limit men's development or future success.[93]

Whereas TBI scientists have lamented how masculine ideals compel athletes to play through injury and underreport concussion symptoms, similar values around toughness and the determination to "get back up when you're knocked down" inform justifications for allowing collisions in youth sports. This contradiction is typically left unaddressed in scientific commentaries recommending that parents conduct their own risk/benefit assessments of their children's participation in collision sports. In fact, parents have reported being conflicted in making these decisions because their assessment is influenced by cultural factors beyond health and scientific findings, including community pressures, family dynamics, and wider social norms.[94] Similar factors shape many boys' choices of specific sports, as do expectations to conform to dominant gender ideologies linking manhood with aggression and physical strength.[95]

Corporate marketing practices and the cultural power of major sports organizations also affect decisions about kids' sports participation. For example, a 2017 poll showed that NFL fandom was a primary variable informing adults' support for youth tackle football.[96] The league sponsors community events and school-based physical educational programs to encourage long-lasting fandom among young people and families. These attachments to the NFL brand, in turn, have the capacity to shape perspectives on tackling and football safety.[97] These strategies are reflected in how the NFL has responded to falling participation in youth tackle leagues by investing heavily in flag football. Reports published in 2018 indicate that there were more kids playing flag football than were registered in tackle football programs.[98] The NFL has sponsored noncontact leagues in community recreation settings and distributes NFL-branded flag football equipment to students in schools.[99] The NFL also markets flag football as a more inclusive version of the sport and one more accessible to young women, who can play in girls' leagues or on mixed-gender teams.[100]

Yet tackle football remains the NFL's core product. The NFL's embrace of flag football can be considered the league's attempt to reimagine its player development pipeline as including tackle and noncontact youth programs.[101] This logic also reflects an assumption that boys who start out playing in flag leagues will transition into tackle programs as they grow older or at least stay invested in the collision version of the sport.[102] Sports Studies scholar Noah Cohan has highlighted how this assumption manifests itself in the marketing of flag football. Whereas advertisements show younger kids of all genders playing flag football, girls are far more prominent in promotional images of older players.[103] The relative absence of older boys in this material implies that they have moved on from flag football to play in tackle leagues. This gendering of flag football demonstrates how tackle is still pushed as the most appropriate version of the sport for older boys and young men, maintaining masculine norms and the violence of the sport.[104]

Other socioeconomic trends impact participation in flag and tackle football. We have discussed how young lower-income Black and Pasifika men in the United States are often drawn to tackle football, which can present an avenue for pursuing opportunities for education and social mobility that might otherwise be unavailable to them. Investigations have shown how lower-income Black and Brown communities, usually those with lower levels of educational attainment, have less access to flag football programs than white, wealthier ones.[105] Kids wanting to play football in these places are more likely to participate in existing tackle leagues, and the NFL has stated that they hope to address these imbalances through financial support for flag programs in these communities.[106] At the same time, however, the league's website emphasizes how tackle football offers young men opportunities for scholarships and educational advancement not available through flag football.[107] These trends, which are informed by systemic disparities, contribute to non-white, lower-income boys being disproportionately exposed to brain trauma through youth sports.[108]

While racial and social class inequities inform who plays tackle football, political ideologies also underlie participation trends. Support for youth tackle football in the United States is strongest among Republican voters, and rates of participation remain higher in traditionally conservative states than in politically liberal regions.[109] Journalists Dave Sheinen and Emily Giambalvo explain that debates around youth tackle football reflect "hallmarks of the larger political divide in America: competing definitions of patriotism, distrust in the media, the fetishization of military symbolism, the trust and distrust of science."[110] These ideological and demographic trends notably contrast with scientific commentaries that claim to denounce political motivations behind calls to restrict tackle football. Indeed, the landscape of youth tackle football and other collision sports is inseparable from cultural politics and social inequities. In chapter 4, we explore these dynamics as they influence TBI knowledge produced through partnerships between sports organizations and the military.

4

The Sport-Military Research Complex

In April 2022, neurosurgeon and NFL team physician Joseph Maroon gave a presentation on chronic traumatic encephalopathy (CTE) for the Vanderbilt University Sports Concussion Center lecture series.[1] After summarizing what he characterized as the limited evidence linking football to CTE, Maroon highlighted the character-building and physical benefits of tackle football. Referencing a slide titled "Football Intangibles," Maroon recounted how US Army General Douglas MacArthur had a plaque erected at the West Point military academy, which stated, "On the fields of friendly strife are sown the seeds that on other days and other fields will bear the fruits of victory." Extending MacArthur's celebration of sports' contribution to military training, Maroon stressed the important life lessons children can learn from participation in team sports. As Maroon's message captures broader understandings of the connections between sport and military values, the societal impacts of this sport-military nexus have come to inform conceptions of traumatic brain injury (TBI).

Let's revisit MacArthur's statement and its implications: it affirms the value of sports for "honing coaching and leadership skills, developing character and grit, and improving fitness" among soldiers.[2] Maroon's use of MacArthur's statement to illustrate the "intangible" benefits of football draws on the sport's history as a requisite activity in military academies starting in the late 1800s.[3] Football's inclusion as a component of military training in the United States overlaps with sport's historical role in the British school system as a method for preparing young men for military service. This approach to military training was exported throughout the British Empire to places like Canada and Australia.[4] For example, in 1900, Australian politician John Thomson explained the bravery of a young lieutenant by asserting how the officer was "prominent in all manly sports" and

63

that "there was no schooling that brought up a man for the battlefield equal to that."[5]

These histories reinforce how the values of athletic and military institutions are often intertwined.[6] This interconnection has manifested itself most visibly as a symbolic relationship: many sporting events serve as public spectacles of militarized nationalism involving the honoring of service members, military color guards carrying flags during national anthems, and warplanes flying over stadiums.[7] Sports also function as sites of military recruiting. The US Armed Forces have for years established a recruiting pipeline through high school and collegiate football.[8] The Australian and Canadian armies have similarly increased their visibility at community sporting events to support their recruitment efforts.[9] While the militarization of sports has a long history, this connection deepened after the attacks on September 11, 2001, and the ensuing "War on Terror." According to cultural studies scholar Samantha King, it marked a new moment of "sport/state synergy" with governments using sport to mobilize support for military action in Afghanistan and Iraq and sports organizations infusing military symbolism into marketing and merchandising strategies.[10] In the United States, the National Football League was foremost among these organizations. The league has widely incorporated military pageantry into its games and initiated military-focused philanthropic efforts (fig. 7).[11]

These spectacles normalize sport as a site for the promotion of wartime politics—even though such displays are presented as apolitical displays of patriotism.[12] Although most closely associated with former President George W. Bush's championing of the War on Terror, the US sport-war nexus continued through the Obama and first Trump presidencies.[13] Yet this symbolic relationship extends beyond US borders. For example, the Canadian government partnered with the NHL to rally support for its military operations in Afghanistan.[14] Across these contexts, the normalization of military spectacles in sports is intertwined with the broader resonance of a post-9/11 "warrior masculinity" built around the celebration of violence, compulsory heterosexuality, antiterrorist vigilance, and a willingness to consume the products of militarization.[15]

Sports and military combat are also linked by the substantial risk of TBI. The more than one hundred years of research into TBI among athletes has been mirrored by over a century of concern about brain injury among soldiers. World War I came with widespread incidence of "shell shock," a condition among soldiers who had sustained head wounds from explosive bombshells and subsequently experienced amnesia, confusion, headaches, and emotional instability.[16] While shell shock was first considered a direct result of brain damage, debates ensued about whether it was instead a type of neurosis or psychological trauma. Shell shock as a term had largely been retired by the start of World War II, yet soldiers continued to report cognitive and psychological difficulties after exposure to powerful artillery blasts. These experiences, identified as postconcussion syndrome, similarly

FIGURE 7. Military pageantry is a key feature of the NFL game experience (AP Photo/Ric Tapia).

sparked questions around their causation, as many of them could not be linked to observable damage in the brain.

TBI continued as a source of military injury into the twenty-first century. Narratives describing sport's concussion crisis through the 2010s came alongside pronouncements that TBI was the signature injury of post-9/11 combat.[17] Soon CTE was diagnosed in the brains of service members with histories of brain trauma and the disease's trademark neurocognitive symptoms.[18] The complex relationship between combat TBI and Post-Traumatic Stress Disorder (PTSD) has made tracing the neuropathological and psychological origins of reported symptoms challenging.[19] Despite these connections between sport and the military, veterans' advocates contend that the public concern around sport's concussion crisis has not extended to combat TBI. Former US Navy Seal Frank Larkin summarized this disparity when he asked the audience at the 2022 Brain Trauma Action Summit, "Do we have to put all our military suffering with TBI in NFL jerseys to get the attention this issue deserves?"[20] A week after he made these comments, Larkin published an op-ed, "Outrage over NFL Brain injuries; Silence over Military Brain Injuries," lamenting the "muted discussion" about service members' brain injuries compared with the "outpouring of concern" for NFL players.[21]

These parallels and discrepancies are the focus of this chapter. We explore the links between the treatment and understanding of TBI across sport and military contexts, acknowledging their connections, as well as their different treatment in public discourse. We first discuss how TBI emerged as a concern related to military action, and then consider how sport and military interests are entangled within TBI research. Given the centrality of the United States in shaping military TBI research, including notable partnerships across US defense and sport organizations, much of our analysis focuses on this national context.

THE SIGNATURE WOUND OF MODERN WARFARE

TBI is widely described as the signature wound of post-9/11 military combat, which is primarily associated with US-led missions in Afghanistan and Iraq.[22] Studies estimate that upward of 23 percent of American active duty service members have sustained mild TBI during Operation Enduring Freedom in Afghanistan and Operation Iraqi Freedom.[23] Research also suggests that nearly 450,000 US service members have sustained a TBI during these periods of conflict, with many reporting multiple TBIs throughout their military careers.[24] Australia and Canada also participated in "War on Terror" operations in Afghanistan, with notable rates of combat TBI documented among members of both countries' militaries.[25]

Early reports about TBI from these missions were primarily concerned with moderate and severe brain injuries involving loss of consciousness and immediate structural damage to the brain. Many of these injuries were caused by bullets, shrapnel, or flying debris from explosions that broke through helmets and penetrated the skull. "Mild" or concussive TBI initially received less attention. Yet these prolonged military operations came with increasing concern about the alarming rates of mild TBI among soldiers.[26] After documenting overwhelming amounts of moderate and severe TBI sustained during the War on Terror, NBC News proclaimed a "silent epidemic" of mild TBI among American military members.[27] Indeed, medical records indicate that over 80 percent of diagnosed TBI in the US military is classified as mild or concussive injuries.[28]

Scientific research has established how military TBI has distinct neurological characteristics since explosive blasts are the cause of most combat TBI. Blast-related TBI occurs when explosions generate immense waves of atmospheric pressure that damage the brain even without objects directly striking the body.[29] Increased rates of milder blast TBI largely stem from advancements in military body armor that have improved soldiers' chances of surviving devastating explosions but cannot fully protect the brain. In addition, hidden improvised explosive devices produce sudden, unexpected blasts that leave little time for soldiers to seek shelter from blast pressure waves.[30] Blast TBI can also result from pressure waves generated when soldiers fire shoulder-mounted weaponry.[31] Journalists and politicians have raised concerns about service members training with heavy artillery and being exposed to TBI before they reach the battlefield.[32] Our research confirmed these apprehensions; military leaders, scientists, and veterans, including those who left active duty because of TBI, expressed the need for strategies to reduce TBI risk during training exercises.

Mild TBI among service members has been associated with poor health outcomes. US studies show that affected military personnel have higher rates of prolonged physical and neurocognitive symptoms—for example, dizziness, headache, and memory problems—than those without a history of TBI. The same is true for functional disabilities, mental health difficulties, and suicidality.[33] Moreover, a study of over 350,000 US veterans found that TBI resulted in a twofold increase in dementia risk.[34] There is substantial evidence that repeated TBI exacerbates these effects.[35] CTE diagnoses in the brains of deceased military service members raise questions about how neurodegeneration might occur differently following blast TBI when compared to the higher frequency of repetitive impacts sustained by athletes.[36] Following calls for athletes to donate their brains for study after they die, campaigns like the Concussion Legacy Foundation's Project Enlist have asked military members to make the same pledge.[37]

Acknowledging the multiple and often concurrent injuries experienced by military members, the U.S. Department of Veterans Affairs maintains the Polytrauma System of Care, which is an interdisciplinary healthcare network with specialized rehabilitation services aimed at addressing TBI alongside other types of injury.[38] Recognizing the multifaceted nature of combat injury is crucial, especially since another distinct feature of military TBI is its strong connection to mental health conditions, particularly PTSD. The relationship between TBI and PTSD is complex because the two conditions can share similar progressions and symptom profiles.[39] The headaches, mood instability, memory issues, and sleep problems characteristic of both PTSD and TBI often develop over similar timelines. The relationship between PTSD and TBI is complicated further by the fact that blast TBI is often an emotionally traumatic experience involving jarring, unanticipated explosions and the maiming or death of other people.[40] In short, PTSD and TBI experiences among military members are often inextricably linked and can be difficult to differentiate in clinical settings.[41]

Researchers have sought to better understand the overlapping cluster of symptoms linking PTSD and TBI by pinpointing their neurobiological or psychological origins. Harkening back to debates about shell shock during World War I, there are conflicting theories about the source of symptoms attributed to PTSD and TBI.[42] Some studies suggest that damage to brain structures from TBI induce neurological changes that increase the likelihood of developing PTSD.[43] Conversely, other research demonstrates that many long-term psychiatric or cognitive symptoms attributed to combat TBI can often be explained by PTSD.[44] Some researchers warn that overdiagnosing military TBI and publicizing its prevalence might create unnecessary anxiety among service members with treatable mental health conditions[45]—a strikingly similar framing to claims made about the culture of fear around CTE, which we discussed in chapter 2. Others have pushed back against this logic, saying it downplays the risk of combat TBI and delegitimizes service members' experiences of brain injury.[46] The challenges in determining specific causes and effects point to the potential benefits of doing away with separate terminology for military PTSD and TBI.[47] Acknowledging how emotional and neurological trauma are often inextricably linked could inform more comprehensive care focused on improving veterans' overall well-being rather than treating isolated symptoms.[48]

Beyond considerations around PTSD, core military values influence how service members respond to TBI. Strong identification with norms of mission focus, self-sacrifice, and unit camaraderie make soldiers less likely to report TBI so they can remain in combat.[49] They may also believe that reporting a TBI could negatively impact their opportunities for advancement through military ranks.[50] These perspectives are interwoven with masculine norms that privilege aggressiveness and warfighting as idealized traits in military personnel.[51] Research highlights how TBI underreporting is shaped by the formation of military identities that value courage, mental toughness, and risk-taking.[52]

Athletes and service members share concerns about how TBI might keep them out of action and be detrimental to their careers, contributing to underreporting in both domains.[53] These similarities point to shared ideologies informing sport and military cultures—in this case, forms of masculinity enacted through bodies pushed to, and often beyond, their limits.[54] As this cultural commonality makes individuals in both contexts vulnerable to TBI, collaborative TBI research combines insights from sport and military domains to improve diagnosis and treatment in these violent settings.

TBI RESEARCH AND THE MILITARY-SPORT NEXUS

Australian, Canadian, and US governments all fund scientific research programs studying TBI in active-duty service members and veterans. The extended military campaigns waged by the United States since the early 1990s necessitated a medical response to a rise in TBI, which included the development of a national research infrastructure. In 1992, the United States Congress mandated the creation of the Traumatic Brain Injury Center of Excellence, a scientific research hub born out of collaboration between the Department of Defense (DoD) and Veterans Affairs (VA).[55] The DoD and VA also initiated the US$50 million Long-Term Impact of Military-Related Brain Injury Consortium (LIMBIC) in 2019, a nationwide network of TBI researchers led by Virginia Commonwealth University.[56] The 2022 Warfighter Brain Health Act required the DoD to launch an initiative dedicated to improving the diagnosis, prevention, and treatment of military TBI.[57]

One especially high profile TBI research collaboration is the DoD/NCAA Grand Alliance, which committed US$28 million to establish the Concussion

Assessment, Research and Education (CARE) Consortium in 2014.[58] The CARE Consortium brings together a national network of researchers to study TBI in college athletes and military cadets and midshipmen across thirty academic institutions. The research assesses TBI in men and women that occurred during twenty-six different military training exercises, sports, and recreational activities. It studies TBI over multiple time periods: the acute injury phase, intermediate stages that might signal early development of chronic effects, and longer-term outcomes. Consortium leaders have explained that the DoD/NCAA partnership is based on the "the realization that military service members, particularly military service academy students, share similar physical and demographic characteristics with NCAA student athletes" in that they are typically performance-driven, physically fit, and relatively young.[59] These commonalities are exemplified by the characterization of military cadets as "tactical athletes" who undergo rigorous fitness regimens similar to elite sports training programs.

Importantly, even with its ties to the DoD, CARE Consortium research does not involve active service members or veterans. The assumption that athletes and cadets share similar TBI experiences makes sense because military academy students are not yet in combat situations where they could be exposed to blasts. The most common causes of TBI in CARE Consortium research are from military training exercises and sports, making the mechanisms of injury across contexts relatively similar. This is a necessary clarification given the differences between the incidence and neurophysiology of TBI in sports as opposed to military contexts. Bodily movements within sports and military training exercises are relatively structured and typically produce a more predictable range of head impacts than those experienced in chaotic combat settings. The powerful pressure waves generated by explosive blasts, also induce neurophysiological responses that are distinct from brain trauma incurred in collision sports and military training.[60]

Despite these differences, much of the knowledge around military TBI has grown out of research on athletes.[61] Sport-military research partnerships are based on the notion that lessons learned about the diagnosis and treatment of sports TBI can be effectively applied to military contexts.[62] This knowledge transfer is largely built around the Sport as Laboratory Assessment Model (SLAM), which supposes that the structured nature of collegiate sport approximates the conditions of a controlled laboratory with unique opportunities to study the same group of individuals over time. Despite ethical concerns around the institutional pressures placed on college athletes to serve as research subjects,[63] findings from these settings are thought to produce rigorous, generalizable data about TBI symptoms and recoveries.[64] TBI diagnosis protocols developed through sports research have also been adapted for use by military organizations.[65]

Political economic ties and shared ideological assumptions underpin sport-military TBI partnerships. The NFL exemplifies these connections; the league's contributions to military TBI research are another dimension of its relationship with the armed forces. In 2012, the league partnered with the United Service Organizations Inc. to raise awareness about concussion among military service members.[66] A US Army Research Laboratory received a one million dollar, NFL-funded research grant in 2015 for the development of new military helmet technologies.[67] In 2017, the NFL awarded $US40 million to the US Army Medical Research and Material Command to fund research on diagnostic tools for TBI detection among soldiers and athletes.[68] These partnerships have been framed as part of the NFL's commitment to championing "independent medical research and engineering advancements" regarding TBI.[69] The NFL's chief medical officer, neurosurgeon Allen Sills, has explained the league's responsibility to share opportunities to advance TBI research with other domains, saying, "Most of the issues we face in the NFL are sport issues, and beyond that they are society issues."[70]

The NFL's support for this TBI research has extended the league's promotional and philanthropic relationship with the armed forces, fortifying the symbolic connection between football and military service. However, this manifestation of "sport/state synergy" goes beyond marketing, philanthropy, and scientific research. It also includes cooperation on the implementation of military technologies and strategies in civilian contexts. Sports sociologist Kim Schimmel has traced how marquee NFL events such as the Super Bowl and annual player draft have become sites for the deployment of military surveillance and securitization methods.[71] The immense scale and popularity of these events serves to justify the use of military tactics, surveillance technology, and weaponry in the name of public safety. Many of these logistical operations are developed through collaboration between the NFL, DoD, Department of Homeland Security, law enforcement, and private sector military contractors. This infrastructure typically remains in place after these one-time NFL events, with host cities retaining military-grade policing tools. The NFL's collaborations with defense organizations on TBI research is therefore intertwined with a larger set of political, economic, and operational structures that support the militarization of everyday life.

As outlined in chapter 2, the NFL's stake in TBI research and reputation for skewing results has sparked concerns about unavoidable conflicts of interest. Public health scholars Kathleen Bachynski and Daniel Goldberg have warned of the tension underlying the NFL's collaboration with the US Centers for Disease Control and Prevention (CDC), arguing the league's private agenda of maintaining the popularity and profitability of tackle football is incompatible with the center's mission to preserve public health.[72] The league's close promotional and economic relationships with military agencies should cast similar skepticism over its involvement in combat TBI research.

University sport practices reveal additional entanglements with the military. The NCAA, for example, has military academies as member institutions and these academies are primary sites for CARE Consortium research studies. Since 2005, the NCAA has held the annual Armed Forces Bowl in Fort Worth, Texas, with military contractors, including Bell Helicopter (2006–13) and Lockheed Martin (2014–present), as title sponsors.[73] These spectacles serve as recruiting tools that mask the violent realities of war: they use sport as a vehicle for promoting military expansion and defusing critiques of supporting policies.[74] The DoD/NCAA Grand Alliance for TBI research thus exists as but one part of a larger set of relationships between the military and sport in the United States.

These research partnerships manifest through the work of university faculty, students, and affiliated scientists within what education scholar Henry Giroux calls the *military-industrial-academic complex:* an alliance of military agencies, defense contractors, and university researchers and administrators.[75] Military funding contributes notably to university research with projects aimed at supporting the armed forces and defense industries. Universities have become prominent sites for devising ways to "wage war better" by supporting research for developing new military technologies and optimizing the performance of military personnel.[76]

Health science departments, for example, have become implicated through US military-funded research seeking improvements in health outcomes among military service members, including those injured in combat. Kinesiology research is similarly mobilized to enhance the training regimens of soldiers to prepare them for engaging in violent conflict.[77] While advancements in TBI rehabilitation among active military personnel and veterans are a benefit of such research, these programs support the broader functions of the military-industrial complex. Increases in military spending are further normalized when the transfer of university-generated knowledge to the armed forces is promoted as an unquestioned good. While allegations of conflicts of interest are a defining concern in the sports TBI landscape, it is similarly important to recognize how the military-industrial-academic complex constrains the focus of TBI research enabled through sport-military partnerships. In the next section, we explore how these dynamics extend into what feminist scholar Jennifer Terry describes as a "biomedicine-war nexus" in which medical advancements born out of the catastrophes of military combat are integrated into everyday life.[78]

BIOMEDICINE-WAR LOGICS AS ECONOMIES OF INJURY

The inevitability of injury is a common element of war and collision sports. Since severe or untreated injuries keep service members and athletes out of action, military and professional sport institutions have a vested interest in keeping their workforces healthy enough to remain productive. Both institutions rely on economies of injury that, to borrow from queer theorist Jasbir Puar, depend on making certain bodies "available for maiming."[79] The NFL's medical infrastructures, including the league's pain and TBI management strategies, prop up the "work machine" of professional football in which injury is normalized as an acceptable part of the game and health is defined primarily by an athlete's ability to return to play—often at the expense of long-term well-being.[80] Anthropologist Ken MacLeith similarly describes how medical rehabilitation practices sustain the violence of war by keeping laboring bodies "in motion" through, out, and often back into the throes of combat.[81] The embodied accumulation of injury and trauma experienced within this cycle, according to MacLeith, tends "toward the debilitation and exhaustion of military lives."[82] TBI is but one condition within these processes.

Ensuring the availability of military labor also involves the strategic framing of injuries as minor and manageable. Many public narratives of mild military TBI downplay its significance compared to other injuries. Take, for example, Iran's 2020 retaliatory missile strike on Ain Al-Asad airbase in Iraq, where US military units were stationed. Official statements from DoD and President Donald Trump assured the American public that no service members were killed or injured in the attack. The Pentagon, however, soon revealed that dozens of service members at the base during the airstrike were subsequently diagnosed with TBI.[83] President Trump characterized the injuries as "headaches" and "not very serious."[84] He then minimized the severity of TBI as "not bad," saying, "I have seen people with no legs and with no arms. I have seen people that were horribly, horribly injured in that area, that war . . . And I consider them to be really bad injuries."[85] Trump's statements reinforce common understandings of TBI as a less significant consequence of war when compared with the amputee veteran whose visible disability is often valorized as a marker of patriotic sacrifice.[86] His comments received criticism, though, as the number of troops diagnosed with TBI from the attack surpassed one hundred.[87] The Pentagon nonetheless declared that over 70 percent of those service members had returned to duty, evincing MacLeish's description of the military cycle of injury, rehabilitation, and redeployment.

Trump's dismissive comments came weeks after he signed a bill approving an unprecedented US$738 billion military budget in late 2019.[88] The timing of the expanded budget reveals tensions between the Trump administration's investments in the military-industrial complex and his public trivializing of TBI. Military-sponsored TBI research is conducted amid this tension. The US$50 million LIMBIC research network was also announced in late 2019, representing a modest contribution compared to the billion-dollar contracts awarded to military weapons and defense contractors. Although advancements in biomedical research have been an outcome of the Global War on Terror, investments in this work are a relatively small component of the economic machinery of war. While such commitments to biomedical research appear informed by an ethics of care rather than violence, advances in the rehabilitation of combat TBI are born out of the need to maintain laboring bodies to continue military operations.[89] Medical innovations gained through military-funded research are developed not only to improve health but also to support infrastructures that enable military violence. Although the subsequent expansion of this medical knowledge into civilian contexts may seem to justify the harms of combat, these health practices remain uncomfortably attached to war.

The resources afforded the biomedicine-war nexus influence whose bodies and brains become priorities in TBI research agendas. Financial support from the DoD and NCAA has allowed the CARE consortium to undertake the most comprehensive and longitudinal study of concussion in athletes and military cadets to date. In contrast, researchers working on issues related to women who experience TBI from intimate partner violence (IPV) have expressed frustration that they have significantly less funding, a concern we discuss further in chapter 6. Although there are scientists who recognize this gap in resources, only a few of them have openly questioned how evidence drawn from research with relatively young, healthy athletes and military trainees is supposed to be generalizable across social groups. Moreover, it is not clear how this research accounts for social inequities that influence TBI outcomes even within its target populations.

Consider, for instance, women who have military affiliations or are veterans. Female service members experience comparatively high rates of IPV over their lifetime. Over the course of our research, participants discussed these concerns, citing statistics that almost 20 percent of the women using US Veterans Affairs (VA) health services do so for IPV.[90] While these trends are likely not unique to the United States, there is notably limited research in other jurisdictions, including Australia and Canada.[91] As one expert explained,

> We need to understand the way in which IPV-related TBI may compound other stresses that are commonly experienced by women who have served in the military such as deployment-related TBI, combat, and military sexual trauma. . . . Clinicians and researchers should use caution when attributing symptoms solely to PTSD.[92]

She went on to explain that women veterans would benefit from access to polytrauma clinics "where they can get a comprehensive TBI evaluation and get treatment recommendations and referrals. . . . And we have many wrap-around services that come to bear, too, like evidence-based mental health interventions for depression and PTSD as well as homelessness services." These compounding considerations highlight a trade-off of the biomedicine-war nexus: while service members may have access to medical care that others do not, these privileges are tied to working in conditions where trauma and violence are prevalent.

Women veterans have acknowledged that VA services are designed to serve men. They have cited how their military experience is often questioned in such medical settings, or how VA services lack care facilities or experts that address women's needs. United States Marine Corps veteran Bambi Bullard stated in an interview that she realized "how dismissive the medical field was towards women vets. Active duty, reserve, it didn't matter what. When most people think of veterans, it's not a woman's face they see."[93] Despite improvements to VA provisions for women, many medical facilities had wards reserved for men, prompting one women veteran to ask, "So what do I do, stay at home and die while you find space?"[94]

Experiencing and seeking treatment for TBI is not isolated from these gendered conditions and the violence of much military work. Reflecting on her own experience with TBI, a former combat veteran explained, "I was hit by a roadside bomb," after which I "was feeling like I had to grovel at the feet of the VA, whether it was a specialist or neurologist, orthopedist, talking to them about needing the care I needed because of the traumas that I experienced." In the process of seeking treatment, additional dimensions emerged:

> And then I was not coping well with the experiences that I had in combat. I had internalized it, the multi layers of trauma, even that one little snippet with, like, all the sexual harassment and all the sort of innuendo and all the things—and the self-inflicted pressures I was putting on myself, and then the external pressures and the external traumas. I was a hot mess. And the VA's answer was to put more drugs on more drugs on more drugs. And suddenly I had this trash bag full of drugs. I was completely disconnected from my friends. . . . I was in a bad place. And I felt like I neither belonged to the military community, and I didn't belong in the veteran community, and I had no identity whatsoever. The military had ripped it from me.[95]

Her reflections capture entanglements of trauma that span brain-specific injury as well as interpersonal and institutional violence. Veterans who were men with TBI had similar stories, albeit not of the same gendered variety. One veteran described his experience as "so bad. . . . No one seems to understand me. I get no help [from the VA]. . . . I wish I had known this [would happen] before I enlisted."[96]

Military-sport research partnerships, such as the DoD-NCAA CARE Consortium, present more sanitized versions of these forms of violence. CARE Consortium research may examine mild TBI, but its focus on noncombat settings means that findings cannot encapsulate the intersecting layers of injury and trauma experienced in active service. This narrow focus, while offering insights into neurological processes of injury and recovery, circumvents important questions about how TBI experiences for service members and veterans are shaped by multiple forms of violence and social inequities. For example, CARE Consortium studies of biological sex differences in TBI outcomes cannot capture the gendered violence and discrimination experienced by the women quoted in this chapter. An approach more sensitive to the ways in which institutionalized violence influences TBI experiences would require examining inequities within the biomedicine-war nexus and how they impact the bodies harmed through military service. This type of investigation remains elusive across sport-military research partnerships embedded in the military-industrial complex.

INSTITUTIONALIZED INEQUITIES
SHAPING MILITARY TBI

So far in this chapter, we have focused on how the biomedicine-war nexus interfaces with TBI research agendas, including partnerships with sport. We have highlighted examples showing how the military-industrial complex relies on the labor of bodies that are perpetually damaged but honored as worthy sacrificial heroes; however, others also emerge as expendable in this calculus.[97] This distinction becomes visible when considering how these hierarchies reflect racialized inequalities that, for example, shape the experiences of non-white US military veterans and citizens in countries affected by US war campaigns such as those in Afghanistan and Iraq.

Military enlistment may promise access to education for people of color from lower-income communities or pathways to citizenship for immigrants, but it comes with the risks of injury, disability, and death. Recruitment strategies targeting lower-income communities frame the potential for social mobility as worth the risks that come with military service.[98] These appeals apply to both US military and football pipelines: for those with limited resources and few educational opportunities, both trajectories are represented as economically promising professions built on masculine heroics and risk-taking.[99] These similarities are pronounced in places like American Sāmoa where, as anthropologist Lisa Uperesa observes, American football and the military are seen as accessible pathways to a better life.[100] Data from the early 2000s indeed points to very high recruitment from Pacific Island territories under the jurisdiction of the United States; they were enlisting in the army at a rate nearly 2.5 times more than that of the US population in general.[101]

Absent from these narratives of social mobility are the persistent inequalities that characterize the treatment of those recruited into military ranks. A concrete example is the accessibility of VA medical facilities. Even though American Sāmoa and Guam are US territories with long-standing political and economic ties to the military, they lack full-service VA facilities. This concern not only raises questions about soldiers' postcombat care but also about a lack of data on TBI outcomes in these places. Available VA data already shows that service members of color are more likely to die from TBI and less likely to seek medical treatment. These trends are even more pronounced among veterans in US territories when compared to their mainland counterparts.[102] Although it is possible that these trends are spillover effects of inaccessible VA services, the minimal TBI-specific data from US territories means that the effects of inequitable patterns remain largely invisible within concussion crisis discourses.

Despite these disparities, there are biomedical systems to address the injuries of US veterans. Narratives promoting the contributions of the biomedicine-war nexus do not extend to include war-damaged Afghani and Iraqi people. During our research, we encountered limited concern and only passing mentions of TBI experienced by civilians in the places most devastated by the War on Terror. This pattern emerged during fieldwork and in reviewing the scientific literature on military TBI. There is little data on the incidence of TBI among civilians throughout the Afghan and Iraq wars. There has, however, been some documentation of civilian TBI in other Middle Eastern countries subject to US-led and supported military violence—for example, in Iran, Lebanon, Palestine, and Syria, including among children.[103] Much of this research concerns moderate and severe TBI that are sometimes fatal or require admission to hospital. In contrast, data for mild TBI is harder to produce given the limited resources for concussion reporting and treatment in many of these countries—a limitation exacerbated by damage and strain to healthcare infrastructure during times of conflict.[104]

Geopolitics underlie the discrepancies between the infrastructure for TBI among US service members and people living in war zones. People caught in the violent crosshairs of the US military-industrial complex are rarely recognized as victims and are almost completely absent from concussion crisis discourses of care extended to military service members.[105] In addition, long-standing observations of colonial power relations point to how these people are rendered as "others" not worthy of medical or political concern. Indeed, disability studies scholar Sona Kazemi situates these dynamics as reflective of imperial framings of a "global-southern body" that is framed as "one that is already dead, and thus a body on whom a full measure of care would be wasted."[106] The injured bodies of residents in war zones are thus easily ignored because their experiences of violence are represented as likely and even necessary collateral damage within military operations. The erasure of these bodies from conceptualizations of military TBI is part of the larger process of concealing the extent of the destruction perpetrated by military occupation and US imperialism.[107]

These and other interlocking systems of oppression underpin the concrete cases of TBI we have examined thus far in this book, even if they are not visible on the surface. In the chapters that follow, we look explicitly at instances of TBI not captured in popular discourses. We consider how advocates and experts have sought to raise awareness of these injuries and how power formations shape the discourses around them. Across these examples, state and structural violence influences how these different manifestations of TBI become features of concussion crisis narratives—if they do at all.

5

Advocating for Women

In December 2017, the US Department of Veteran Affairs (VA) announced it would actively recruit women as posthumous brain donors to advance the work of the National Posttraumatic Stress Disorder (PTSD) Brain Bank—an initiative later referred to as the Female Brain Bank. According to Carolyn Clancy, then the executive in charge of the Veterans Health Administration, the move would address the lack of female brains available for research. "In the past, the focus of TBI and PTSD brain research has primarily been based on male brains," she stated. "We have a lot to learn about how the female brain deals with TBI and PTSD, which makes this effort long overdue."[1] PINK Concussions, a non-profit organization dedicated to raising awareness about brain injury in women and girls, has highlighted several issues that the Female Brain Bank could help address: the underrepresentation of women in TBI clinical trials, differential rates of TBI among women compared to men, exclusion of female subjects from preclinical trials, and wider concerns about the quality of data on TBI in women and their health outcomes.

Support from high-profile athletes has bolstered awareness of these efforts. Briana Scurry, an Olympic medalist and the first Black woman inducted into the US National Soccer Hall of Fame, has been a long-time brain injury advocate after a career-ending concussion in 2010. In an interview, she recalls the profound effects of her injury: "My whole life changed from that moment."[2] Her concussion cascaded into debilitating symptoms, suicidal thoughts, trauma, and significant financial strain, with Scurry pawning her Olympic gold medals to pay rent. Scurry's story is similar to narratives from some NFL and NHL players, but it has not informed popular concussion crisis narratives in the same ways men's experiences have.

The comparative lack of attention paid to Scurry's experience, even though she is a known brain injury advocate and has testified before Congress, fits within the wider dominance of men's sports in media coverage. Other considerations influence public narratives, though. Consider Scurry's role in elite US women's soccer, which is a sport known for strategically appealing to white, middle-class conceptions of femininity.[3] Her position as a Black woman within this normative culture was apparent in media coverage of the national team's World Cup championship in 1999. Her game-saving performances were overshadowed by teammate Brandi Chastain's championship-winning penalty kick and her now-iconic shirtless celebration.[4] The images of Chastain solidified the link between US women's soccer and white, middle-class femininity, with Scurry often portrayed as testament to her white teammates' inclusiveness.[5]

These dynamics carried over into appeals to address TBI among women. When Chastain pledged to donate her brain to CTE research in 2016, Scurry remained relatively absent within reports, even though she had also pledged to donate her brain. Chastain's pledge was heralded as a "courageous act that will ultimately improve the future health of female athletes, military veterans, and other women who experience repetitive brain trauma."[6] Other former US women's national soccer team players, including Megan Rapinoe and Abby Wambach, have subsequently announced their intention to donate their brains for CTE research, receiving praise for their contributions. Scurry's relative absence from this coverage shows how something as seemingly straightforward as celebrity support for TBI awareness can reflect cultural norms and exclusions.

This chapter examines framings of TBI among women. We highlight how proposals to remedy the lack of attention to women with TBI have involved the production of not only new knowledge, but also *nonknowledge*—that is, absences of information about gendered bodies, which carry over into understandings of health and well-being.[7] Drawing on discussions from a 2017 US NIH agenda-setting workshop on TBI among women, similar subsequent events, and relevant research, we consider how such efforts often revolve around limited conceptions of women's bodies (and brains) as inherently distinct from men's bodies (and brains). This distinction informs the category of *female TBI*, which is typically represented as a specific condition distinct from male TBI. We reflect on how conceptions of "female TBI" and "female brains" tend to focus on biological attributes understood as inherent. Although well-intended, such appeals often evoke narrow, binary constructions of sex and gender. As research on female TBI constructs sex and gender as separate, albeit related variables, we demonstrate how this distinction departs from the increasing recognition of "sex/gender" as a concept capturing the entanglement of biological and social factors.

Biological and social interconnections are shaped by historical contexts and societal structures, meaning that sex/gender is not only constituted through lived experience but also experienced in distinct ways.[8] We explain how biological constructions of female TBI overlook social considerations that can affect women differently than men and that affect groups of women differently. As illustrated through Scurry's relative absence from media narratives surrounding brain donation pledges from women's soccer players, these framings also contribute to certain women's bodies becoming more visible than others in concussion crisis narratives. In the pages that follow, we explore how the category of female TBI negates how women's diverse experiences of brain injury are influenced by social concerns and inequities.

RAISING AWARENESS ABOUT THE TBI GAP BETWEEN WOMEN AND MEN

The cultural visibility of TBI sustained in violent spectacles of men and masculinity has contributed to women being historically excluded from public conversations about these injuries. Gendered assumptions operating within medicine and science have reinforced this disparity. Despite growing awareness of violence against women throughout the 1970s, TBI was often mistaken "as emotional and psychological rather than physical and neurological."[9] Effects of brain injury among male boxers and other collision sport athletes became matters of scientific concern while the struggles of women who had experienced blunt force trauma to the head through abuse by a partner were commonly diagnosed as psychiatric complaints.

Addressing the systemic inattention to TBI among women required documenting neurological injuries that women sustained. A major wave of this research came from studies of concussion among women athletes in the early to mid-2000s. Findings from this work—and from many subsequent sports-specific studies—have been oriented around three main claims: (1) that women suffer concussions at higher rates than men, (2) that they experience symptoms differently from men, and (3) that they require more time to recover from concussion than men.[10] These assertions informed the basis for growing media coverage on the lack of TBI research specific to women. For example, a 2017 ESPN headline asked, "Why Does It Seem Like Nobody Cares about Female Concussions?" The ensuing article acknowledged "women suffer more concussions than men in the sports that both play with an injury rate 50 percent higher."[11] Although receiving limited attention compared to the concussion crisis in men's sports, TBI among women athletes is increasingly framed as an overlooked but significant issue. Recent news stories have portrayed scientists as "playing catch up in women's concussion research," reiterating how "there has, until recently, been little attention paid to concussions suffered by women, despite research that suggests women suffer concussions differently than men, including experiencing worse symptoms and requiring longer recovery times."[12] Some media reports consider whether these susceptibilities could extend to long-term consequences of brain trauma, including CTE, among women athletes.[13]

When mapping future research agendas for TBI among women, the 2017 NIH workshop included cases beyond sports, including intimate partner violence (IPV) and the military. Experts at the meeting acknowledged several knowledge gaps and expressed concern that sports TBI was overrepresented in current research. The lack of understanding of women's experiences of TBI, particularly how they might differ from men's experiences, underpinned calls for more research related to female subjects and women in different contexts.[14] For example, women may sustain fewer TBI during military deployments than men, but the growing number of women in active military service is likely to translate into higher rates of combat-related TBI in this group. Similarly, advocates focusing on survivors of IPV, at the NIH meeting and elsewhere during our fieldwork, explicitly stated more research is necessary to capture the distinct experiences of these women. To quote one expert in the field:

> We cannot just take what we know from the military studies that we have on military personnel, or from what we know about sports, and say, "Well, we can just apply that to this group of women." We simply can't do that. There are so many different variables that make this population very unique that we need to specifically study these women . . . the whole IPV TBI area is the gap in the literature. There's not anything specific about it. We know very little about it. There's literally a handful of studies that are looking at IPV-related TBI specifically.[15]

These comments clearly acknowledge that nonknowledge about TBI among women was an important issue to remedy.

Even when highlighting multiple contexts and TBI experiences, many experts, including those at the NIH meeting, advocated for biomedical research and framed TBI-related issues as matters of sex difference. In doing so, they emphasized distinctions between female and male subjects in animal studies, not just women and men in human studies.[16] This focus carried over into the published report on the workshop, which summarizes the discussions as being "centered on the existing knowledge regarding sex differences in TBI research and how these differences could be incorporated in preclinical and clinical efforts going forward . . . despite some progress, there remains an abundance of research focused on males and relatively little explicitly on females."[17]

The Female Brain Bank was one response to this inequity, and it has been praised for ensuring that research accounts for such differences. In a 2016 interview, Ann McKee, director of Boston University's CTE Center, explained, "There is great concern that the female brain may, in fact, be more prone to injury and adverse long-term outcome than the male brain . . . but the rate of brain donation from women has been exceedingly low."[18] The attention on sex difference acknowledges imbalances in TBI knowledge about men and women; however, this focus tends to evoke engrained notions of binary sex/gender. The resulting knowledge produced about TBI conceals important complexities constituting gendered experiences of brain injury.

FEMALE TBI AND SEXING THE BRAIN

In *Sexing the Body*, feminist science studies scholar Anne Fausto-Sterling illustrates how biological claims about the body, particularly assertions of binary sex, reflect societal beliefs.[19] Scientific research is not excluded from this observation. For example, the NIH introduced research guidelines in 2015 specifying the inclusion of "sex as a biological variable" (SABV), a policy that remains in place, though was briefly reclassified as a "historic document" in January 2025 following the Trump administration's prohibition of diversity, equity, and inclusion work in federally funded programs.[20] This policy was made in response to "the over-reliance on male animals and cells" in preclinical biomedical research.[21] The director of the NIH Office of Research on Women's Health, Janine Clayton, presented the SABV policy as a necessary reform to ensure better health outcomes for women. While heralded by some, it has attracted criticism for suggesting that findings attributed to sex will apply across multiple animal species. Indeed, this assumption fails to capture the biological variability within and between species.[22] The policy also implies that sex can be studied as an isolated variable and distinguished from environmental considerations. When "female" is used to describe a person as having inherent biological vulnerabilities, the category can minimize recognition of material and social conditions that affect well-being—a manifestation of nonknowledge. Such categorizations can inform conclusions that make complex interactions of biological and environmental factors appear to be simply outcomes of binary sex difference. The SABV policy seemingly legitimates these beliefs by providing government recognition and support.

The emphasis on sex to advance women's health has influenced the study of TBI. Consider how the NIH workshop aimed "to identify knowledge gaps, best practices, and target populations in research on females and/or sex differences within the field of TBI."[23] This statement reaffirmed the centrality of female/male difference and biomedical research—though gender was recognized at the workshop. Many participants made distinctions between conceptions of sex and gender. They described sex as concerned with biological features observed distinctly in relation to female and male bodies. They framed gender as inclusive of feminine and masculine attributes, classifying it as a separate consideration reflective of human cultures and societies.[24]

To quote one participant considered an expert on sex differences:

> Gender is a purely human construct . . . I have a lot of colleagues who like to argue with me about whether animals have gender . . . But to this point, we pretty much are in agreement that animals, if they do have gender, they can't tell us. So, our quest to

> improve sex as a biological variable usage is to get the reviewers of journal articles to remind researchers that [if] you're [studying] animals you are studying sex.[25]

The statement was not unique in terms of characterizing laboratory animals as lacking gender. It reflects how scientific norms often construct animals as technologies—instrumental tools within biomedical systems of knowledge production.[26] The participant's observations also reveal how sex can be used to stand in for what cannot be explained through accepted scientific methods—such as whether animals have gender. This example shows how sex is not a stable set of biological attributes as common framings might suggest. What sex categories come to represent in scientific practice is indeed subject to interpretation.

Feminist scholars have long acknowledged the shortcomings of understanding sex and gender as distinct categories. Rather than consider sex as limited to the domain of biology, or gender as confined to the social, there is a wider recognition that sex/gender are inextricably linked.[27] This approach challenges the notion that biological sex is uninfluenced by social factors. Scientific efforts have failed to detect a clear biological marker delineating women from men and have in fact revealed more variability than originally anticipated.[28] Such findings reinforce how understandings of sex as inherent and fixed are indeed socially constructed. Accordingly, many feminist inquiries have shifted to address "the co-constitution of nature and culture."[29] In contrast, many neuroscientific conceptions of sex difference tend to generate more homogenous accounts of male and female brains that overlook the variations within and across each category—when such complexity should call the stability of these categories into question.[30] This focus on sex tends to privilege explanations that reflect preconceived binary distinctions without critically investigating how they embody material and social complexities.

At the NIH workshop, many participants framed preclinical research as providing insights into sex difference, with animals serving an instrumental purpose for extracting such knowledge. Despite some statements about the importance of understanding the interplay between sex and gender, the ways in which participants spoke about how they studied sex—and did not intend to study gender—made sex the central lens for establishing research priorities related to TBI in women. Most participants did not question how these categories were used, even when some expressed concerns about findings from animal models not translating to human studies. Throughout the agenda-setting process, their explanations reproduced binary distinctions between female and male and between sex and gender despite making statements that acknowledged complexities around these concepts.

These slippages became clear when participants discussed preclinical models as providing insights specific to sex but made gendered interpretations to explain them. For example, one researcher described findings that female mice were less likely than male mice to engage in open-field exploration or to participate in play following mild TBI. The researcher explained this "more avoidant behavior" as showing how "outcome measures might be different" and "sex specific."[31] While framing this observation as a matter of sex, the explanation evoked stereotypically feminine traits of hesitancy and passivity to describe the female mice, distinguishing them from more active male mice.[32] This example demonstrates how gendered ideas and language can seep into scientific findings attributed to binary constructions of sex difference—even in animal studies.[33]

The privileging of sex over gender at the NIH meeting carried over into discussions of human studies, including clinical, epidemiological, and rehabilitation research. During discussions about clinical trials, participants acknowledged the underrepresentation of women as opposed to men in TBI studies as another shortcoming hindering the translation of research from the lab to clinical settings. Their observations conveyed a preoccupation with the inclusion of women as research subjects, with many comments critiquing the low number and percentage of women in TBI studies. Participants justified this position by emphasizing the observable differences in TBI outcomes between women and men. Far less attention was paid to how studies including women might account for factors beyond sex, such as gender influences and other social conditions that affect health.

This biological emphasis was especially evident in reflections on how menstrual cycles and sex hormones affect women's experiences of TBI. Scientists pointed to research indicating that women with raised levels of progesterone at the time of injury often have better outcomes than women with high levels of estrogen when injured. Progesterone is also a possible treatment for women who are struggling with TBI symptoms, something one advocate described as saving her from "unbearable pain where I've felt my head separate from my body every single month . . . Within a few weeks of having a natural progesterone cream that I rubbed into my head every day, twice a day, it was the first time I actually got rid of my migraines." Many researchers emphasized these findings as having breakthrough implications, seemingly justifying the explanatory power and potential of research attentive to sex difference. These imaginings of progress, however, were limited to specific scientific fields and postinjury interventions. They rarely explored broader questions of how women sustain TBI and what could be done to prevent them. As such, there were missed opportunities to draw connections between TBI outcomes among women and the social conditions and inequalities that shape them.

As a result, the NIH workshop retained a targeted focus on individual attributes that were often depicted as being inherent to women's bodies and distinct from men's. Many explanations reified the divide between women and men as seemingly based on biological differences.[34] They often described observed differences across genders as stemming from innate characteristics and negated the social processes that contribute to these differences. The construction of sex difference as a "natural" phenomenon reflects a convergence of scientific and ideological processes that shape gendered explanations of TBI among women. An emphasis on sex difference can, as sociologist Victoria Pitts-Taylor cautions, "deny the complexity, specificity, and multiplicity of lives."[35] Indeed, both TBI research and advocacy tend to overlook how social forces contribute to making some bodies prone to experiencing TBI and its severe long-term effects.

HOW BINARY SEX/GENDER SHAPES TBI EVIDENCE

Public claims about the higher rates and greater severity of TBI symptoms in women similarly draw on sex difference as an explanation.[36] The causes of these disparities are still largely uncertain: research points to a combination of physiological distinctions, symptom-reporting behaviors, and psychological characteristics along binary gender distinctions. Scientific studies have indicated that sex differences in TBI can be found in biomolecular and cellular responses in the brain linked to processes of neurological repair and recovery. Experts propose that these neurological differences between men and women could help predict disparities in recovery outcomes between the sexes.[37]

Sex difference is also a focal point of sports-specific findings, which remain central within the TBI knowledge base. Studies involving women athletes have proposed that hormonal changes linked to menstrual cycle phases can increase both the intensity and duration of TBI symptoms.[38] Other sports research highlights sex-based neurological distinctions, with men tending to have greater volumes of white matter in the brain while "female axons in the central nervous system are smaller in diameter and mechanically more prone to stretch injury than male axons."[39] Scientific studies continue to suggest that higher rates of TBI in girls and women are outcomes of their inferior neck strength compared to that of boys and men.[40] This popular claim persists even though, as one systematic review puts it, there is "limited evidence regarding direct associations between neck strength and concussion."[41] The framings of this claim reveal an important tension within many calls for increased research on TBI in women. For example, a 2021 study acknowledges that research on head impact biomechanics among rugby players has been mostly conducted with men and suggests that "focusing on female-specific injury mechanisms and epidemiology is required to safely advance the women's game." Yet the study also highlights that research should investigate "the extent to which cervical spine weaknesses and instabilities" contribute to concussion in women's rugby.[42] This is a trend we noticed throughout our research: many calls for gender equity in TBI research also evoke assumptions about women's inherent "weaknesses and instabilities."

Common approaches to sports injury tend to portray biological risks as connected to female anatomy and distinct from social circumstances. Work by sociologist Nancy Theberge illustrates how explanations of different rates and experiences of sports-related injuries often privilege physiological distinctions between men and women, overlooking contextually specific patterns or environmental conditions that influence injury. Perhaps most notably, these concerns manifest themselves in explanations regarding knee injuries, particularly anterior cruciate ligament (ACL) tears, among women in sports. The emphasis on sex difference implies that female bodies are more susceptible to these kinds of injuries even though emergent research provides more comprehensive explanations that address how entanglements of sex/gender shape them.[43]

As Theberge observes, presenting gendered concerns as "biological risk factors" might be well-intended, but it can revive "notions of female frailty and unsuitability for vigorous physical activity."[44] Despite greater acceptance of women in sports and the military, this underlying logic can reinscribe refuted beliefs that female bodies are inherently weaker than—or dysfunctional compared to—male bodies, a generalization that "female athletes and feminists have worked hard to dispel."[45] Although TBI is certainly distinct from ACL tears, sex-focused attempts to understand both injuries can evoke an imagined female subject who has particular needs determined by biology. These approaches also negate the full diversity of bodies that are women.

This is not to say that proponents of sex difference research view TBI in women as a one-dimensional concern. Although privileging a focus on sex, the NIH workshop did not convey female TBI as a singular thing. Even though speakers used similar language to emphasize the importance of sex in understanding TBI, they drew on very different examples to make sense of it—afflictions experienced by animal subjects, including mice and pigs, and by women in the military, sports, and situations of interpersonal and family violence. The process of developing an agenda around TBI in women captured how female TBI came into being through collaborative practices that spanned different contexts and research paradigms. To borrow Annmarie Mol's language, female TBI is *multiple*, brought together and made legible through various techniques of clinical and preclinical scientific research, available evidence, and tacit knowledge about sex/gender.[46] Female TBI is thus a gendered creation: its assertion of biological difference is grounded in cultural notions of binary gender that depict women as fundamentally different from their male counterparts.

There were some, albeit limited, explorations of gender at the 2017 NIH workshop. They tended to focus on individual behavior, which one expert described as the "place where biological sex, cultural gender, self-expression, personal outward expressions of identity, sexual orientation—all these things are really mixed together."[47] There were similarly few explorations of how women's TBI experiences might be shaped by other dimensions of social location beyond gender. An epidemiologist raised questions about the role of factors such as age, immigration, race and ethnicity, sexual orientation, and socioeconomic status, but few participants reflected on the relevance of social categories of difference in depth. Instead, there were comments acknowledging their connections loosely, including, for instance, the need to recognize the "amalgamation of biological sex and gender identity and gender expression."[48] Moreover, experts at the workshop suggested experimental or quasi-experimental designs to isolate sex and gender in order to infer causal relationships regarding TBI outcomes. In short, few participants in the workshop advocated for a more intersectional approach—or even recognized what such an approach might involve.

Instead, the framings tended to present gender as distinct between men and women, a pattern that can yield productive insights but that also raises more questions. Consider, for instance, research on how gender affects whether athletes report TBI symptoms to coaches or medical staff. As diagnoses and assessments of symptom severity are largely reliant on self-reported data, many explanations for discrepancies in TBI outcomes among men and women focus on gender differences in reporting behaviors. It is widely reported that women are more likely than men to disclose TBI symptoms and seek medical care.[49] While it is possible that a susceptibility to more severe symptoms may prompt women to report their injury and pursue treatment, this discrepancy could also reflect women's tendency to be more forthright than men when discussing their health.[50] Research in other contexts suggests cultural expectations around toughness and self-reliance make men more likely than women to downplay illness or injury and avoid addressing medical problems.[51] In settings where there are high risks of injury, such as sports, men are believed to be more likely to hide injuries to demonstrate strength and commitment. Women, in contrast, are thought to be "more concerned about the effects of an injury on their future health, and may be more honest in reporting, and not as affected as male athletes when told they cannot participate."[52]

While these kinds of generalized claims may portray women's presumed honesty in reporting TBI as a positive trend, they can overlook how traditionally masculine norms around toughness and playing through injury are celebrated as essential to athletic success, irrespective of gender. A study led by medical scientist Emily Kroshus concludes it is more productive to examine how masculine ideals "are contributing to unsafe concussion care-seeking behaviors" across genders rather than focusing on sex differences.[53] This emphasis draws attention to the complex influence of cultural and gendered norms rather than framing social behaviors according to predetermined sex/gender categories. It also reveals how straightforward assertions about reporting can reinforce long-standing ideas about women athletes being more passive and less competitive than men—stereotypes that are frequently used to delegitimize women's sports and women athletes.[54] Moreover, racism can shape assumptions about women's sports: Black, Brown, and Indigenous women are often characterized as hyper-aggressive and transgressive of traditional gender norms, whereas white women are more often understood as representing an idealized notion of passive femininity that aligns with observed trends in concussion reporting.[55]

Interpreting patterns of behavior according to binary sex/gender categories obscures other contextual factors that influence TBI reporting. When reflecting on military-specific data, one expert at the NIH meeting reiterated that self-reported symptoms are subjective and shaped by multiple considerations:

> Some people will tend to tell you everything that's bothering them. Other people will really not report much at all. Intentional over- and under-reporting is also an issue. So, in service members and veterans specifically, over-reporting can be an issue if patients want to get out of the military or if they want to receive more compensation for their injuries, and under-reporting can be an issue if patients want to stay in the military, [or] they want to stay on the mission, stay on deployment, or get promoted.

This comment was not intended to cast doubt on individuals' claims about their symptoms, but was instead meant to highlight the various influences that can shape self-report data irrespective of gender. Further, findings from military personnel indicate that "controlling for PTSD and symptom validity resulted in fewer gender-based differences in post-concussive symptoms than previously demonstrated in the literature."[56] In short, when contextualized, the presumed differences between men and women are not as powerful as initially assumed.

These observations are borne out in recent empirical research enabled by the Concussion Assessment, Research and Education (CARE) Consortium, a partnership supported by the US Department of Defense (DoD) and the NCAA. One large-scale study—the largest on women's concussion recovery to date—suggests no significant evidence of sex difference in concussion recovery among university athletes when women have equitable access to care and resources.[57] According to lead author Jaclyn Caccese,

> Historically, some women's sports didn't have the same on-site access to health care, and what that does is result in delayed evaluation, delayed initiation of treatment, and prolonged recovery . . . Student-athletes at the institutions in this study receive immediate access to the best sports medicine evaluation and treatment. I think that could be one of the driving factors in why we didn't see much of a sex difference.[58]

In sum, addressing environmental and social conditions not only promotes better outcomes for women but also highlights the limitations of using sex as the primary lens for research agendas on TBI among women.

FROM THE RECOGNITION OF FEMALE TBI TO BRAIN INJURIES IN WOMEN AND GIRLS

Advocacy efforts around TBI in women reflect dynamic changes and negotiations around how sex/gender is framed in relation to brain trauma. Over the course of our research for this book, we have observed a growing shift, particularly since 2020, in recognizing a wider range of gendered considerations. Consider how Katherine Snedaker, the founder of PINK Concussions, has explained how and why women's experiences of TBI are different from men's. Through 2019, the PINK

Concussions website emphasized sex-based approaches that seek "to improve the research, medical care, and community support for females with brain injury including concussion." A statement from Snedaker read, "I believe females with brain injuries ARE the invisible patients."[59] In keeping with this focus, the PINK Concussions website drew attention to how "female and male brains differ in more than 100 ways in structure, activity, chemistry, and blood flow, and so it is logical that damage to the brain would also manifest differently in women and men."[60] More recently, the organization has adopted more gender-responsive language and added events addressing how different societal inequalities affect brain injury.[61] Its Partner-Inflicted Brain Injury Taskforce hosts regular meetings, an increasing number of which focus on how social conditions, including intersections between sexism and racism, affect lived experiences of violence and TBI among different groups of women.

Others have mobilized to counter implicit beliefs about the fragility of female bodies and brains. A documentary produced by the University of Minnesota Tucker Center for Research on Women and Girls in Sport, working with Twin Cities Public Television, offers a case in point.[62] It highlights how gendered dimensions of women's sports participation inform experiences of concussion, with expert commentaries highlighting various considerations: competitive and sport-specific norms; age-related, cognitive, and physiological differences; and wider regulatory challenges that administrators, coaches, referees, and support staff face. Some of its featured commentators also draw attention to how the violence embraced in men's collision sports reinforces beliefs that men are naturally stronger and more resilient than female athletes. They acknowledge how this point is seemingly validated by higher concussion rates in more aggressive women's sports, like women's ice hockey, compared to rates in similar men's sports. The emphasis on such a trend, however, becomes especially troubling when the discrepancy is exclusively attributed to biological sex differences rather than accounting for environmental influences or women's higher rates of reporting. In response to these concerns, the documentary advocates for multidisciplinary inquiries into how concussion symptoms and health outcomes can vary greatly by individual and for examinations of how societal and sport-specific conditions contribute to making participants in women's sports more vulnerable to TBI.

The documentary's recommendations align with a vocal minority of experts observed during the research for this book. In the 2017 NIH meeting, for instance, a researcher dedicated a presentation to explaining the importance of studying broader patterns of difference in sports-related concussion, stating explicitly that "we must use epidemiological data to drive prevention efforts so that we can keep athletes as safe as possible while they get the benefit of that physical activity while playing sports."[63] She presented prevention as a necessary priority: "I know if I prevent that direct blow—that direct transfer of force to the head—or the blow to the body . . . that causes the acceleration/deceleration of the rotational forces of the brain within the skull, [we] can prevent the concussion." She emphasized, "Primary prevention efforts largely are just as effective in female athletes as they are [in] male athletes, whether it's banning heading [the ball in soccer] or eliminating athlete-athlete contact or putting a helmet on both girls and boys lacrosse players." In other words, sports offer multiple opportunities for intervention that are not necessarily gender specific. As the speaker elaborated, the same data showing how men and women experience concussion symptoms differently also illustrates that those gaps are shrinking. The decreasing disparity suggests that improving women's avenues for postconcussion identification and treatment might have a profound impact.

These observations point to the significance of environmental considerations, which scholars have observed are gendered in ways that influence sports-related injuries. As sexist norms pervade institutions and structures, health scholars Joanne Parsons, Stephanie Coen, and Sheree Bekker emphasize the importance of not presenting sex/gender as an inherent source of injury risk. Instead, they argue how one might better capture how environmental, material, and social conditions could make women more likely to experience and report injury. Taking these issues seriously enables scrutiny of how injury patterns are linked to gender norms around physical activity, the systematic underfunding of women's sports compared to men's sports, and other pressures athletes might experience, such as perceived competitive or financial stakes. Importantly, as Parsons and colleagues argue, "we cannot simply tell girls/women to 'get stronger' to reduce injury risk if society and the environment do not support those types of activities for everyone. Work in public health tells us that prevention efforts are most effective when broader society and cultural norms are targeted."[64] Such an approach would attend to interpersonal relationships, social networks, and sport-specific conditions, which often sustain cultures of risk that encourage participants to play through injury and have both gendered and racialized contours.[65]

Accordingly, it is essential to better understand the practices and systems contributing to rates of concussion, data collection, reporting, and treatment so that high-risk environments can be identified and changed. Despite signs that advocates and researchers are looking for more holistic understandings and assessments of gender and TBI, much of the available population-level data does not provide the necessary information on the diversity of groups affected by brain trauma. The lack of data, in turn, contributes to reifying the centrality of differences between women and men while rendering other distinctions, like geographic disparities, racialized differences, and socioeconomic inequalities, seemingly irrelevant. Only one speaker at the 2017 NIH meeting of experts drew attention to these specific considerations and how this shortcoming meant researchers knew little about the social contours of risk, even as they claimed to identify TBI risk factors among individuals based on available data.

Gendered data that does exist largely falls within binary divisions. The limited focus on concussions among intersex and transgender people persists, despite the growing visibility of their participation in sports and in the military, as well as evidence that transgender individuals are more likely to experience interpersonal violence than their cisgender counterparts.[66] As with other calls to protect women under the guise that they are the weaker sex, gender diverse, nonbinary, and transgender people remain marginalized within gendered discussions of TBI.[67] The overall lack of data and analysis attending to differences among and between bodies prevents the possibility of accounting for variations that do not fit ideal types. Bodies "regularly run afoul of neat categorization," as Pitts-Taylor argues. An ideal body "has to be recognized as such; it is not a real, living, enacting, or perceiving body, but a construct."[68] In contrast, the mainstay of TBI research remains biomedical with a focus on binary sex/gender, the privileging of which can negate the range of intersectional considerations that can impact the prevalence of TBI.

TBI BEYOND THE GAZE OF BINARY SEX/GENDER

Significant questions remain regarding how interlocking systems of inequality and marginalization contribute to experiences of TBI. Although sociologists contend that social categories of difference, such as age, ethnicity, gender, and race, are more prominent in modern medicine, they are relatively emergent considerations in TBI research.[69] Experts increasingly recognize the importance of these considerations in their work. Tatyana Mollayeva and colleagues contend that sex and gender are generative of "intersecting" vulnerabilities to TBI, writing that "certain groups of men and women are more vulnerable to TBI than others, owing to the unique interactions between their biological, behavioral, social and cultural conditions preceding injury and at the time of injury."[70] Research by Samira Omar, Stephanie Nixon, and Angela Colantonio documents systematic oversights in TBI research, noting that studies rarely attend to "sex, gender, and race . . . as demographic variables" let alone as interlocking systems that shape care pathways.[71]

In the absence of systematic investigation into these considerations, research on cisgender men points to patterns that demonstrate how racism can contribute to TBI risk. For example, analyses of men's collision sports reveal that athletes from ethnic and racial minority backgrounds are often channeled into sport-specific positions that require greater levels of physical contact, which could contribute to higher rates of TBI.[72] Research on health disparities also illustrates that racism and socioeconomic inequalities have a cumulative effect on mental and physical health outcomes. In the United States, the health threat posed by race-related discrimination "may be more systematic, insidious, and constant than other stressors."[73] In fact, public health research demonstrates that inequitable social forces manifest themselves in human bodies. This is especially the case within the stress paradigm, where people who experience racial discrimination are thought to distinctly experience "cumulative wear and tear on the body's systems owing to repeated adaptation to stressors."[74] In short, racism contributes to health deterioration earlier in life for Black people compared to their white counterparts. This observation aligns with sociological findings, which have detailed the continued failure to recognize and remedy how Black people, particularly Black women, have borne the brunt of systemic racism in US health care—a pattern that spans historical forms of dehumanization to contemporary practices of mistreatment.[75]

The limited TBI research attentive to these concerns points to disparities in health outcomes following injury.[76] Despite observations of how racism uniquely contributes to and exacerbates health disparities, these discussions remain largely absent from the discourse of TBI among women, because the focus on "female TBI" prioritizes sex/gender—and sex more so than gender—as the primary lens for distinguishing differences in TBI-related symptoms and experiences. This focus reveals a classic intersectional dilemma: focusing on one axis of social difference tends to overlook and misrepresent the experiences of women of color, as they can experience forms of marginalization that exceed the scope of sex/gender.[77]

Attention to intersectionality and societal power is only beginning to take shape in TBI-related advocacy and research. Such studies have found that structural violence by institutions prevents women who have experienced domestic and family violence from receiving formal TBI diagnoses or treatment even though they have symptoms.[78] Scientists, too, have begun to acknowledge the need for TBI studies to better address diverse, intersecting identities. As conveyed by a neuroscientist, the range of "gender effects on brain injury is underappreciated . . . So, the discussions I have in my lab, the discussions I have with all colleagues is, 'Is gender binary?' And the answer is, 'Not a chance.' Like we cannot put people into categories, and it goes well beyond gender as well."[79] Instead of offering more "categorical approaches" to studying TBI, he pointed to the need for greater recognition of diverse gender identities and racial backgrounds, particularly among groups who experience higher rates of violence.

These efforts reflect early steps toward developing more nuanced understandings of how intersecting forms of marginalization come to shape and mediate experiences of TBI, as well as the level and quality of diagnosis and treatment that individuals receive. This focus departs from the more commonly used lens of sex difference and points to the dual roles of knowledge and nonknowledge. While research addressing sex difference can generate important forms of knowledge, its privileging can yield notable gaps related to the structural conditions that position certain groups as more likely to experience brain trauma than others. This includes important factors that public health scholars often frame as "social determinants of health," a term that draws attention to how embedded inequalities yield disproportionate health outcomes for populations that experience marginalization.[80]

Many TBI initiatives purport to close the knowledge gap between men and women, but they often fail to consider how multiple gaps—not simply one along the lines of binary sex/gender—co-exist. They can miss an important opportunity to attend to the complex ways gender informs TBI and intersects with other social categories of difference, including their material effects on individual bodies and brains. There are opportunities, however, to expand the scope. Distinct from biomedical framings, there have been recent calls to amend social determinants of health frameworks, so they better capture how structural ableism, classism, racism, and sexism are root causes of health inequities. Such improvements would enable the centering of certain groups' disproportionate exposure to violence.[81] The Female Brain Bank could also be used to support analyses that are not limited to sex difference, as recruitment efforts have encouraged a diverse sample of donors—although they face challenges in the United States, given the Trump administration's orders to end diversity and inclusion initiatives in federally funded research. In the next chapter, we explore how advocates work to address TBI and its relationships to gendered forms of violence. We examine assumptions and tensions that emerge when making appeals to recognize and respond to partner-inflicted TBI as a social problem.

6

A Hidden Epidemic at Home

Concussion crisis narratives, as we have illustrated throughout this book, often focus on sports, particularly men's sports. Despite growing awareness of the risks associated with TBI, research remains primarily focused on sports, the military, and men. In chapter 5, we explored the growing interest in TBI among women athletes. Relatively few studies, however, focus on TBI in relation to where women are most likely to endure violence: at home and at the hands of people they know—that is, until relatively recently. A 2022 *New York Times Magazine* article, "The Hidden Epidemic of Brain Injuries from Domestic Violence," profiles experts advocating to raise awareness about TBI among women with histories of domestic violence.[1] The piece reflects on nearly twenty years of research in the United States by Eve M. Valera, an expert based at Harvard Medical School, stating, "Every year, hundreds of concussions occur in the NFL; thousands occur in the military. Valera's estimated number of annual brain injuries among survivors of domestic abuse: 1.6 million."[2] Similarly, a 2023 Australian Broadcasting Corporation article cites "experts estimating up to 20 million women in the US sustain TBIs through partner violence every year—11 to 12 times the number experienced by athletes and military personnel combined."[3]

These figures bolster advocates' claims that TBI from domestic violence is a significant issue, even though it receives limited public attention compared to sports TBI. According to Katherine Snedaker, the founder of PINK Concussions, an organization dedicated to raising awareness of and educating people about brain injury in women and girls, "If brain injury is the 'invisible illness' of our time, then within this invisible injury, women have been the invisible patients."[4] Although many groups have argued for stronger responses to violence endured in private spaces, including the home, it is perhaps not surprising this form of

TBI has received little attention or funding. As concussion crisis narratives gained traction in Australia, Canada, and the United States over the course of the 2010s and early 2020s, we have observed advocates in each country work to center victim-survivors within understandings of TBI.[5] To do so, they have attempted to build coalitions with different groups: other brain injury advocates, experts studying TBI, and emergency management and law enforcement officials who are often first responders in cases of domestic and family violence. In a workshop dedicated to these issues, many scientists stated how "raising awareness is critical," emphasizing the need to engage with and educate police and paramedics, judges, support staff, and victim-survivors to cultivate better understandings of TBI from partner-inflicted violence.[6]

Although the intentions of building these coalitions is to effect positive change for victim-survivors with TBI, tensions and tradeoffs can emerge. This is especially the case in campaigns against domestic violence, a space that sociolegal scholar Jonathan Simon identifies as a clear instance of a movement pursuing social justice by turning to mechanisms of criminalization such as incarceration and policing.[7] This shift involves what sociologist Renee Shelby calls "fellow traveler discourses," which are ways of thinking that accompany interventions aimed at social problems.[8] When it comes to domestic and family violence, criminalization is a pervasive fellow traveler discourse, at least in the countries studied here. It is also difficult to evade. Even anti-violence responses that try to avoid criminalization practices can fail to consider how the intersections of heteronormativity, racism, sexism, and socioeconomic inequalities shape domestic and family violence.[9] In doing so, such responses can inadvertently uphold power imbalances and inequities.

Accordingly, anti-violence strategies are often not responsive to the distinct experiences of Black, Brown, and First Nations people. Such practices can invite *carceral creep*—a process through which criminalization and legal punishment come to shape responses to social problems—because they do not appreciate how state-sanctioned interventions often punish communities of color.[10] Carceral creep is not something that happens immediately. It involves, as abolitionist scholar Mimi Kim elaborates, "the incremental and often imperceptible advance of carceral forces," including legal punishment, policing, and surveillance, into everyday life. Kim explains how processes of carceral creep have come to dominate a feminist anti-violence movement that once mostly lacked the presence of law enforcement.[11] This trend exemplifies how advocacy that fails to acknowledge structural forces contributing to domestic and family violence can perpetuate additional forms of punishment and violence onto victim-survivors in the name of supporting them. This shortcoming especially impacts those already experiencing interlocking forms of oppression.

This chapter examines how appeals for greater visibility of TBI among victim-survivors intersects with fellow traveler discourses from law, science, and social services—all of which can enable carceral creep. While many advocates recognize that inequality affects victim-survivors, particularly between women and men, fellow traveler discourses often minimize the consideration of how power shapes agendas for social change and TBI responses. Specifically in this case, we illustrate how biomedical conceptions of TBI seep into framings of victim-survivors' injuries and legal responses to them. In particular, we explore how law enforcement approaches to domestic and family violence leak into advocacy efforts. These approaches can fail to support—and further victimize—Black, Brown, and First Nations women as well as queer and trans people, all of whom experience higher rates of intimate partner violence (IPV) than their white, heterosexual, and cisgender counterparts.[12]

ADVOCATING FOR RECOGNITION OF TBI AMONG VICTIM-SURVIVORS OF DOMESTIC VIOLENCE

As we discussed in chapter 5, research on TBI and its symptoms reflects gendered discrepancies. Medical historians Stephen Casper and Kelly O'Donnell have documented how the formal recognition of brain injury from domestic violence has primarily taken shape since 1990 after a woman with a long history of partner abuse was diagnosed with CTE.[13] The 1990s were also a period in which the criminalization of domestic violence expanded.[14] Prior to that time, recognized symptoms among victim-survivors were often depicted as psychiatric issues, even though campaigns throughout the 1970s raised awareness of physical violence against women and TBI research on men highlighted long-term neurological effects of direct blows to the head.

Partner-inflicted TBI continues to receive less attention than TBI in men's collision sports and the military. According to Michelle Fitts, an Australian researcher who has worked with Aboriginal and Torres Strait Islander communities on issues related to disability and TBI, despite the growing recognition of concussions and their harmful effects, there is limited media coverage or information "about women who've experienced concussion repeatedly as a result of violence. We need to raise the profile and visibility of head injury in relationships" and "educate the community about the potential long-term harm and disability you can cause someone."[15] In the United States, some have drawn direct comparisons with sports, characterizing TBI in the NFL as "miniscule" by comparison, arguing that for "every NFL player that sustains a concussion, you could nearly fill an NFL stadium with IPV victims with probable concussion symptoms."[16] Others have described professional athletes as "the luckiest people in the world" compared to others with TBI: "the second you get a brain injury, *boom*, you're yanked off the field" to prevent further injury and receive treatment.[17] In short, the comparative lack of visibility and support for victim-survivors with TBI is emblematic of the stark inequalities underpinning the concussion crisis.

Many advocacy efforts are built around proving how this form of TBI occurs at scale and has long-term health effects. Increasing scientific knowledge and literacy has been one such approach to providing this kind of evidence. A 2021 report by experts concerned with female TBI and sex difference considered how science could support greater awareness of TBI resulting from interpersonal violence. The authors stress the need for better data and estimates of population-level rates, more assessments of women's neural, cognitive, psychological, and social functioning, better biomarkers for diagnosing TBI and understanding comorbidities, more research into chronic symptoms and disorders, and attention to the perceived needs of women with TBI.[18] This work has not been limited to research; it has also involved cultivating cross-country networks, including, for example, through the creation of the Partner-Inflicted TBI Task Force by PINK Concussions in 2019.

Activists and researchers have built and maintained connections with other anti-violence campaigns. The Survivors of Abuse and Brain Injury through Research (SOAR) initiative in British Columbia, Canada, for instance, aims to support survivors of abuse who experience brain injury by bringing together the expertise of both social workers and TBI researchers.[19] Similarly, Standing Courageous is a survivor-led nonprofit organization in the United States that works with researchers to provide education to frontline workers on how to respond to trauma and overlooked injuries from interpersonal violence, including brain injury and strangulation.[20]

These kinds of partnerships are often enabled by advocates, many of whom are women, working in professional roles that span anti-violence organizations, nonprofit management, and research. As such, many coalitions reflect a pattern of professionalization that is markedly different from the social movement origins of the battered women's movement. This shift has given rise to an agenda primarily focused on providing services and treatment, which represents a noticeable departure from the "social change agenda" associated with the origins of the battered women's movement.[21] The trend toward professionalization maps onto a long-standing tension—namely, that the domestic violence movement remains predominantly middle- to upper-middle class and white and so has failed to address interlocking issues of class and race, while still not collaborating meaningfully with Black, Brown, or First Nations communities to support transformative change.[22]

Professionalization is only one aspect of the dynamics shaping the domestic violence movement in North America. It is intertwined with neoliberal changes that have promoted individualized treatment and carceral creep.[23] The partnerships supporting TBI advocacy are materializing in an era where carceral logics pervade mainstream anti-violence strategies. While civil society organizations mobilizing against domestic violence once selectively engaged with police, they now maintain sustained connections with criminal legal actors. These once distinct domains have come to reflect hybrid arrangements that enable law enforcement approaches to significantly influence the activities of anti-violence coalitions.[24] Accordingly, feminist organizations engaging with state actors have contributed to what Kim describes as "the architecture undergirding the construction of the expanding punitive state."[25]

These forces produce powerful fellow traveler discourses that TBI advocates negotiate, both consciously and unconsciously, in their attempts to effect change. Throughout our research we observed meetings of several North American anti-violence professionals and TBI researchers involved in approaches for addressing brain injury among victim-survivors, including sessions on improving scientific knowledge, legal responses, and support services. During a 2020 meeting, a session on survivor support services centered the health and well-being of women with histories of physical injury, trauma, and violence.[26] At the same meeting, discussions of legal responses tended to focus more narrowly on law enforcement, including the development of tools to help police better identify TBI when responding to domestic disputes and strategies for prosecution that use evidence of TBI to punish perpetrators of violence. In short, a focus on care emerged alongside a preoccupation with punishment. Across these conversations, there was limited attention to the varying experiences of survivors of violence, experiences that shape whether or how they engage with—or are recognized by—the criminal legal system, emergency responders, and health services. The negative dimensions of these interactions can be stark for people whose identities are not cisgender, middle-class, or white.

People within anti-violence advocacy networks are not oblivious to these differences as they affect Black women and women from culturally and linguistically diverse backgrounds. Some advocates for victim-survivors with TBI, including PINK Concussions, began formally acknowledging intersectional issues related to violence following the police killing of George Floyd, an unarmed Black man arrested by Minneapolis police for allegedly using a counterfeit twenty-dollar bill.[27] Beyond the United States, Australia and Canada were also notable sites of protest highlighting how Floyd's death exemplified the wider harms of police violence against Black and Brown communities. In both countries, these movements drew attention to how colonialism cannot be disentangled from violence against First Nations peoples—who remain among the groups disproportionately targeted by law enforcement and state violence.

The wider recognition of how colonialism and racism shape violence has not yet translated into TBI agendas. At a 2020 meeting we observed regarding partner-inflicted TBI, some speakers acknowledged the need to account for intersectional concerns to enhance support for victim-survivors. In fact, it was noticeably more explicit than what we had seen when carrying out research for this book in the early and mid-2010s.[28] This awareness, however, did not necessarily overcome or correct for the institutionalized frames through which many experts conceptualize

TBI. Their lenses reflected dominant approaches (discussed in chapters 2 and 5), which do not recognize racism as a structural influence on health and rates of violence.

Consider, for instance, one Native American expert's commentary at the event. When asked to discuss partner-inflicted TBI before a predominantly white audience, she made explicit connections to structural violence, including the violence that institutions tasked with supporting victim-survivors can inflict. Structural violence captures the political and social conditions contributing to specific groups and people experiencing higher levels of bodily and psychological harms, including, but not limited to, physical injuries.[29] Her reflection emphasized patterns of gendered colonial violence instead of addressing specific requests to speak about brain injury among Indigenous women. Within her explanation, TBI emerged as a symptom of larger issues that required priority—such as the lack of meaningful action by Canadian and US governments in relation to missing and murdered Indigenous women, even though a Canadian inquiry presented findings that were acknowledged to amount to genocide.[30] Rather than focusing on TBI-specific services, she expressed greater concern about how Indigenous communities did not have adequate health services, citing only a few Native American specialty nurses where she lives, even though the area is home to hundreds of thousands of Native American people. Importantly, her explanation made clear how the challenges of addressing violence and accessing healthcare services were inextricably linked to the complicated relationships between First Nations peoples and settler-colonial governments.

This focus on structural dynamics diverges significantly from most TBI-related advocacy, which is concerned with improving research on victim-survivors of domestic violence and enhancing service provision. An emphasis on structural violence aids in understanding intersectional patterns of TBI captured in the prevalence of interpersonal violence and the influence of structural and state violence underpinning them. For example, in Australia, where data indicates that First Nations women are sixty-nine times more likely to experience a head injury after being physically assaulted, there remains a lack of appropriate services for Aboriginal and Torres Strait Islander women, particularly in remote areas.[31] Research led by Fitts traces systemic failures in providing care, documenting instances of these disparities materializing in practice: women not receiving referrals for neuropsychological assessment, patients who presented less severe symptoms not receiving follow-up communications, and the high turnover of staff affecting the overall ability to identify TBI.[32] As Fitts and colleagues stress, addressing these issues requires First Nations women having a valued voice in the development of responses to guarantee adequate and long-term care. While improving research and supporting frontline staff are important measures, those recommendations alone would not address what are fundamentally structural inequities.

Structural dimensions, however, are rarely central in discussions of TBI as a social problem. Instead, fellow traveler discourses, particularly those informed by law and science, often foreground understandings of TBI in relation to individual bodies. Institutional responses, in turn, tend to share this focus. This limitation reflects a critical observation made by other social scientists—namely, that scientific claims about the brain carry over into other domains but fail to account for the ways science can perpetuate social inequalities.[33] In the examples that follow, we examine how science and law become enrolled in TBI advocacy, often bringing with them beliefs and principles that negate the complexities of economic, gender, and racial oppression. As these discourses have been recognized as sustaining carceral creep in the name of helping victim-survivors, we explore the distinct contours of these dynamics in relation to partner-inflicted TBI.

ADVANCING SCIENTIFIC UNDERSTANDINGS OF TBI RESULTING FROM DOMESTIC VIOLENCE

As we have discussed in other chapters of this book, neuroscientific knowledge about sports and military TBI has been mobilized in advocacy for safer sports, support for veterans, and legal recourse for those experiencing the long-term consequences of repeated brain injury. Even as some critics have characterized this evidence base as inconclusive, the attention given to neuropathological studies of athletes' and soldiers' brains has been central to the formation of concussion crisis narratives. In relation to domestic and family violence, TBI among victim-survivors is often understood as "a public health secret" in that it is, according to neuroscientist William Stewart, "remarkable that up to 30 percent of women may experience IPV over their lifetime, yet so little is understood. . . . Sadly, studies and pathology of IPV-related TBI are vanishingly small."[34] Moreover, estimates regarding the prevalence of brain injury among victim-survivors have limitations. Much of this research relies on small convenience data samples that are prone to biases and inconsistencies. Experts thus suggest that more robust epidemiological or longitudinal research would be more generalizable to a larger population.[35]

Despite these observations and continued efforts, science alone does not provide a complete or clear picture of the health risks or long-term disability burden of TBI among victim-survivors. As Stewart acknowledges, "At Glasgow, we have the largest archive of brain tissue for research globally," which is about "25 percent to 30 percent female. Undoubtedly, we must have many cases of unrecognized IPV-related brain injury in our archive, but the stories remain hidden."[36] Biomedical research nonetheless remains a central pillar in calls for more robust data about TBI in women. Many such justifications evoke understandings of women as fundamentally different from men and represent women's experiences of TBI as inherently distinct as well.

The lack of attention paid to women with TBI, particularly those with histories of domestic and family violence, reflects gendered inequities. "We live in a patriarchal society and women are still second class," Valera has stated publicly. "We aren't given the same appreciation in science. Males, including in animal research, are studied far more than females."[37] The push for women in clinical trials and female subjects in preclinical research is one clear way that institutions have moved to address such disparities. When the US NIH Sex as a Biological Variable policy introduced requirements to ensure that both sexes receive "adequate consideration" in preclinical biomedical research on animals, it built on assumptions that sex-balanced studies would support better health research for women.[38] However, as we outlined in chapter 5, such approaches to addressing inequity have other effects. They reinforce sex difference as a dominant mode of explaining TBI-related findings at the expense of more complex, intersectional considerations of gender.

In response, scholars have worked to create better measures to assist with explaining gender's impact on TBI rates and responses, including ways that aim to better account for the relationships between gender, interpersonal violence, and TBI.[39] Although neuroscientists seek better ways of demonstrating how biological and social dimensions of the brain are "not separable but interlaced," there still remains limited engagement with other formations of power that materialize along social categories of ability, ethnicity, gender, race, and sexuality.[40] Continued efforts to separate and distinguish sex and gender as research variables are one such outcome of this tension. Although intended to be more precise, they nonetheless reaffirm the binary constructions of gender and collapse the intersection of multiple social forces under the universal category of gender.

Failing to capture these complexities has material effects for victim-survivors.[41] As Kim writes regarding anti-violence campaigns, these dynamics have "masked the dramatically unequal impact of pro-criminalization policies" because campaigns and policies have focused on "white female victimization while neglecting the consequences of criminalization on targeted and marginalized racial communities."[42] These insights illustrate how narrow scientific and legal framings of domestic and family violence align in the way they negate the influence of structural violence rooted in entanglements of economic, gendered, and racial oppression. Instead, these framings elevate imagined notions of homogenous victimhood that ignore how women do not share a universal experience.

In recent years, an active movement to better address the interrelations between gender and sex in TBI advocacy and research has emerged. A growing number of TBI experts have sought to explicitly consider how racism and sexism interact when considering partner-inflicted TBI. For example, in 2023, PINK Concussions conceded it had maintained a "lack of diversity, equity, and inclusion in its formal leadership" and pledged to ensure its advocacy supports "women who have been systematically marginalized and traditionally unheard, including women of color, women in the LGBTQ+ community, and women in the criminal justice system."[43] The organization has sought to showcase research and interventions into the various forms of discrimination and vulnerability that victim-survivors often navigate, including economic precarity, housing insecurity, and racism. These are factors that cannot be captured using binary constructs of gender and sex.[44] While these statements acknowledge past failures and suggest a commitment to change, such recognition does not guarantee more equitable outcomes. Proclamations often fall short when efforts focus on TBI at the individual level and do not address structural barriers that are the outgrowth of deep-seated and historical inequalities.[45]

Gender-diverse people remain at the periphery of many such efforts. Over the course of our research, relatively few individuals acknowledged the particularities of partner-inflicted TBI among people who are not cisgender. Those who did draw on data regarding rates of violence to non-cisgender people called for greater focus on groups and identities overlooked in mainstream TBI discourse. For example, when speaking on the nature of interpersonal violence, a practitioner working with brain injury-affected people acknowledged the prevalence of violence against women, while also sharing information about how First Nations women and transgender people are twice as likely as their white or cisgender counterparts to experience domestic violence over the course of their lives.[46]

In a similar vein, when addressing the limitations of research in a 2020 forum on TBI and domestic violence, a presenter raised targeted questions about the need to recognize "intersectional genders" and the forms of marginalization experienced by the wide range of people, including people of color, who identify as LGBTQIA+.[47] This point, the presenter argued, was particularly relevant when considering the high rates of interpersonal and systemic violence targeting transgender people. He then called for a better accounting of the spectrum of gendered identities and expressions that do not align with binary constructs associated with female/male categories. He affirmed that doing so would enhance both research and support services, especially because healthcare can be a discriminatory space for nonbinary, queer, and transgender people.

This recognition emerges in tension with scientific conventions that emphasize sex difference, which, as discussed in chapter 5, tacitly contribute to constructions of a universal female subject. Female TBI might draw attention to the prevalence of male-centric approaches to scientific research on TBI, but it does not aid in responding to the range of gendered social forces that shape domestic and family violence. As biomedical research remains a dominant component of concussion crisis narratives, it contributes to limited engagement with the powerful influence of structural violence on TBI rates. It also means advocates trying to raise awareness of partner-inflicted TBI must navigate the impact of such narrow constructions in at least two capacities: in TBI research practice and in domestic violence movements.

FRONTLINE SERVICES AND THE CHALLENGES OF TBI DIAGNOSIS AMONG VICTIM-SURVIVORS

Frontline responses to domestic violence highlight how universalized ideas about women and victimhood contribute to practical shortcomings in response to partner-inflicted TBI. These limitations begin with widely varying estimates of TBI rates among victim-survivors of domestic violence. Some research suggests that not even a quarter of domestic violence victim-survivors in emergency departments are identified as having TBI symptoms, despite evidence of physical harm.[48] This pattern contrasts with research highlighting significant rates of brain injury—as high as 90 percent among women who seek emergency or support services after incidents of domestic violence.[49] As a US-based epidemiologist explained, "30 to 74 percent, depending on the study, have found women to have a history of TBI. Other studies have looked at physical violence by an intimate partner, and around 90 percent involve some type of injury to the head or neck. . . . However, as I mentioned, there's no current national-level prevalence estimates."[50] In fact, a 2020 Government Accountability Office report acknowledges this lack of federal data and recommends improvements to data collection so that resources could be better channeled to address partner-inflicted TBI.[51]

This trend reflects an underlying concern expressed by experts: a lack of professional training in TBI makes it difficult to identify the cause and nature of symptoms that victim-survivors present. Consider, for instance, how this pattern manifests itself in shelters and refuges intended to support victim-survivors of domestic and family violence. As Valera explains, "If you think of the resources shelters provide, they may have a social worker, a therapist, somebody with some legal experience. But there's no neuro-rehab, no one's thinking about anything like that."[52] Shelters are often not equipped to conduct formal screening for TBI, with staff likely to attribute symptoms to behavioral or psychological conditions, such as depression or trauma, instead of brain injury.[53] These limitations make it difficult for support staff to differentiate TBI or postconcussion symptoms from, for example, post-traumatic stress related to violence. Similarly, in Australia and Canada, many frontline workers and general physicians lack TBI-specific education or training. As Fitts has explained, these shortcomings contribute to symptoms being attributed to "mental health or drugs and alcohol or a combination of those things" without considering the possibility of brain injury.[54]

Specialist organizations such as Standing Courageous aim to fill this gap through consciousness-raising talks about domestic violence-related TBI and by training professionals such as first responders and police. Its mission is informed by the experiences of its founder, Paula Walters, whose TBI-related conditions were diagnosed thirteen years after being caused by a violent partner. She not only had health consequences, including irritability, light and noise sensitivity, and memory loss, but she also suffered under the stress of financial debt and unemployment after losing her job as a paramedic.[55] In addition to training, other suggestions focus on improving tools for first responders to identify symptoms of brain injury, including the use of on-site hand-held devices with eye-tracking technology that helps determine whether someone is concussed.[56] Experts, including Australian neuropathologist and founder of the Australian Sports Brain Bank Michael Buckland, have also emphasized the need to mainstream CTE screening to better understand and raise awareness of the long-term harms of physical violence, particularly when it is repeatedly inflicted by partners.[57]

Prioritizing these kinds of scientifically informed interventions is understandable given the challenges of diagnosing TBI in victim-survivors, but they do not necessarily mean appropriate services flow to those in need. In fact, the targeted focus on identifying TBI in individuals risks not engaging more deeply with the challenges presented by the systems and spaces that victim-survivors occupy. For example, there is ample analysis of how shelter rules can undermine women's agency and psychological well-being, discriminate against women of color, and ostracize gender nonconforming, queer, and transgender people.[58] Recognition of TBI arguably does little in these contexts without institutional and structural reform. In addition, technologies adopted in the hope of better identifying and helping victim-survivors, including those with TBI, do not overcome the well-documented shortcomings of police approaches to domestic and family violence. Body cameras offer a case in point. Despite seeming to provide objective documentation of events, this evidence is still subject to interpretation. Authorities often perceive victim-survivors as suspect and unreliable if they deviate from stereotypes associated with ideal victims. Research demonstrates that interpretations of video evidence often reify—instead of challenge—these subjective beliefs.[59] Collectively, these examples attest to the ways in which individualized interventions alone are unlikely to benefit victim-survivors with (and without) TBI.

This pattern is concerning when considering how different victim-survivors interact with healthcare and criminal legal systems. For example, many First Nations women not only face higher rates of violence, including homicide, but also must navigate legal and social service responses that often compound—rather than address—these forms of violence. Fitts and colleagues' work has shown how these effects deter Aboriginal women in Australia from reporting domestic and family violence, because, to quote one of her participants, "if there is any words that come from the woman that children were there, children are considered at risk and so they are taken."[60] Such risks reflect the material consequences of structural violence for victim-survivors, particularly if their identities and experiences do not align with imagined notions of victimhood associated with middle-class, white women. It is these and other entanglements with criminal legal systems that make reliance on formal institutions precarious—even perilous—for many victim-survivors.

While many advocates did not convey an appreciation of these intersections during our research, many would acknowledge funding limitations. This was especially of concern in the United States, where a downward trend in resourcing for domestic violence services has been documented in many states.[61] To illustrate the need to better fund services, they often refer to successful interventions for victim-survivors. The Domestic Violence Brain Injury Program at the Barrow Neurological Institute in Phoenix, Arizona was the first program of its kind and was a highly praised example during our research—both within and beyond the United States. The program provides a multidisciplinary approach to concussion rehabilitation, accounting for distinct physiological afflictions associated with domestic violence, such as strangulation. Trained social workers provide additional support—for example, assistance with child custody, employment, and housing—and the program fully covers treatment costs thanks in large part to philanthropic funding.

Only a few such programs have been piloted elsewhere, including one at a survivor-led antiviolence organization in Toronto, Ontario.[62] According to the Barrow program's medical director, Glynnis Zieman, these combined services are essential, because, to use her words, "I can give patients all kinds of explanations for their migraines, but if they don't know where they're sleeping next week, their priority is somewhere else."[63] Despite its success, the Barrow model has not proliferated, which Zieman attributes to a lack of "in-house medical expertise or the funds to acquire it." One limitation of evoking an isolated exemplar to follow, though, is that it leaves questions about how to overcome structural barriers. They include, but are not limited to, funding inadequacies and difficulties determining how to tailor services for the diverse needs of victim-survivors. Moreover, it is not easy to anticipate the prospective influence of fellow traveler discourses. As we show next, calls for legal recognition of partner-inflicted TBI offer some insight into the pervasive influence of carceral creep.

ADVOCACY FOR LEGAL RECOGNITION AND THE RISKS OF APPEALING FOR PUNISHMENT

Advocacy around partner-inflicted TBI is not limited to healthcare and service provision for victim-survivors. Law represents a resource and tool for responding to TBI. Even though many people who experience domestic and family violence do not report it to police, appeals to legal authority are not surprising: criminalized logics have strongly influenced approaches to domestic violence, and family-related conflict often involves legal complications, particularly if there are attempts to separate from a partner or if children are affected. Law, as an arena for addressing domestic and family violence-related harms, is not always straightforward or conducive to the needs of victimized people.

While the punitive edge of law is commonly envisioned as targeting only those charged with abuse, it often affects victim-survivors by perpetuating further victimization, particularly for people of color disproportionately criminalized by these systems.[64] These patterns demonstrate how the power of law reflects patriarchal values and relies on binary logic, which threatens to aggravate harms among groups facing other forms of social exclusion and marginalization.[65] Further, as disability studies scholars have documented, law is often complicit in committing injustices against people with disabilities—an observation that is particularly relevant for victim-survivors who suffer longer-term effects of TBI.[66]

During our research, law emerged as an influential fellow traveler discourse within TBI frameworks. It informed many framings of remedies for victim-survivors with TBI, although people who worked in the domestic and family violence sector tended to prioritize the need for improved service provision and support rather than engage in debates about law and punishment. In fact, some participants in the United States explicitly cited the devastating consequences of criminal legal proceedings for women they had worked with previously.[67] In contrast, many TBI experts tended to both embrace and underestimate carceral creep. Their imaginings of law often upheld criminal punishments as strategies for addressing the harms of partner-inflicted TBI without fully appreciating the potential negative impacts of legally recognizing victim-survivors who have had multiple concussions.

One illustrative example comes from an observed discussion between experts about how to better convey the effects of sustained violence and repeated TBI in court proceedings. The conversation focused on how to apply research insights to document the needs of victim-survivors and ensure they received adequate legal protections. Some were surprised when one participant asked if there were potentially unintended consequences for victim-survivors: could such evidence be used *against* the people this group had hoped to support?[68] In response, at least one expert admitted she had assumed the legal recognition of brain damage would be good for women with histories of domestic violence. She and others conceded that such findings could serve as grounds for questioning whether a victim-survivor has sufficient cognition or capacity to care for children or maintain regular employment. In fact, such information could be used to prevent victim-survivors from working in some professions.

Advocates have increasingly acknowledged this tension. While a diagnosis is often necessary for victim-survivors to be eligible for TBI-specific medical treatment and rehabilitation, it may not have empowering effects, especially given the lack of resources for partner-inflicted TBI. A 2022 *Globe and Mail* piece captures this potential catch-22: "Without adequate services to direct women to, some experts believe that even informal brain injury diagnoses can be pointless—or even dangerous; for example, it could be weaponized against a woman during child custody proceedings."[69] Despite the inclination to imagine law as an important arbiter of justice for victim-survivors, the history of the domestic violence move-ment suggests the realities of legal practices yield highly variable outcomes.

Similar contradictions emerged around advocacy efforts aimed at improving law enforcement responses, as participants often negated how these partner-ships come with the risk of state-sanctioned violence. In Phoenix, Arizona, for example, where the Barrow Domestic Violence Brain Injury Program is based, recent investigations into law enforcement officer misconduct have revealed how gender-based violence, including sexual assault, occurs with impunity despite com-plaints.[70] In other parts of North America, as well as Australia, expressed concerns about police brutality include forms of gender-based violence, including domestic and family violence, in addition to outcries about racial oppression.[71] These move-ments point to a deeper phenomenon in which criminal legal systems are normal-ized as the response to domestic and family violence.[72] These logics present state institutions as allies targeting individual perpetrators as the purveyors of violence, even though system responses are more likely to treat women and queer people of color, particularly Black women, as criminals rather than as victims. We revisit these themes in chapter 7, considering how state violence is a source of TBI-related harms, as evinced in Australian cases of Indigenous deaths in police custody. In relation to concerns about partner-inflicted TBI, the limitations of law enforcement responses to domestic and family violence were largely absent.

Instead, proposed reforms to police practice focused primarily on improving the recognition of TBI among victim-survivors. Although well-intended, these expressions conveyed foundational assumptions that law enforcement officials would perceive women with partner-inflicted TBI as victims. Testimonials of victim-survivors who have navigated institutional responses to partner-inflicted TBI illuminate more complicated dynamics, some of which have featured in PINK Concussions' advocacy efforts. In one such statement, a participant explained that even though she had been hospitalized,

> not a single person, other than the ambulance driver who was with my husband standing at the end of ambulance, asked me, "Did your husband do this to you?" Not a single person looked at me and said, "Hmm, something's not right here about what this woman came into the hospital with." So, I need you guys to think outside of the box . . . I have never had any treatment to this time, and so that's what I really need for you guys to do in the future.[73]

Her explanation depicts how institutions charged with caring for patients are not necessarily responsive to victim-survivors' circumstances. It also highlights barri-ers to disclosing domestic violence to healthcare practitioners, including fears that medical personnel would not understand or respond to violence appropriately and that a perpetrator (in this case, her husband) would retaliate if he were to find out.[74]

Her observation nonetheless puts the onus on institutions to find solutions. Developing such responses, as scholars of violence against women convincingly argue, cannot be limited to strategies that focus on individual acts of physical violence.[75] It requires naming and addressing patriarchal structures that foster violence and how such violence also includes nonphysical dimensions. Focusing on technological interventions that aim to improve first responders' concussion diagnoses—for example, eye-tracking devices—do not target such structures or recognize the multifaceted nature of violence affecting victim-survivors. In fact, technologies intended to collect evidence of domestic violence harms can be used to stand in for the voices of victim-survivors in court—even when those survivors want to disengage from criminal legal proceedings.[76] Such data, particularly when interpreted by law enforcement officials, can be understood as more credible and trustworthy than accounts made by the women who experienced the violence firsthand. These problems should serve as cautionary examples for responses to partner-inflicted TBI. While the acknowledgement of cognitive impairment may help in explaining a victim-survivor's behavior and circumstances, it can also serve as grounds to undermine their agency.

The underappreciation of structural inequities emerges in some advocates' calls for more punitive approaches to partner-inflicted TBI. In prioritizing legal forms of punishment, such recommendations reflect an embrace of what scholars describe as *carceral feminism*. Carceral feminism, as feminist sociologist Elizabeth Bernstein explains, entails the overreliance on criminal legal systems like police and prisons to advance feminist goals, such as addressing partner-inflicted violence.[77] Appeals to cite TBI in criminal sentencing is one prominent example of this approach. With many US states increasingly recognizing strangulation as a distinct criminal offence, experts have considered the benefits of affording TBI similar status. Given the nature and complexity of TBI and its effects, the need for persuasive medical testimony and evidence is a major concern. In one such discussion, experts contemplated several proposals: from creating specialty exams for medical practitioners to implementing a forensic system that would store biomarker data.[78] They speculated on the challenges of obtaining a conviction for partner-inflicted TBI, which included how to draft TBI-specific statutes, how to develop reliable yet affordable medical tests, how to train law enforcement to recognize TBI, and how to ensure that the timing and severity of a TBI could be documented.

During our research, many well-meaning participants in North America would often frame these efforts as a partnership in which legal and scientific experts could work together to enhance the formal recognition of the harms perpetrated by men who abuse their partners. While this is an understandable goal given the widespread failures to meaningfully address domestic and family violence, such strategies follow a longstanding pattern of pushing for criminal punishment in the name of protecting victim-survivors. Yet these kinds of approaches should not be prioritized over others that could, for instance, assist in alleviating economic and housing challenges that make it difficult for victim-survivors to leave abusive relationships.[79] In contrast, many Australian experts working in this area demonstrated a clearer awareness that punitive responses do not guarantee resources for victim-survivors—and that law enforcement responses would not always lead to supportive pathways, especially for Indigenous women with TBI. If anything, they understood further revictimization through criminal legal processes can involve apathetic or harmful responses from police, as well as discrimination by health, housing, and legal institutions. In short, advocacy concerned primarily with punishment negates how many victim-survivors endure forms of violence beyond that which is inflicted by partners.

CONCLUSION

The growing recognition of partner-inflicted TBI reflects ongoing challenges in responding to domestic and family violence. Although the increased acknowledgement of intersecting axes of oppression suggests promise for developing responses tailored for the diverse needs of victim-survivors, fellow traveler discourses can sustain forms of gender essentialism and undermine these efforts. In this case, the privileging of sex difference and biomedical research discussed in chapter 5 means much of the evidence base on TBI among women does not capture interlocking systems of inequality. In addition, many proposals for institutional interventions can evoke narrow conceptions of how legal, medical, and social services respond to partner-inflicted TBI. For example, a notable number of North American participants focused on how systems should support victims without necessarily acknowledging the differential practices that occur in cases of domestic and family violence. Given how government support has contributed to embedding law enforcement approaches within domestic violence responses, it is perhaps unsurprising that many appeals for funding do not question the value of criminal legal practices.

These conditions undermine critical engagement with how interlocking formations of oppression shape domestic and family violence. The resulting situation showcases a well-established intersectional dilemma: that the recognition of only one axis of oppression (in this case, gender) fails to adequately capture and respond to the systems of domination that victim-survivors experience.[80] Gender oppression is not isolated from ableism, classism, heteronormativity, and racism; they are entangled. These entanglements become visible when accounting for the varying experiences of victim-survivors, particularly those who are not middle-class or white. In practice, failing to recognize those differences can harm groups whose experiences cannot be captured by a singular focus on gender. This trend contributes to the carceral creep exemplified by the US domestic violence movement.

In relation to partner-inflicted TBI advocacy, an embrace of specific notions of victimhood may offer promising rhetoric for raising awareness of the patriarchal norms in TBI research and response, but it does not necessarily translate into comprehensive action that benefits victim-survivors. For example, proposed sentencing enhancements for partner-inflicted TBI focus on individualized forms of violence, not the broader patterns of violence that victim-survivors experience, including through criminal legal systems. The emphasis on punishment can direct attention and resources away from the need for structurally attuned responses that support victim-survivors more holistically and address violence more widely in society. As we have traced in other chapters of this book, the linkages between masculinity and violence are not limited to the actions of individuals. They are socially embedded. Embracing criminalized logics leaves little space for counteracting the deeper connections between masculinity and violence, including those expressed in spaces of law and policing. Thus, in the next chapter, we explore state violence as an overlooked and underappreciated force within concussion crisis discourses.

7

From Criminal Minds
to Deviant Brains

In 2017, at the age of twenty-seven, former NFL star Aaron Hernandez died by suicide in his prison cell. He was two years into a life sentence without parole for the murder of Odin Lloyd. Within six months of Hernandez's death, neuroscientists from Boston University announced he had been diagnosed with CTE. In a press conference, Ann McKee, the neuropathologist whose work has been central to understanding CTE, announced that Hernandez had Stage III CTE (with Stage IV being the most severe). His brain, she explained, represented the most extreme case of the disease her lab had observed in a person under the age of forty-six. Throughout her presentation, brain images flashed on the large projector screen behind her, displaying slides that juxtaposed Hernandez's atrophied, discolored brain tissue with the larger, healthier brain of a normal twenty-seven-year-old (see fig. 5, page 39). As we explained in chapter 2, the comparative images provided a visual basis for non-expert audiences to see the magnitude of a CTE diagnosis. They enabled an explanatory connection between Hernandez's deviant behavior in life and the deviance observed in his brain. Their presentation reinforces the significance of McKee's claims, which seemed to verify speculations about Hernandez's actions in life: although he had been a standout American football player at the University of Florida and as a member of the New England Patriots, Hernandez was often perceived as "a ticking time bomb."[1]

Many media representations of Hernandez had drawn heavily on racialized tropes, depicting him as a "thug" who lacked self-control over his criminalistic tendencies.[2] The brain images emerged as a different way to make sense of his deviance. As McKee highlighted the severe degeneration specific to the brain's frontal lobes, she described how these regions are "very important for decision-making, judgment, and cognition."[3] Although she stated that she could not confirm

110

whether the damage was the cause of Hernandez's violent actions, McKee stated that individuals with CTE of the same severity would have "difficulty with impulse control, decision-making, inhibition of impulses for aggression, emotional volatility, [and] rage behaviors."[4] With no evidence of other brain diseases, such as Alzheimer's, every aspect of the analysis conducted by McKee and her colleagues uncovered what she described as "classic CTE."[5]

This brain-focused narrative would carry over into public commentaries on Aaron Hernandez's life and death. In addition to news media, Hernandez's story was the subject of a popular 2020 Netflix true crime series, *Killer Inside: The Mind of Aaron Hernandez*. The production suggested that CTE exacerbated an inherent deviance in Hernandez that manifested as violence after he spent years wrestling with his closeted homosexuality in a notoriously homophobic football culture.[6] CTE has since emerged as the suspected cause of other violent acts by former professional collision sports athletes, including former NFL player Phillip Adams, who killed six people before taking his own life in 2021 and who was later diagnosed with Stage II CTE.[7] We consider these and similar cases as representative of the "CTE defense," an explanation for criminal actions that frames CTE as an uncontrollable condition that can cause violent behaviors.

These kinds of causal explanations for acts of violence misdirect focus away from social problems contributing to crime and deviance. By locating the source of violence in the brain, these accounts stifle engagement with complex societal issues related to violence, which are informed by inequality, marginalization, and trauma. In attributing the source of deviance to the body rather than society, these explanations negate how social inequities, institutions, and structures shape manifestations of crime and deviance.

Aaron Hernandez emerged as a unique case where American football-related CTE was proposed as the cause of his violent behavior, which had been previously attributed to his character flaws. Connections between TBI and crime, however, are more common than this discourse insinuates. There are disproportionately high rates of TBI among criminalized persons in the United States, a population in which nonwhite and poor people are overrepresented. Estimates for rates of TBI among criminalized people range between 25 percent and 87 percent (versus 8 percent in the general population).[8] Research also suggests high rates of TBI among incarcerated people.[9] Similarly, people experiencing homelessness or housing insecurity are ten times more likely to experience moderate or severe TBI than the general population, with self-report data indicating higher rates of poor "physical and mental health, higher suicidality and suicide risk, memory concerns, and increased health service use and criminal justice involvement."[10] Yet, in contrast to high-profile evocations of the CTE defense, there remains little recognition of these trends within and beyond legal systems. There is even less scrutiny of the societal forms of violence that contribute to these groups experiencing TBI at such rates.

In this chapter, we explore these disparities, looking at how TBI-related afflictions have been treated differentially by law and state authorities. To illustrate, we draw from research carried out across our research sites, first focusing on US discourses proclaiming how the CTE defense can change legal practices, then highlighting connections between brain injury and state violence observed in both Australia and the United States, and finally reflecting on legal challenges related to compensation for TBI-related injuries, which have been most pronounced in the United States. Across these examples, legal documents, media narratives, and scholarly research provide an archive of how damaged brains have been assessed and understood. Taken together, they facilitate closer scrutiny of how law becomes intertwined with other forms of oppression and structural violence. Racism, in particular, comes to the fore.

Scholars have explained how law does not simply interact with violence; it is a field built on violence.[11] Law does not seek to end violence; it harnesses and controls its distribution. In some legal cases, like that of Hernandez, connections between TBI and crime are visible, discussed, and debated as part of the concussion crisis discourse. In other circumstances, such as when the state mobilizes violence against people—for example, through law enforcement—public recognition of these harms is often invisible or framed as separate from concussion crisis rhetoric. This selective recognition of TBI in relation to crime and deviance is reflective of law's capacity to channel and shape violence. These processes, both overt and implicit, communicate values and understandings not just about TBI but about different social groups. As sociologist Oliver Rollins has noted in relation to the wider influence of neurobiological knowledge, the discourse contributes to shaping explanations of how brain function contributes to the likelihood of actions that are understood as normal or violent.[12] Here, we examine how law, including the violence it wields, informs what—and how—injured brains become enrolled in and excluded in discussions of violence within concussion crisis narratives.

THE RISE OF THE CTE DEFENSE

As we elaborate in chapter 2, scientific definitions typically describe CTE as a neurodegenerative condition associated with repeated exposure to TBI. Although the capacity to connect CTE pathology to lived symptoms is still developing, existing work has observed that individuals diagnosed with CTE can exhibit noticeable cognitive and emotional decline, as well as problems with aggression and impulse control, before their death.[13] The CTE defense connects two causal logics: that repetitive head impacts sustained through sports produce measurable brain damage *and* that this brain damage can provoke criminal actions. As Hernandez's crimes were connected to his CTE diagnosis following McKee's announcement, the postmortem framings of his wrongdoings exemplify these connections. In fact, Hernandez's attorney, Jose Baez, has since expressed regret for not introducing arguments around CTE during the murder trials, stating that, in hindsight, he had witnessed Hernandez display many behaviors linked to CTE.[14]

Law professors Amy Dillard and Lisa Tucker concur that such an approach might have made a difference. In a *New York Times* editorial, published under the provocative headline, "Is CTE a Defense for Murder?", they argue that information about the behavioral manifestations of CTE could have swayed the jury's thinking in Hernandez's murder trial.[15] Their commentary questions whether Hernandez should have been held responsible for his actions when CTE is known to compromise a person's cognitive and emotional state. They conclude: "We now know there was substantial evidence that Mr. Hernandez should not have been convicted of first-degree murder. Given the conclusive diagnosis of Stage III CTE, it is likely that a lifetime of playing football—not Mr. Hernandez's will—was to blame." Their reasoning suggests that CTE is grounds for recognizing the accused's incapacity for self-control. Like the insanity defense, this would require expert witnesses to establish (or refute) a defendant's diminished capacity or responsibility.

CTE has yet to be deployed successfully as a legal defense, but the articulation of the CTE defense has nonetheless informed cultural imaginings of criminal, particularly violent, behavior. Immediately after Hernandez's death, and months before McKee's formal diagnosis, journalists speculated about how a future CTE diagnosis might change his status under the law.[16] They also posed questions about whether lawyers would incorporate CTE into their defense of Kellen Winslow Jr., a former NFL player convicted of kidnapping, rape, and sexual assault. Although Winslow was thirty-five years old and had not been formally diagnosed with CTE, the notion that brain damage could contribute to reduced mental capacity informed media coverage of his trial.[17] Commentators considered the viability of this legal strategy for Winslow through direct comparisons with Hernandez, and they presented both men's crimes as particularly egregious and lacking in self-control.

Evoking CTE in this way offers a neuroscientific explanation for spectacular forms of violence. Consider, for example, ex-NFL player Phillip Adams, who killed six people and died by a self-inflicted shotgun wound. Family members quoted in the media indicated that his "mental health degraded fast and [was] terribly bad" prior to his death, demonstrating "'extremely concerning' signs of mental illness, including an escalating temper and personal hygiene neglect."[18] The family's statement about his postmortem CTE diagnosis conveyed an appreciation for obtaining a "better understanding of the mental turmoil that Phillip was dealing with during the last moments of his life." They elaborated on how he had sought assistance but to no avail:

> After going through medical records from his football career, we do know that he was desperately seeking help from the NFL but was denied all claims due to his inability to remember things and to handle seemingly simple tasks such as traveling hours away to see doctors and going through extensive evaluations.[19]

Despite a history of documented concussions during his professional career, Adams was not eligible for compensation as part of the NFL settlement because he had not retired by 2014.[20]

These observations, while centered on making sense of violence committed by former professional American football players, reflect a wider shift in understandings of the brain. Beyond questions of legal adjudication and culpability, neuroscience and neuropathology have gained traction as explanations for various social problems, including crime and violence. This logic, which has been referred to as *neurocriminology*, locates the basis for deviant behavior inside the brain so that criminal actions can be explained as matters of neurological dysfunction.[21] Along these lines, the focus on Hernandez's brain effectively recoded his crimes, repositioning him as a victim of violence in addition to being a perpetrator of crime. As this notion of victimhood informed assertions that Hernandez should not be held fully responsible for his violent actions, his damaged brain also became physical evidence that could implicate institutions, such as the NFL and NCAA, as failing to protect him from the harms of football.[22]

Yet there are pitfalls to such neurocriminological reasoning. The CTE defense constructs neurological explanations for crime, which gloss over the behavioral, environmental, and social processes surrounding violent acts.[23] Athletes' relationships with violence are manifestations of more than brain dysfunction: they can be shaped by involvement in sports cultures, the status and privileges that often accompany athletic careers, possible histories of trauma and exploitation, or experiences of discrimination and social marginalization. Neurocriminology, however, sidesteps investigation into the complex confluence of biographical and societal considerations that shape behaviors. It approaches violence as something perpetrated by individuals, ignoring how structural inequalities create conditions for interpersonal violence. In chapter 1, we explored how sports violence is a multidimensional phenomenon involving media spectacles, political economic relations, and social values that materialize through the damage inflicted on athletes' bodies. Common neurocriminological accounts, in contrast, do not conceptualize sports violence beyond the accumulation of trauma in athletes' brains. By locating deviance in the brain, such explanations lose sight of how behaviors, even those associated with CTE, are not isolated from the social conditions that influence athletes' relationships with violence. Importantly, the CTE defense does not reckon with contradictions between the celebration of athletes' aggression on the field and their unsettling acts of violence away from their sport.

Despite the perceived potential of the CTE defense for holding powerful institutions to account, its limitations hinder such efforts. Since this particular defense relies on establishing neurobiological links between TBI, CTE, and deviant behavior, it is susceptible to familiar arguments that refute causal connections by citing scientific uncertainty or the intricacies of athletes' lives. For instance, NFL spokesperson Joe Lockhart affirmed that Hernandez's "personal story is complex. It doesn't lend itself to simple answers."[24] While such statements point to the legitimate problems with using CTE as the sole explanation for acts of violence, they also support the manufacture of doubt around the connection between football and brain damage.[25] Neurocriminological reasoning can thus help organizations disavow culpability because its impression of straightforward causality can be undermined by questioning CTE's connection to collision sports. In the Hernandez story and similar cases, the CTE defense overlooks how the institution of American football—dominated by the NFL and the NCAA—impacts players' lives beyond the harm inflicted on their bodies and brains. As players must navigate a sports culture that rewards masculine aggression and celebrates violence, the physical toll of a football career is intertwined with players' embodiment of the sport's cultural values. The focus on neurobiological causation draws attention away from the role of sports organizations in shaping athletes' dispositions and overall well-being including, but not limited to, brain trauma.

These observations point to tensions within practices of law and science. The law may present science as a category of knowledge characterized by factual certainty, but scientific findings are often questioned or challenged during legal proceedings.[26] The credibility of science is not taken for granted in court; its claims are subject to critical scrutiny through proceedings.[27] Building a criminal defense around the incapacitating effects of TBI or CTE requires navigating the interpretative logics of law, not simply making assertions of fact. Classist, gendered, and racialized beliefs can also come to bear on how scientific findings and other evidence are assessed across criminal legal systems. Discriminatory assumptions can prevent many people who experience TBI from having their injuries recognized when they encounter law or other forms of state authority. As we discuss in the pages that follow, power relationships often foreclose the possibility of identifying the consequences of brain damage in certain people and can perpetuate forms of violence in doing so.

THE NONRECOGNITION OF BRAIN TRAUMA AS VIOLENCE

Although the Aaron Hernandez story may appear to be a distinctive case linking TBI and deviance, data on wider patterns of brain injury among incarcerated persons suggest otherwise. What makes the Hernandez story unique is not necessarily his criminalization but his athletic success. Indeed, two trends are notable when comparing estimated rates of TBI among incarcerated persons to the general population: (1) that justice-involved people—who are disproportionately Black, Brown, Indigenous, and poor—experience higher rates of TBI; and (2) that their exposure to violence can be nearly ten times greater over their life course.[28] While researchers have not established a "direct causal relationship" between criminal legal involvement and TBI, they have observed a connection between rates of brain injury and exposure to violence.[29] These rates, particularly as they correlate with incarceration, are imprints of violence beyond acts inflicted by individuals; they reflect how state and structural violence harm certain types of bodies more than others.

Common conceptions of violence tend to focus on acts of crime and interpersonal violence. They often overlook enactments of state violence, which can be perpetrated by government or state institutions and include acts of police brutality, or violence and self-harm occurring under the direct supervision of state systems. As sociologist Aaron Roussell and colleagues explain, the state "is the unnamed elephant in the room" within assessments of crime and violence.[30] State violence is particularly hard to pin down. Current and historical crime measures rarely capture the impact of state violence and conceal how certain populations are at "elevated risk for violence from civilians *and* the state."[31]

In recent years, though, the actions of state agents, particularly law enforcement, have received greater public attention—and in concrete ways. Consider, for instance, the impact of bystander video recordings showing the killing of George Floyd, an unarmed Black man arrested by Minneapolis police for allegedly using a counterfeit twenty-dollar bill, and of Eric Garner, a Black man whom police attempted to arrest on suspicion of selling individual cigarettes without tax stamps. These deaths prompted significant social mobilization and sparked protests nationally and globally. Both men experienced lethal forms of neck compression—Floyd owing to an officer's knee on his neck and Garner owing to a prohibited chokehold—as they repeated their last words, "I can't breathe."

These and other killings have raised awareness about not only connections between racism and police brutality, but also the use of chokeholds specifically. Chokeholds, a term often used to capture two use-of-force tactics (chokeholds and carotid holds), can block someone's breathing or slow blood flow to the brain to render the person unconscious. They can result in significant brain damage. This observation, following George Floyd's death, prompted some neurologists to refute suggestions that law enforcement can safely use these techniques, stating any such claims are "simply false."[32] Pressure to change use-of-force policies has induced a notable uptick in curtailing or prohibiting chokeholds in many North American jurisdictions, despite legal challenges by police unions.[33] The US Department of Justice announced a ban on their use in 2021 (except in cases where deadly force is authorized); the Royal Canadian Mounted Police, however, continues to allow their use, even though the federal government in Ottawa called for an end to these practices.[34] Despite being a substantial shift in policy, the progress on chokeholds reflects the impact of focusing on individualized notions of law enforcement violence. This focus negates how police brutality is a structural phenomenon and not simply violence committed by rogue police officers acting out their own racial hostilities.[35]

Critics have expressed cautionary warnings about narrowly targeted interventions that focus on monitoring and controlling individual officers' behavior. Research shows that reforms to curb or deter violence such as body cameras do not address structures that enable state violence. Criminologist Katheryn Russell-Brown highlights the unintended consequences of embracing these technologies: the evidence they collect often stands in for the voices of communities that experience high levels of police violence.[36] This move, although often done to increase police accountability, demonstrates governments' continued disregard of community proposals to counter such violence. Recordings of police violence have not led to structural changes but instead re-entrench social inequalities. While the online circulation of these videos creates space for the collective witnessing of police violence, it also means that affected communities can be retraumatized through the broadcasting of harms suffered by their own people.[37] These images and videos, particularly police body camera footage, have also become digital commodities that increase website traffic and generate revenue for internet users and platforms.[38] In this way, visibility has not meant accountability—or even meaningful recognition of the multifaceted harms caused by police violence.[39] Instead, it creates new modes of trauma for communities already managing various forms of violence.

Against this backdrop, it is perhaps not surprising that groups who disproportionately bear the brunt of state violence remain disconnected from concussion crisis narratives, even as experts increasingly frame police violence as a "public health crisis" and call for greater investment in community-centered approaches to safety and security.[40] When brain injury is recognized among these groups, responses obscure how these individuals are more likely to experience *both* interpersonal and state violence. For example, as we discussed in chapter 6, advocates have suggested using knowledge about TBI among victims of domestic and family violence to strengthen mechanisms for punishment or to ensure the incarceration of perpetrators. Doing so risks creating further exposure to trauma and violence through the criminal legal system and may not guarantee appropriate support or resources for victim-survivors. Proposals to acknowledge the harms of domestic and family violence through legally binding TBI-sentencing enhancements, which would use evidence of TBI to pursue harsher sentences, serve as a case in point. In practice, prioritizing legal punishment requires victim-survivors' engagement with the police, which can result in them experiencing forms of revictimization and may not deliver the legal outcomes they desire. Focusing primarily on sentencing enhancements not only negates victim-survivors' needs, but also risks disregarding the impacts of interpersonal and state violence on the lives of people, including women and children, in abusive situations.

The complexity of responding to overlapping patterns of violence becomes clear in instances when the state has failed people who have experienced TBI in its custody. Consider, for example, the fifty-five-year-old Yorta Yorta woman Tanya

Day.[41] Day is one of the hundreds of Indigenous persons who have died in Australian jails and detention facilities since 1991, when the Royal Commission into Aboriginal Deaths in Custody issued its final report and made 339 recommendations to prevent such deaths.[42] In December 2017, Day fell asleep on a train traveling to Melbourne. Instead of reaching her destination, she was detained by police and sustained a TBI later that evening while confined to a prison cell. She died seventeen days later in a Melbourne hospital.[43] Day was arrested for public drunkenness after the conductor called police to assist with managing an "unruly" passenger; her legs had allegedly blocked the aisle while she slept. After being awakened by police, Day was transferred to a prison for a four-hour "sobering up" period, during which she fell a total of five times, hitting her head on the cell wall. Despite protocols to physically check on detainees every thirty minutes, police returned hours later to find Day appearing unwell, with a large bruise on her forehead.[44] An ambulance arrived an hour later and transported Day to a local hospital. A scan revealed bleeding on her brain because her head hit the wall while in police custody. Day was then airlifted to a larger hospital, where she was admitted for surgery and later died.

The coroner's inquiry indicated that Day's death resulted from a "left cerebral haemorrhage of traumatic origin" and "was clearly preventable had she not been arrested and taken into custody."[45] The coroner, Caitlin English, acknowledged the family's request to consider whether Day's death was the result of negligent manslaughter and whether systemic racism was an attributable cause—making it the first Australian investigation into a death in custody to acknowledge racism in this way. English's assessment stopped short of attributing the death to systemic racism but did not deny the role of "unconscious bias" in Day's death. English specifically highlighted how Day's arrest for public drunkenness compared to the treatment of a non-Indigenous woman who was also found intoxicated on a train the same day. The other woman was taken home and did not receive a fine.

English also described the conductor's "decision to consider [Day] unruly and to call police in preference to other options was influenced by her Aboriginality," citing that Day was the "only sleeping passenger he has ever called police to remove from the train, although he comes across three sleeping passengers a week."[46] She reported that the officers responsible for Day's arrest had not adhered to police policies and protocols, failing to treat her "with dignity and humanity" as required by the state's human rights charter.[47] English found that "an indictable offence may have been committed," as the evidence suggested officers had not adequately attended to Day's health or safety while she was in custody.[48] Months later, however, the police announced they would not pursue charges against the officers. Their decision prompted criticisms about the government's failure to address police impunity.

The circumstances of Day's death point to a longer-standing set of issues related to police violence. Day's family expressed such concerns when responding to the decision not to pursue charges: "In the last 30 years, hundreds of Aboriginal people . . . have died at the hands of the police, yet no police officer has ever been held criminally responsible. Aboriginal people will keep dying in custody until the legal system changes and police are held accountable."[49] While the state government has not embraced Indigenous calls for broader community-led reforms,[50] it has decriminalized public drunkenness, which was one of the recommendations from the Royal Commission into Aboriginal Deaths in Custody. Decriminalization alone, however, does not acknowledge the deeper patterns of structural violence that underpin this offence and its enforcement. As Gomeroi legal scholar Amanda Whittaker explains, public drunkenness is a "highly discretionary" and "highly racialized offense" in Australia; nearly a third of people incarcerated for public order offenses are of Aboriginal or Torres Strait Islander heritage.[51]

Similarly, Aboriginal and Torres Strait Islander peoples make up 32 percent of the average daily population incarcerated in Australia despite being only 3 percent of the overall population.[52] Experts have traced this pattern as interconnected with experiences of abuse and trauma.[53] State violence often exacerbates these conditions by selectively recognizing them. For example, an analysis of coroners' inquests over nearly thirty years reveals that police have rarely recognized or protected women, particularly Indigenous women, as victims of interpersonal violence. Police have instead dismissed women's health and safety concerns while sometimes scorning them when doing so.[54] Medical professionals have directed women experiencing violence, including those in states of mental crisis, to carceral settings rather than culturally appropriate care and treatment facilities. Coroners' reports reveal evidence of trauma from domestic and family violence, systemic racism, and grief from the loss of loved ones. The causes of physical injuries like TBI cannot be disentangled from these conditions.

In highlighting patterns among women who have died in custody, there is a tendency to focus on the individual characteristics associated with criminalization, incarceration, and death. Yet such an emphasis distracts from how inequitable systems frame these women as "criminal," "disturbed," and "sick" in the first place.[55] Such characterizations have been used to reinforce perceptions of Black and Indigenous peoples as inherently deviant or susceptible to violence. Formal explanations of Indigenous deaths in custody can reproduce underlying assumptions and judgments that critical race and feminist scholar Sherene Razack has described in depth—that is, medicalized explanations can represent the dead person as "an inherently sick body" who was "responsible for [their] own demise."[56] This framing reflects the shortcomings of using death rates as indicators of racial inequality without also accounting for the impacts of systemic racism in shaping these disparities.

These limitations extend to broader health concerns. Indigenous health experts Chelsea Watego, a Munanjahli and South Sea Islander woman, and Lisa J. Whop, a Goemulgal person of the Wagadagam tribe of Mabuiag Island in the Torres Strait, warn that an over-emphasis on individual characteristics "risks perpetuating racialized imaginings of Indigenous peoples as 'destined to die.'"[57] They highlight the consequences of health professionals' inclination to cite behavioral explanations for Aboriginal and Torres Strait Islander health outcomes. In other words, such explanations minimize how health and legal systems perpetuate racial violence that contributes to illness, injury, and death.[58] This tendency directs attention away from how institutions inflict structural violence and enable it to persist.

TBI among Indigenous peoples is a case in point. Keeping with the Australian context, studies highlight assault as a key cause of TBI among Aboriginal and Torres Strait Islander peoples, a trend that is notably higher compared to non-Indigenous peoples.[59] Available data suggests Aboriginal and Torres Strait Islander peoples living in central, southern, and western parts of the country are up to twenty times more likely than non-Indigenous persons to be admitted to hospital for a brain injury, with estimates pointing to TBI rates double those of non-Indigenous persons.[60] Some researchers, including Marcia Langton, a distinguished professor of Yiman and Bidjara heritage, have explained how these disparities reflect the stressors managed by Indigenous peoples including "poor housing and overcrowding, financial difficulties and unemployment" but also "intergenerational trauma."[61] She and others acknowledge these experiences are inextricably linked to historical and structural inequalities that persist in Australia.

These connections manifest themselves in patterns of brain injury. Studies show how high rates of TBI are linked to forms of intergenerational trauma like those experienced by many Aboriginal and Torres Strait Islander communities.[62] Despite these trends, service providers often fail to identify TBI among Indigenous peoples. This concern is compounded in rural and remote areas with limited access to specialist treatment for brain injuries. These patterns represent a system of geographic healthcare inequity that is etched and shaped by structural violence.[63] This is violence that, in keeping with sociologist Johan Galtung's observations, leaves "marks not only on the human body but also on the mind and the spirit."[64] Such violence becomes justified—or at least understood as not wrong—through institutionalized healthcare practices.

Structural violence has direct implications for Indigenous peoples' health, particularly regarding their interactions with institutions such as the police. During the COVID-19 pandemic, thousands of people in Australia joined mass gatherings to denounce racial profiling and police brutality in Australia and globally. They called for action to curb Aboriginal and Torres Strait Islander deaths in custody and expressed support for the Black Lives Matter movement. Despite these efforts, Indigenous adults and minors continue to sustain injuries during encounters with law enforcement. In 2022, for instance, the hospitalization of a teenage Indigenous boy who sustained a TBI during an arrest in New South Wales received national media coverage.[65] TBI among Aboriginal and Torres Strait Islander peoples are usually only diagnosed—that is, *if* they are diagnosed—after they are engaged by the criminal legal system as perpetrators or victim-survivors of violence.[66] In addition, authorities often misidentify brain injury symptoms as signs of drug and alcohol consumption, which increases the likelihood of injured people becoming subject to criminal legal processes instead of receiving medical care—let alone participating in culturally appropriate preventative measures.[67]

These responses to brain trauma reflect structural violence affecting the health of Aboriginal and Torres Strait Islander peoples. The systemic inequalities illustrate Ruth Wilson Gilmore's argument that racism instigates premature death among targeted groups. First Nations advocates and health experts have called for approaches that recognize and work to redress racist systems. One such approach, Indigenist Health Humanities, foregrounds Indigenous sovereignty in health contexts and attends to "how race operates in the everyday, from birth to death."[68] Unveiling racism's tangled relationship with structural violence remains a persistent challenge, which we discuss next in relation to compensation claims related to TBI.

RACIALIZING BRAINS AS DEVIANT FROM THE NORM

Outcomes of high-profile lawsuits illustrate how racism can influence how injuries are assessed and how brains are understood. After the NFL reached a billion-dollar settlement with retired players experiencing long-term effects of TBI, questions about discrepancies in payouts emerged, even as awards had been capped at a maximum of five million dollars per player. In 2020, two former players, Kevin Henry and Najeh Davenport, accused the NFL of discriminating against Black players seeking compensation through the process established by the settlement.[69] Their lawsuit asserted that medical assessments relied on "a discriminatory testing regime," where doctors would apply different standards for Black and white players.[70] This approach made it harder for Black applicants to demonstrate they suffered severe enough cognitive impairment to qualify for compensation. Henry and Davenport's case, in turn, exposed embedded forms of scientific racism within assessments made about individual brains and their cognitive function.

Henry and Davenport, both Black men who played professionally for the Pittsburgh Steelers, alleged that race-based adjustments to their neurocognitive test scores resulted in their ineligibility for dementia-related payments. At that time, retired players had received around 720 million US dollars for neurocognitive problems, including more than three hundred million dollars for dementia. More than two-thirds of the approximately three thousand dementia-related claims, however, had been denied, often because the NFL challenged them.[71] Davenport and Henry alleged:

> Black former players are automatically assumed (through a statistical manipulation called "race-norming") to have started with worse cognitive functioning than white former players. As a result, if a Black former player and a white former player receive

the exact same raw scores on a battery of tests designed to measure their current cognitive functioning, the Black player is presumed to have suffered less impairment, and he is therefore less likely to qualify for compensation.[72]

This assertion is troubling given that most NFL retirees are Black.[73] As anthropologists Tracie Canada and Chelsey R. Carter explain, the application of race norming in this context reflects an embedded notion of race as "a binary, biological concept." It assumes that distinctions between white and nonwhite bodies and brains are "not only existent, but quantifiable."[74] In addition to these neuropsychological tools relying on an inaccurate construction of race, their use provides grounds for denying Black athletes compensation to which they would otherwise have been entitled from the NFL—an organization that relies on a business model that profited from their injuries.[75]

Beyond the NFL compensation claims process, race norming is a practice in neuropsychology that seeks to account for historical trends showing Black people may have lower average scores on cognitive tests than white people do. The rationale for creating these lower benchmark scores is to prevent Black people from being subject to overdiagnosis of cognitive impairment. While race norming attempts to adjust for racial biases within cognitive tests, it does not eliminate them. Instead, it creates scientific categories that serve as proxies for more complicated patterns of social difference. This process can result in misinterpretations, suggesting that neuropsychological commonalities reflect "genetic or cultural homogeneity" across an identified group.[76] By design, race norming glosses over the diversity of experiences within racialized groups and can thus perpetuate sweeping generalizations about inherent differences between races.

As part of the NFL settlement, race norming had a key place within the assessments of dementia claims by creating a different baseline measure for Black claimants' cognitive function. Testing focused on skills across five elements: "complex attention/processing speed, executive functioning, language, learning and memory, and visual perception."[77] A player with a notable decline in two of these areas would be entitled to an award, the assessment of which was made in relation to three categories of neurocognitive impairments (levels 1.0, 1.5, 2.0). An example documented by the Associated Press illustrates how the adjusted scoring worked:

> One player's raw score of 19 for "letter-number sequencing" in the processing section was adjusted using "race-norming" and became 42 for whites and 46 for Blacks. The raw score of 15 for naming animals in the language section became a 35 for whites and 41 for Blacks. And the raw score of 51 for "block design" in the visual perception section became a 53 for whites but 60 for Blacks. Taking the 24 scores together, either a white or Black player would have scored low enough to reach the settlement's 1.5-level of early dementia in "processing speed." However, in the language section, the scores would have qualified a white man for a 2.0-level, or moderate, dementia finding—but shown no impairment for Blacks. Overall, the scores would result in a

1.5-level dementia award for whites—but nothing for Blacks. Those awards average more than $400,000 but can reach $1.5 million for men under 45, while 2.0-level dementia yields an average payout of more than $600,000 but can reach $3 million.[78]

Players classified as 1.0-level would not qualify for compensation.

Race norming led to tangible differences in award assessments because it upheld whiteness as the normative default. Brains of Black players were treated as inherently deviant from that norm and thus evaluated differently. They were assumed to have inferior baseline cognitive capacities compared to white players. The adjusted norms meant that Black players had to demonstrate more significant cognitive impairment to qualify for a comparable award. Henry and Davenport's complaint emphasized that, without the application of race norming, their scores warranted compensation.

The resulting media attention around these seemingly overt racial inequities prompted four US lawmakers to write to NFL commissioner Roger Goodell. In expressing concerns that the assessment process violated equal protection requirements, the letter stated:

> If these allegations are true . . . the algorithm used to modify the results of your cognitive evaluations appear to have the effect of denying Black players—a historically disadvantaged and legally protected group—compensation to which they would otherwise be entitled. This would raise serious questions about the NFL's commitment to racial justice and compliance with the Federal law that mandates equal protection.[79]

In a technical sense, race norming translates social difference into neuropsychological categories. Yet the comments from these four US congressmen highlight how the practice is inextricably linked to structural inequities recognized as discriminatory before the law. In drawing attention to this form of racism, their statement also reflects how the relationship between race and racism has changed with the rise of computational methods and algorithmic analysis. Calculations were designed around an inaccurate conception of race as a fixed attribute to be universally applied to people from certain social groups. They were set up as if whiteness represents a neuropsychological norm from which other racial groups deviate.[80]

A judge dismissed Henry and Davenport's lawsuit in 2021, ordering mediation as the avenue for resolution.[81] The widespread criticism of the NFL, however, prompted the league to stop this specific use of race norming. Even so, the NFL concussion-related awards underscore broader concerns around the misuse of race in medicine and science. As the public outcry around the claims made by Henry and Davenport played out in the media, a letter published in *Science* called on the NIH to address the misguided tendency to analyze race categories as if they are indicators of inherent differences.[82] The focus on race, the authors contended, fails to attend to how racism reflects and interacts with environmental, social, and structural disparities, which are key drivers of poorer health outcomes for Black and Indigenous peoples, as well as for many other people racialized as nonwhite. By using the category of race to stand in for cultural, educational, and socio-economic experiences, the NFL's baseline for measuring neurocognitive damage was a misleading representation of differences between groups of players.

The NFL's use of race norming demonstrates the very real consequences of misrepresenting observed discrepancies in brain health and function. As sociologist Victoria Pitts-Taylor argues, neuroscience is often applied to correct inequitable health or social outcomes among groups experiencing multiple forms of marginalization, as if the roots of these problems are neurobiological rather than social in nature.[83] Referring to this tendency as *biosocial determinism*, she argues that such explanations ignore how social structures create inequality and instead propose that inequalities are products of inherent biological features.[84] In this example, scientific practices built on the assumption of Black brains being deviant from a white norm—itself an outgrowth of anti-Black sentiments—served to justify inequities that materialized through legal practices surrounding workplace compensation claims.

The discrepancies in concussion-related NFL compensation awards attest that science can reinforce deceptively inaccurate notions of race, especially as they articulate assumptions of whiteness as normality. The downstream effects resonate with criticisms of neurocriminology, as both forms of knowledge production look inside the brain and body for explanations of deviance and, in doing so, "simultaneously produce ignorance regarding the social."[85] This particular use of race norming upholds racial inequities by maintaining formations of structural violence. These patterns and practices exemplify concerns about conceptions of scientific neutrality in the face of systemic health injustices. The veneer of neutrality hides how scientific institutions typically avoid investigating state-sanctioned violence and oppression, even though such examinations could thoroughly reveal and explain the origins of health inequities.[86] Instead, the belief in neutral objectivity provides a smokescreen for science's lack of engagement with structural violence and its implicit entrenchment of whiteness as normatively superior. Addressing these and other forms of structural violence across health systems is an essential project that encompasses, but also surpasses, questions about TBI.

TRACING IMPRINTS OF VIOLENCE
ON BRAINS AND BODIES

This chapter has explored how racialized power asymmetries underpin the selective recognition of TBI-related harms. In discussing examples spanning health and law, we have sought to trace how violence affects TBI in different ways. Violence in this instance is not limited to individual acts or experiences; it includes structural manifestations enacted through institutions, often in ways beyond physical force. Narrow formulations of neurocriminological arguments, the prevalence of systemic racism within criminal legal practices, the maintenance of racial and geographic health inequities, and the use of racially biased scientific categories are indeed forms of violence that produce disparities in TBI outcomes. Most concussion crisis narratives fail to consider how these dimensions of structural violence shape TBI rates and experiences. The examples presented in this chapter illustrate how concussion crisis discourses also neglect many groups with high rates of TBI or examine the structural conditions contributing to these harms.

In pointing to these patterns, we offer two sets of insights. The first is a reminder that explanations presenting deviant behaviors as originating in the brain often serve to depoliticize crime and violence. In other words, the framing of deviance as manifested *in* the body often directs attention away from *how* institutions both enable and enact violence. Second, the recognition of CTE and TBI poses potentially complicated challenges for advocates and experts. Their diagnosis might be an indicator of violence's imprints, but they—and the proposals to address them— are nonetheless subject to interpretative processes that do not necessarily escape classist, gendered, and racist norms. Accordingly, explanations of scientifically observed phenomena can still evoke and rely on implicit assumptions about social categories of difference. When these beliefs are accepted as fact, they can incorrectly represent health inequities as outcomes of inherent attributes rather than as entanglements of biological and societal circumstances. Having foregrounded the impact of structural forces, we conclude this book by reflecting on how concussion crisis narratives direct attention away from important social conditions that contribute to inequality and violence. We then explain how critical social sciences can support efforts to recalibrate TBI-related agendas to support health equity.

Epilogue

We completed this book in late 2024, a time when high-profile concussion crisis events remained a regular part of the news cycle. In the United States, an analysis by Ann McKee, director of the Boston University CTE Center, had showed evidence of TBI in a US Army reservist who had committed a mass shooting in Maine that killed eighteen people and injured many more. McKee's findings suggested that brain trauma could have contributed to the reservist's behavior changes in the ten months prior to the shooting.[1] ESPN had recently published an article questioning "how fears about CTE and football outpaced what researchers actually know."[2] There were limited actions undertaken in response to the Australian Government Senate Inquiry into Concussions and Repeated Head Trauma in Contact Sports, even though a growing number of collision sports athletes cited concussion as their primary reason for retiring. In Canada, Chris Simon, former NHL enforcer and member of Michipicoten First Nation in Northern Ontario, had died by suicide at the age of fifty-two. Simon's family subsequently expressed their belief that his suicide was linked to CTE.[3] The NHL, however, continued to deny any connection between the disease and a career in professional hockey.

After over a decade of research, we find ourselves struck that concussion crisis narratives haven't changed that much. Like stories surrounding the deaths of NFL players Jovan Belcher (2012) and Aaron Hernandez (2017), histories of brain trauma are still proposed as biological explanations for men's acts of violence. Concerns about CTE in collision sports remain clouded by claims that media distort scientific facts in sensationalized stories about the disease. Athlete deaths and CTE diagnoses continue to evoke public sympathy while many sports organizations attempt to sidestep accountability. Despite government hearings, the self-regulation of TBI in sports often leaves athletes to deliberate whether extending their career is worth jeopardizing their neurological health.

At the time of writing, other instances of brain trauma have still not received the same kind of mainstream attention as sports TBI does, particularly in relation to victim-survivors of violence caused by partners and state agents, such as law enforcement. As we discussed in chapter 4, military servicemembers, too, express frustration regarding the lack of support for the polytrauma they have experienced in their roles as state agents, even though they continue to manage the effects daily. To paraphrase a former combat veteran we spoke to during our research:

> I don't know what's going on. I can't get answers at the VA. I get nothing, because they don't care. I had my second TBI more than six years ago and still have issues. They found bleeding [on my brain] years after. I can't remember why I walk somewhere. I get headaches. But I get nothing from the VA. . . . I always had a [short] fuse, but now I can't control it like I used to. I rage over little things. . . . I just get pushed around at the VA. They do nothing. I hear some drugs work. I can't really find anything on the internet. If something could give me even one percent relief from this, it'd be worth it. I don't want to be an Aaron Hernandez, but I can see how it happens.[4]

Despite efforts to develop better medical interventions for TBI and related forms of trauma, many of the people we spoke to described how the systems for delivering such services did not enable access to treatment. Instead, they often felt many clinicians misunderstood or disbelieved their descriptions of their symptoms.

Although it has been more than a decade since the concussion crisis discourse took hold in the United States, certain men's bodies and brains remain central to narratives about TBI. Calls to include women and girls, both as sports participants and as survivors of violence, are more visible, but they emerge primarily as punctuated examples of how they receive little attention compared to men. People who endure state and structural violence are largely absent—except in cases where TBI is linked to exceptional acts of male violence, such as the Maine mass killing. Even then, those cases are framed as individual instances of violence connected to pathology in the brain, with limited recognition of the societal conditions that contribute to them.

Despite growing awareness of TBI-related harms, including connections to CTE, nonknowledge remains significant in shaping concussion crisis rhetoric and TBI responses. As sociologist Rene Almeling explains, nonknowledge is not simply a lack of biomedical research on certain topics; it reflects cultural and social processes that support the development of deep knowledge in some areas while producing knowledge gaps in others.[5] Within concussion crisis debates, nonknowledge manifests in claims that frame the science around TBI's effects as unsettled and insufficient for justifying action beyond incremental measures to protect the brain. More broadly, the dominant focus on biomedical knowledge has reproduced scientific gender biases and contributed to a lack of knowledge regarding women and TBI. It also impacts the relative absence of research on a range of societal considerations shaping TBI, including inequities that materialize along social categories of difference, such as ethnicity, gender, geographic location, and race. In short, nonknowledge is a key element of narratives that continue to privilege collision sports and men's bodies and brains—despite the prevalence of TBI far exceeding sports-related concussion.

The centrality of men's collision sports in concussion crisis discourses contributes to narrow understandings of TBI. This constrained conception of TBI illustrates how popular culture, including sports, influence social problems. In the 1980s, prominent sociolegal scholar Stewart Macauley argued how sports constitute a powerful domain of legal culture that shapes foundational beliefs about authority and societal rules, even though people rarely recognize its influence in everyday life.[6] Acknowledging the importance of this observation, we conclude by emphasizing that concussion crisis discourses convey not only important messages about sports and TBI, but also implicit assumptions about bodies, brains, and injury. Our hope is to encourage continued critical engagement with questions of structural violence and brain injury, which public health scholar Daniel Goldberg has emphasized in relation to sports TBI.[7] Here, we contend that such queries should not be limited to sports and popular culture; rather, they should be understood as starting points for scrutinizing larger patterns of violence in society.

CONSTRUCTIONS OF THE CONCUSSION CRISIS

Throughout *Violent Impacts*, we have analyzed how biomedicine and collision sports profoundly shape popular imaginings of the concussion crisis, at least in the countries we have studied here—Australia, Canada, and the United States. Notions of a concussion crisis that first materialized in the context of sports remain central, even as specific narratives point to advances in research or highlight TBI in other domains. As TBI has been most visible within the violent spectacles of men's collision sports, the concussion crisis is grafted to a domain of social activity where violence is expected and often celebrated. Despite greater acknowledgement of sports TBI among children and women in recent years, understandings of these injuries still tend to reference the default experiences of men.

The strength of the public association between TBI and sports has kept other forms of violence out of conversations that aim to respond to the concussion crisis. The emergence of collision sports as the cultural and scientific touchstone for understanding TBI has established the parameters for conceptualizing these injuries: they are understood primarily as isolated events framed in terms of linear, cause-and-effect relationships, which are typically studied using the tools of neuroscience and sports science. Sociological concerns sometimes inform concussion crisis narratives. They consider athlete suicides or off-the-field violence, corporate conflicts of interest, and the connections between gender norms and concussion reporting, yet these issues have been largely subsumed by scientific logics that stopped short of examining the social forces contributing to these problems. Perhaps most influential among these developments, at least in terms of response, is how sports have normalized the construction of TBI as something that can be managed through medical, rule-based, and technological interventions. Importantly, this understanding of TBI has made calls to drastically reduce or eliminate violent collisions in sports seem extreme or unnecessary. The dominance of this approach, which includes interventions that are not applicable beyond specific sport contexts, forecloses deeper engagement with the structural violence behind TBI in everyday life.

Throughout *Violent Impacts*, we have highlighted how biomedicine and neuroscience are positioned as the primary—and sometimes exclusive—sources of knowledge about TBI. This dominance carries over into the development of solutions to the societal problem of this so-called invisible injury. Biomedical framings of TBI construct definitive knowledge as emerging from microscopic exploration of neurobiology and impacts of biomechanical forces. They contribute to making the brain the presumed site of intervention to treat TBI, whether it be through medical or other technoscientific capacities. Claims about scientific uncertainty entrench the reliance on biomedicine rather than opening these conversations to different forms of knowledge and analysis that consider how cultural and structural conditions shape brain injury and trauma. Privileging a biomedical approach threatens to foreclose opportunities to advance health equity for more populations affected by TBI.

In this book, we have questioned the accepted inclination toward biomedical knowledge by illustrating the valuable insights that come from adopting an analytical lens attentive to power and inequality. Each chapter has shown how the concussion crisis reflects a wider assemblage of bodies, economies, and values than what is currently captured by neuroscientific approaches to TBI. We have emphasized the need to examine the underlying social conditions that not only make repetitive brain trauma possible but also more likely for some groups compared to others—and not just among athletes. Chapters 1 through 3 analyze how sports influence concussion crisis discourses and research agendas. Chapters 4 through 7 illustrate the people and practices that are not captured in most public imaginings of the concussion crisis. Across these chapters, we point to how patriarchal norms, political economy, and racism contribute to the overall inattention to the violence that causes many instances of TBI. We hope the pages of this book showcase the value of looking at TBI beyond biomedical lenses and thinking creatively about how to bridge neuroscientific and sociological concerns.

We reiterate this approach in considering explanations of CTE, which tend to frame the disease as a neurological outcome of repeated impacts to the head. In contrast, CTE is better understood as the embodiment of social conditions that make repeated hits to the head possible: economic incentives, gender norms, political investments, racial hierarchies, scientific knowledge, and societal values. These forces can materialize in sports that normalize head impacts as part of competitions and games, and they could be targeted to make structural changes to aid in preventing TBI from happening in the first place. The most extensive TBI and CTE prevention strategies would involve unmaking this assemblage: addressing economic inequalities that incentivize participation in collision sports, creating rigorous processes of informed consent to play sports with high exposure to TBI, providing more thorough media coverage of TBI that draws critical attention to sports violence and its potentially negative effects, and conducting transparent TBI research that better manages conflicts of interest.

This focus would depart significantly from the narrow neuroscientific framing of CTE causation that constructs tau as an agent that operates within the brain independent of social context. Socially attuned research need not replace biomedicine. It can complement existing efforts to diagnose CTE in living people and to develop pharmaceutical treatments to stop or reverse the accumulation of abnormal tau.[8] A socially oriented research agenda can help explain why TBI happens in different contexts while informing cultural changes to help prevent TBI. Biomedicine cannot achieve this alone because it does not have the analytical tools to center and address certain groups' disproportionate exposure to violence.

TBI AS A SYMPTOM OF INEQUALITY AND STRUCTURAL VIOLENCE

We have presented critical analyses of biomedicine in *Violent Impacts* not to debunk neuroscientific contributions but to highlight their limitations and propose methods for addressing these shortcomings. Responses to TBI would benefit from efforts that focus on the social determinants of health and how embedded inequalities result in disproportionate health outcomes for populations that experience forms of marginalization and oppression.[9] A key dimension of such work entails making the role of social forces—and their complicated nature—visible. Amid calls for enhancing social determinants of health frameworks to better capture how ableism, classism, racism, and sexism are causes of health inequities,[10] we have written this book to showcase how critical traditions in the humanities, law, and social sciences can support public health efforts. Specifically, we highlight how critical race theory, feminist studies, and science and technology studies (STS) offer tools for understanding and targeting the complexities of interlocking formations of marginalization and oppression.

In pointing to the importance of considering societal inequities from critical vantage points, we have pursued two interrelated aims in this book: (1) to illustrate how gendered and racialized social forces contribute to popular representations of TBI captured in concussion crisis discourse, and (2) to show how these power relationships direct attention away from many forms of TBI resulting from state and structural violence. Structural violence in this case captures the societal configurations that render certain individuals and groups more likely to experience harm—in short, making them more prone to injury and undermining their quality of life. In a foundational sense, structural violence is integrally linked to institutions and social structures that enable interlocking systems of oppression. Thus, *Violent Impacts* has not only traced how gendered norms around violence make certain men's experiences of TBI more visible than others in society; the book has also explored how racialized inequities contribute to the likelihood of TBI and its recognition.

Overall, our aim has been not to isolate the causes for why and how men and women from different backgrounds sustain TBI; rather, it has been to draw on lived experiences to illustrate the myriad ways through which TBI is a symptom of structural violence that disproportionately targets certain segments of society. While experts have drawn attention to gender disparities in TBI agendas, there remains limited scrutiny of racism and its influence on TBI discourse, rates, and research. Our analysis of racism highlights how high-profile US collision sports may prominently showcase non-white athletes in ways that increase their exposure to TBI. Further, as demonstrated in the NFL concussion settlement, racism also contributes to the unfair treatment and compensation for their injuries.

Just as importantly, the influence of racism on TBI outcomes is not limited to athletes. Racism is pervasive in how other people with TBI are seen and understood. In chapter 3, whiteness is central in depictions of the harms of TBI in children's sports. In Chapters 6 and 7, racialized inequities interact with criminal legal systems that make Black, Brown, and Indigenous people less likely to be recognized as victims of violence and more likely to face punitive measures or institutional neglect, even when those survivors have TBI. These dynamics are not unique to the United States. We have drawn on examples from Australia and Canada to illustrate the similarities—and distinct contours—of racial formations shaped by colonial and national conditions. Taken together, they point to the many ways that racism influences how TBI is recognized and how adjoining forms of nonknowledge around TBI persist.

Violent Impacts does not capture the full range of people who experience TBI because of structural violence. That task exceeds the scope of this book. We invite others to continue that work. The insights captured in this book do, however, attest to the importance of approaching interlocking systems of inequality and structural violence as dynamic forces—that is, as assemblages with contingent features that are not fixed as clearly as the language of "structural determinants" might suggest. We have endeavored to illuminate power formations that are not always visible in TBI debates, but, given the centrality of the United States in our analysis, it is not comprehensive in scope. Of the estimated sixty-nine million people who experience TBI globally, most live in low- and middle-income countries, with the greatest disease burden in Southeast Asian and Western Pacific regions.[11] These patterns point to transnational power dynamics in need of further scrutiny. As disability researcher Nirmala Erevelles explains, colonial and geopolitical power relations are significant influences on disability and injury.[12]

The impacts of war-related violence associated with US-led operations in Afghanistan and Iraq, which we discuss in chapter 4, are one such example. Instead of framing disability as a private matter concerning individual bodies, scholars like Erevelles and Sona Kazemi stress how the disabling acts of military violence are manifestations of global forces that make such violence appear necessary or inevitable. For people living in conflict zones, the process of becoming disabled does not begin with an isolated event. It is initiated through the workings of economic and political agendas that support military campaigns and provoke regional conflict. Taking shape against the backdrop of postcolonial and globalized inequality, structural violence often materializes as physical violence that affects people across borders. While US servicemembers and veterans are often associated with TBI as the signature wound of post-9/11 conflict, they are certainly not alone. Their heightened visibility in these discourses reflects US investments in the biomedicine-war nexus identified by feminist scholar Jennifer Terry, which has largely ignored residents of war-torn areas.[13] These dynamics reflect how TBI injury and disability are inextricability linked to fundamental questions about whose bodies are valued in certain spheres—and for what purpose.

The critical insights of experts who specialize in deconstructing disability, injury, and structural violence are essential for meaningfully addressing the structural determinants of TBI and promoting health equity. Such an approach would necessitate two shifts in common approaches to TBI: (1) it would require extending popular concern beyond sports; and (2) it would encourage critically engaging how the dominant focus on sports TBI contributes to structural violence by relegating consideration of societal inequities to the margins of public interest, scientific inquiry, and social response. Doing so would not downplay the significance of sports TBI as a public health issue. Rather, it would recognize how an emphasis on sports directs attention away from the broader patterns of structural violence that make TBI more likely—and more debilitating—for some people and not others. *Violent Impacts* is one attempt at making visible some of the power dynamics shaping how TBI is understood as a social problem. We have sought to shed light on the cultural and scientific parameters established through the dominance of sports within the concussion crisis. We hope that in highlighting forms of TBI underappreciated in popular discourse and understudied in scientific practice, this book points to possibilities for approaches that explicitly address TBI as an outcome of structural violence.

NOTES

INTRODUCTION

1. "Chiefs' Belcher Kills Girlfriend, Self, Police Say," ESPN.com News Services, December 2, 2012, https://www.espn.com/nfl/story/_/id/8697360/kansas-city-chiefs-jovan-belcher -kills-girlfriend-commits-suicide-police-say; Joe Saraceno, "Victim Called Birth of Daughter 'Best Day of My Life,'" *USA Today*, December 12, 2012, https://www.usatoday .com/story/sports/nfl/2012/12/01/kansas-city-chiefs-belcher-perkins-murder-suicide /1739303/.

2. "Panthers Vs. Chiefs Will Be Played Sunday as Scheduled," *USA Today*, December 1, 2012, https://www.usatoday.com/story/gameon/2012/12/01/jovan-belcher-statement-kansas -city-chiefs-vs-carolina-panthers/1739235/.

3. Jay Busbee, "The Timeline of the Kansas City Chiefs Tragedy," Yahoo! Sports, December 5, 2012, accessed June 14, 2021, https://sports.yahoo.com/blogs/shutdown-corner /timeline-kansas-city-chiefs-tragedy-211218126-nfl.html.; Houston Mitchell, "Jovan Belcher's Last Moments are Recounted by Kansas City Star," *Los Angeles Times*, December 4, 2012, https://www.latimes.com/sports/la-xpm-2012-dec-04-la-sp-sn-last-moments-of-jovan -belcher-20121204-story.html.

4. Matt Williams, "Kansas City Chiefs Observe Moment of Silence for Domestic Violence Victims," *Guardian*, December 3, 2012, https://www.theguardian.com/world/2012 /dec/02/kansas-city-chiefs-moment-silence.

5. David J. Leonard, "Kasandra Michelle Perkins: We Must Say Her Name," The Feminist Wire, December 3, 2012, https://thefeministwire.com/2012/12/kasandra-michelle-perkins/; Justin Peters, "No, Seriously, the NFL Really Does Have a Domestic Violence Problem," Slate, December 4, 2012, https://slate.com/news-and-politics/2012/12/jovan-belcher-murder -suicide-no-seriously-the-nfl-really-does-have-a-domestic-violence-problem.html; Diana Reese, "Kasandra Perkins Forgotten Victim in Jovan Belcher Murder-Suicide,"

Washington Post, December 3, 2012, https://www.washingtonpost.com/blogs/she-the-people/wp/2012/12/03/kasandra-perkins-forgotten-victim-in-jovan-belcher-murder-suicide/.

6. Derek Flood, "Jovan Belcher's Murder-Suicide Raises Questions of Traumatic Brain Injury in the NFL," Huffington Post, December 3, 2012, https://www.huffpost.com/entry/jovan-belchers-murdersuic_b_2229009; Sydney Lupkin, "Jovan Belcher Didn't Have 'Long Concussion History,' Team Says," ABC News, December 2, 2012, https://abcnews.go.com/Health/jovan-belcher-long-concussion-history-team/story?id=17857167.

7. Ann C. McKee et al., "The Spectrum of Disease in Chronic Traumatic Encephalopathy," *Brain* 136, no. 1 (2013): e255; Sydney Lupkin, "CTE, a Degenerative Brain Disease, Found in 34 Pro Football Players," ABC News, December 4, 2012, https://abcnews.go.com/Health/cte-degenerative-brain-disease-found-34-pro-football/story?id=17869457.

8. "Chiefs' Belcher Kills Girlfriend, Self, Police Say"; Lupkin, "Jovan Belcher Didn't Have 'Long Concussion History,' Team Says"; Andrew O'Hehir, "Football's Death Spiral," Salon, February 3, 2013, https://www.salon.com/2013/02/03/footballs_death_spiral/; Ta-Nehisi Coates, "Junior Seau Had CTE, *Atlantic*, January 11, 2013, https://www.theatlantic.com/entertainment/archive/2013/01/junior-seau-had-cte/267025/.

9. "Mother of Jovan Belcher Sues Chiefs for Wrongful Death," *USA Today*, December 31, 2013, https://www.usatoday.com/story/sports/nfl/chiefs/2013/12/31/mother-of-jovan-belcher-sues-chiefs-for-wrongful-death/4273091/.

10. Steve Delsohn, "Doctor Says Belcher Had CTE Signs," ESPN, September 30, 2014, https://www.espn.com/espn/otl/story/_/id/11612386/jovan-belcher-brain-showed-signs-cte-doctor-says-report.

11. Cindy Boren, "Jovan Belcher Likely Had CTE, a Study of His Brain Shows, *Washington Post*, September 29, 2014, https://www.washingtonpost.com/news/early-lead/wp/2014/09/29/jovan-belcher-likely-had-cte-a-study-of-his-brain-shows/; Tyler Conway, "Jovan Belcher Reportedly Showed Signs of CTE," Bleacher Report, September 30, 2014, https://bleacherreport.com/articles/2214846-jovan-belcher-reportedly-showed-signs-of-cte; Delsohn, "Doctor Says Belcher Had CTE Signs."

12. Sean Gregory, "Are NFL Head Injuries Causing Domestic Violence?" *Time*, September 30, 2014, https://time.com/3450441/nfl-head-injuries-domestic-violence-jovan-belcher/.

13. Sam Mellinger, "Jovan Belcher's Brain Showed Signs of CTE, According to Post-Mortem Exam," *Kansas City Star*, September 30, 2014, https://www.kansascity.com/sports/nfl/kansas-city-chiefs/article2296030.html.

14. See, for example, Robert A. Stern et al., "Long-Term Consequences of Repetitive Brain Trauma: Chronic Traumatic Encephalopathy," *PM & R* 3, no. 10 (2011): S460–67.

15. *Head Games: The Global Concussion Crisis*, directed by Steve James (2012, Variance Films); Alan Schwarz, "New Signs of Brain Damage in Football," *New York Times*, January 27, 2009, https://www.nytimes.com/2009/01/28/sports/football/28brain.html.

16. Mark Faul et al., *Traumatic Brain Injury in the United States: Emergency Department Visits, Hospitalizations, and Deaths* (Centers for Disease Control and Prevention, National Center for Injury Prevention and Control, 2010).

17. Mersine A. Bryan, Ali Rowhani-Rahbar, R. Dawn Comstock, and Frederick Rivara, "Sports- and Recreation-Related Concussions in U.S. Youth," *Pediatrics* 138, no. 1 (2016): e20154635.

18. Jason Breslow, "New: 87 Deceased NFL Players Test Positive for Brain Disease," Frontline, September 18, 2015, http://www.pbs.org/wgbh/frontline/article/new-87-deceased

-nfl-players-test-positive-for-brain-disease/; Jesse Mez et al., "Clinicopathological Evaluation of Chronic Traumatic Encephalopathy in Players of American Football," *Journal of the American Medical Association* 318, no. 4 (2017): 360–70.

19. The term "sub-concussive" is also used to describe impacts that do not produce symptoms. We follow Nowinski and colleagues' recommendation, using "nonconcussive" to describe these impacts, since the term does not imply that they are less dangerous than concussive impacts. See Christopher J. Nowinski et al., "'Subconcussive' Is a Dangerous Misnomer: Hits of Greater Magnitude than Concussive Impacts May Not Cause Symptoms," *British Journal of Sports Medicine* (2024), doi: https://doi.org/10.1136/bjsports-2023-107413.

20. Mireille E. Kelley et al., "Analysis of Longitudinal Head Impact Exposure and White Matter Integrity in Returning Youth Football Players," *Journal of Neurosurgery: Pediatrics* 28, no. 2 (2021): 196–205.

21. Kathleen E. Bachynski and Daniel S. Goldberg, "Youth Sports & Public Health: Framing Risks of Mild Traumatic Brain Injury in American Football and Ice Hockey," *Journal of Law, Medicine & Ethics* 42, no. 3 (2014): 323–33; Jonathan T. Macy et al., "Fewer U.S. Adolescents Playing Football and Public Health: A Review of Measures to Improve Safety and an Analysis of Gaps in the Literature." *Public Health Reports* 136, no. 5 (2021): 562–74.

22. Travis R. Bell and Janelle Applequist, "Do the Things You're Gonna Do on Game Day, Just Don't Get Hurt": A Narrative Analysis of the NFL's 'Future of Football' Advertising Campaign," *Journal of Broadcasting & Electronic Media* 6, no. 1 (2022): 110–28; Donna Spencer, "World Rugby Funds Canadian Injury, Concussion Research, Co-led by Player," *Globe and Mail*, August 3, 2022, https://www.theglobeandmail.com/sports/article-world-rugby-funds-canadian-injury-concussion-research-co-led-by-player-2/.

23. Katherine M. Helmick et al., "Traumatic Brain Injury in the U.S. Military: Epidemiology and Key Clinical and Research Programs," *Brain Imaging and Behavior* 9, no. 3 (2015): 358–66.

24. Stephen T. Chen et al., "FDDNP-PET Tau Brain Protein Binding Patterns in Military Personnel with Suspected Chronic Traumatic Encephalopathy," *Journal of Alzheimer's Disease* 65, no. 1 (2018): 79–88.

25. Centers for Disease Control and Prevention, *Surveillance Report of Traumatic Brain Injury-Related Emergency Department Visits, Hospitalizations, and Deaths—United States, 2014* (Department of Health and Human Services, 2014); Elizabeth Thomas, Melinda Fitzgerald, and Gill Cowen, "Post-Concussion States: How Do We Improve Our Patients' Outcomes? An Australian Perspective," *Journal of Concussion* 4 (2020): doi: https://doi.org/10.1177/2059700220960313.

26. Michael C. Dewan et al., "Estimating the Global Incidence of Traumatic Brain Injury," *Journal of Neurosurgery* 130, no. 4 (2018): 1080–97; Maria Pia Tropeano et al., "A Comparison of Publication to TBI Burden Ratio of Low- and Middle-Income Countries Versus High-Income Countries: How Can We Improve Worldwide Care of TBI?" *Neurosurgical Focus* 47, no. 5 (2019): E5.

27. Zachary Y. Kerr et al., "Agreement Between Athlete-Recalled and Clinically Documented Concussion Histories in Former Collegiate Athletes," *American Journal of Sports Medicine* 43, no. 3 (2015): 606–13.

28. Centers for Disease Control and Prevention, *Traumatic Brain Injury In the United States: Epidemiology and Rehabilitation* (US Department of Health and Human Services, 2015); Helene Lefebvre, Genevieve Cloutier, and Marie Josée Levert, "Perspectives of

Survivors of Traumatic Brain Injury and Their Caregivers on Long-Term Social Integration," *Brain Injury* 22, no. 7–8 (2008): 535–43.

29. Kathleen E. Bachynski and Daniel S. Goldberg, "Time Out: NFL Conflicts of Interest with Public Health Efforts to Prevent TBI," *Injury Prevention* 24, no. 3 (2018): 180–84.

30. Victoria Pitts-Taylor, *The Brain's Body: Neuroscience and Corporeal Politics* (Durham: Duke University Press, 2016); Oliver Rollins, *Conviction: The Making and Unmaking of the Violent Brain* (Stanford University Press, 2021).

31. Pitts-Taylor, *The Brain's Body*, 6.

32. Rollins, *Conviction*, 2.

33. Bandy X. Lee, "Causes and Cures VII: Structural Violence," *Aggression and Violent Behavior* 28 (2016): 109–14. See also Paul E. Farmer et al., "Structural Violence and Clinical Medicine," *PLOS Medicine* 3, no. 10 (2006): e449. For an analysis of structural violence and sports TBI, see Daniel S. Goldberg, *Tackle Football and Traumatic Brain Injuries: Law, Ethics, and Public Health* (Johns Hopkins University Press, 2024).

34. Peter L. Berger and Thomas Luckmann, *The Social Construction of Reality* (Penguin Press, 1967).

35. Phil Brown, "Naming and Framing: The Social Construction of Diagnosis and Illness," *Journal of Health and Social Behavior* 35 (1995): 36.

36. Steve Woolgar and Dorothy Pawluch, "Ontological Gerrymandering: The Anatomy of Social Problems Explanations," *Social Problems* 32, no. 3 (1985): 214–27.

37. S. Lochlann Jain, *Malignant: How Cancer Becomes Us* (University of California Press, 2013), 24.

38. Gilles Deleuze and Félix Guattari, *A Thousand Plateaus: Capitalism and Schizophrenia* (Athlone, 1988).

39. George E. Marcus and Erkan Saka, "Assemblage," *Theory, Culture & Society* 23, no. 2–3 (2006): 102.

40. Jasbir Puar, *Terrorist Assemblages: Homonationalism in Queer Times* (Duke University Press, 2007), 211.

41. Ben Anderson et al., "On Assemblages and Geography," *Dialogues in Human Geography* 2, no. 2 (2012): 175.

42. Daniel M. Morrison and Monica J. Casper, "Gender, Violence, and Brain Injury in and out of the NFL: What Counts as Harm?" in *Football, Culture, and Power*, ed., David J. Leonard, Kimberly B. George, and Wade Davis (Routledge), 165.

43. Cornelia Vismann, *Files: Law and Media Technology*, trans. Geoffrey Winthrop-Young (Stanford University Press, 2008).

44. Iris Marion Young, *Justice and the Politics of Difference* (Princeton University Press, 1990).

45. Patricia Hill Collins, *Black Feminist Thought: Knowledge, Consciousness, and the Politics of Empowerment* (Unwin Hyman, 1990).

46. Ruth Wilson Gilmore, Golden Gulag: Prisons, Surplus, Crisis, and Opposition in Globalizing California (University of California Press, 2007).

47. Matt Ventresca, "The Tangled Multiplicities of CTE: Scientific Uncertainty and the Infrastructures of Traumatic Brain Injury," in *Sports, Society, and Technology*, ed. Jennifer J. Sterling and Mary G. McDonald (Palgrave Macmillan, 2020), 73–98.

48. Christine Hine, "Strategies for Reflexive Ethnography in the Smart Home: Autoethnography of Silence and Emotion," *Sociology* 54, no. 1 (2000): 27.

49. Bachynski and Goldberg, "Time Out"; Kathleen E. Bachynski and Daniel S. Goldberg, "Youth Sports & Public Health; Peter Benson, "Big Football: Corporate Social Responsibility and the Culture and Color of Injury in America's Most Popular Sport," *Journal of Sport and Social Issues* 41, no. 4 (2017): 307–334; Daniel S. Goldberg, "Mild Traumatic Brain Injury, the National Football League, and the Manufacture of Doubt: An Ethical, Legal, and Historical Analysis," *Journal of Legal Medicine* 34, no. 2 (2013): 157–91.

50. Bachynski and Goldberg, "Time Out."

51. Sean Brayton et al., "Exploring the Missing Link between the Concussion 'Crisis' and Labor Politics in Professional Sports," *Communication & Sport* 7, no. 1 (2019): 110–31; Daniel A. Grano, "Football after Fragmentation: Brain Banking, Chronic Traumatic Encephalopathy, and Racial Biosociality in the NFL," *Communication and Critical/Cultural Studies* 17, no. 4 (2020): 339–59.

52. Brendan S. Hokowhitu, John Sullivan, and Les R. Tumoana Williams, "Rugby Culture, Ethnicity, and Concussion," *MAI Review* 1, no. 1 (2008): 9; see also Kathryn Henne and Matt Ventresca, "A Criminal Mind? A Damaged Brain? Narratives of Criminality and Culpability in the Celebrated Case of Aaron Hernandez," *Crime, Media, Culture* 16, no. 3 (2020): 395–413; Kathryn Henne, "Brain Politics: Gendered Difference and Traumatic Brain Injury in Sport," in *Sociocultural Examinations of Sports Concussions*, ed. Matt Ventresca and Mary G. McDonald (Routledge, 2019), 151–69.

53. D. Goldberg, "Mild Traumatic Brain Injury."

54. Hyunkag Cho, "Racial Differences in the Prevalence of Intimate Partner Violence against Women and Associated Factors," *Journal of Interpersonal Violence* 27, no. 2 (2012): 344–63; Jamila K. Stockman, Hitomi Hayashi, and Jacquelyn C. Campbell, "Intimate Partner Violence and its Health Impact on Ethnic Minority Women," *Journal of Women's Health* 24, no. 1 (2015): 62–79.

55. Donna Haraway. "Situated Knowledges: The Science Question in Feminism and the Privilege of Partial Perspective," *Feminist Studies* 14, no. 3 (1988): 585.

56. Kathryn Henne and Rita Shah, "Feminist Criminology and the Visual," in *Oxford Research Encyclopedia of Crime, Media, and Popular Culture*, ed. Michelle Brown (Oxford University Press, 2016).

57. See Michelle Brown, "Visual Criminology and Carceral Studies: Counter-Images in the Carceral Age," *Theoretical Criminology* 18, no. 2 (2014), 176–97.

58. Mieke Bal, "Visual Essentialism and the Object of Visual Culture," *Journal of Visual Culture* 2, no. 1 (2003): 22.

59. Woolgar and Lezaun, "The Wrong Bin Bag," 323–24.

60. Henne, "Multi-Sited Fieldwork in Regulatory Studies," in *Regulatory Theory: Foundations and Applications*, ed., Peter Drahos (ANU Press, 2017), 99.

61. George Marcus, "Ethnography in/of the World System: The Emergence of Multi-Sited Ethnography," *Annual Review of Anthropology* 24 (1995): 95–117.

1. SPECTACLES OF VIOLENCE IN SPORT

1. Lynda Nead, "Stilling the Punch: Boxing, Violence, and the Photographic Image," *Journal of Visual Culture* 10, no. 3 (2011): 305–23.

2. Susan Sontag, *Regarding the Pain of Others* (Farrar, Straus, and Giroux, 2003), 104.

3. Stephen Casper, "Concussion: A History of Science and Medicine, 1870–2005," *Headache: The Journal of Head and Face Pain* 58, no. 6 (2018): 795–810; Stephen Casper, "How the 1950s Changed our Understanding of Traumatic Encephalopathy and its Sequelae," *Canadian Medical Association Journal* 190, no. 5 (2018): E140–42; Stephen Townsend, "'The Tragedy of the Punch Drunk': Reading Concussion in Australian Sporting Newspapers, 1843–1954," *Frontiers in Sports and Active Living* 3 (2021): doi: https://doi.org/10.3389/fspor.2021.676463.

4. Varda Burstyn, *The Rites of Men* (University of Toronto Press, 1999); Michael Messner, *Power at Play: Sports and the Problem of Masculinity* (Beacon, 1992); Kevin Young, *Sport, Violence and Society* (Routledge, 2013).

5. John L. Jackson, "Lights, Camera, Police Action!" *Public Culture* 28, no. 1 (2016): 6.

6. "Infographic: Is Football Too Violent For Our Youth?" Slate, accessed April 23, 2022, https://www.slate.com/articles/sports/esquire_fnt/2015/01/infographic_is_football_too_violent_for_our_youth.html; CBC News, "NHL Concussion Reignites Debate about Violence in Hockey," October 3, 2013, YouTube, https://www.youtube.com/watch?v=pDn8Y3s4IcQo.

7. Young, *Sport, Violence and Society*, 1.

8. Kathryn Henne and Rita Shah, "Feminist Criminology and the Visual," *Oxford Research Encyclopedia of Crime, Media and Popular Culture* (2016): doi: https://doi.org/10.1093/acrefore/9780190264079.013.56.

9. Casper, "Concussion"; Casper, "How the 1950s Changed our Understanding"; K. G. Sheard, "'Brutal and Degrading': The Medical Profession and Boxing, 1838–1984," *International Journal of the History of Sport* 15, no. 3 (1998): 74–102.

10. Emily A. Harrison, "The First Concussion Crisis: Head Injury and Evidence in Early American Football," *American Journal of Public Health* 104, no. 5 (2014): 822–33.

11. Stacy L. Lorenz and Geraint B. Osborne, "'Nothing More Than the Usual Injury': Debating Hockey Violence During the Manslaughter Trials of Allan Loney (1905) and Charles Masson (1907)," *Journal of Historical Sociology* 30, no. 4 (2017): 698–723.

12. Richard Gruneau and David Whitson, *Hockey Night in Canada: Sport, Identities and Cultural Politics* (University of Toronto Press, 1993); Harrison, "The First Concussion Crisis"; Kevin B. Wamsley and David Whitson, "Celebrating Violent Masculinities: The Boxing Death of Luther McCarty," *Journal of Sport History* 25, no. 3 (1998): 419–31.

13. Burstyn, *The Rites of Men*; Nathan Kalman-Lamb, *Game Misconduct: Injury, Fandom, and the Business of Sport* (Fernwood, 2018); Young, *Sport, Violence and Society*.

14. Grant T. Baldwin, Matthew J. Breiding, and R. Dawn Comstock, "Epidemiology of Sports Concussion in the United States," *Sports Neurology*, ed. Brian Hainline and Robert A. Stern (Elsevier, 2018), 63–74.

15. Sean Brayton et al., "Exploring the Missing Link Between the Concussion 'Crisis' and Labor Politics in Professional Sports," *Communication & Sport* 7, no. 1 (2019): 110–31; Aryn Martin and Alasdair McMillan, "Concussion Killjoys: CTE, Violence, and the Brain's Becoming," *BioSocieties* 17, no. 2 (2022): 229–50.

16. Kerry R. McGannon, Sarah M. Cunningham, and Robert J. Schinke, "Understanding Concussion in Socio-Cultural Context: A Media Analysis of a National Hockey League Star's Concussion," *Psychology of Sport and Exercise* 14 (2013): 891–99.

17. John Branch, *Boy on Ice: The Life and Death of Derek Boogaard* (HarperCollins, 2014); Mark Fainaru-Wada and Steve Fainaru, *League of Denial: The NFL, Concussions, and the Battle for Truth* (Crown Archetype, 2013); Kathryn Henne and Matt Ventresca,

"A Criminal Mind? A Damaged Brain? Narratives of Criminality and Culpability in the Celebrated Case of Aaron Hernandez," *Crime, Media, Culture* 16, no. 3 (2020): 395–413; Matt Ventresca, "The Curious Case of CTE: Mediating Materialities of Traumatic Brain Injury," *Communication & Sport* 7, no. 2 (2019): 135–56.

18. Anita Lam, "Decoding the Crime Scene Photograph: Seeing and Narrating the Death of a Gangster," *International Journal for the Semiotics of Law* 34, no. 1 (2021): 173–90.

19. Kalman-Lamb, *Game Misconduct*; Christopher Matthews and Alex Channon, "'It's Only Sport'—The Symbolic Neutralization of 'Violence,'" *Symbolic Interaction* 39, no. 4 (2016): 557–76; Messner, *Power at Play*.

20. Rich McHugh, "Call for DOJ to Investigate Possible Civil Rights Violation in NFL's Brain Injury Settlement," *Donlon Report*, July 26, 2021, https://www.newsnationnow.com/the-donlon-report/call-for-doj-to-investigate-possible-civil-rights-violation-in-nfls-brain-injury-settlement/.

21. Dominic DiMattia, "How Much Brain Deterioration Do You Need to Get into Court: Analyzing the Issue of Statutes of Limitations for Athletes' Concussion-Related Injury Litigation through the Lens of Toxic Tort Law," *University of Baltimore Law Review* 48, no. 3 (2019): 435–52.

22. Richard Sherman, "We Chose This Profession," *Sports Illustrated*, October 23, 2013, https://www.si.com/nfl/2013/10/23/richard-sherman-seahawks-concussions-in-the-nfl.

23. Reuters, "All Blacks Captain Sam Cane Says He Worries about Concussion Health Risks," *Guardian*, December 18, 2020, https://www.theguardian.com/sport/2020/dec/18/all-blacks-captain-sam-cane-says-he-worries-about-concussion-health-risks.

24. Christopher Matthews and Alex Channon, "Understanding Sports Violence: Revisiting Foundational Explorations," *Sport in Society* 20, no. 7 (2017): 751–67.

25. Jill D. Weinberg, *Consensual Violence: Sex, Sports, and the Politics of Injury* (University of California Press, 2016).

26. Jeff Hearn, *The Violences of Men: How Men Talk about and How Agencies Respond to Men's Violence to Women* (Sage, 1998); Michael Messner, "Sports and Male Domination: The Female Athlete as Contested Ideological Terrain," *Sociology of Sport Journal* 5, no. 3 (1988): 208.

27. "Fighters Not Swayed by Risk of Head Trauma in Combat Sports like Boxing and MMA," *Canadian Press*, December 6, 2018, https://www.tsn.ca/fighters-not-swayed-by-risk-of-head-trauma-in-combat-sports-like-boxing-and-mma-1.1222148.

28. Kath Woodward, *Boxing, Masculinity, and Identity: The 'I' of the Tiger* (Routledge, 2007).

29. Joe Yerdon, "Krys Barch Says Players Can Deal with Concussions Because They're Not Soldiers Fighting War," NBC Sports, March 13, 2012, https://nhl.nbcsports.com/2012/03/13/krys-barch-says-players-can-deal-with-concussions-because-theyre-not-soldiers-fighting-war/.

30. Dave Birkett, "Calvin Johnson: Playing through Concussions is Part of NFL Life," *Detroit Free Press*, May 22, 2017, https://www.freep.com/story/sports/nfl/lions/2017/05/21/calvin-johnson-nfl-concussions/335165001/.

31. Scott W. Ruston et al., "Performance Versus Safety: Understanding the Logics of Cultural Narratives Influencing Concussion Reporting Behaviors," *Communication & Sport* 7, no. 4 (2019): 529–48.

32. Josh Alper, "Ed Reed: Junior Seau Knew What He Was Signing Up For," NBC Sports, January 30, 2013, https://profootballtalk.nbcsports.com/2013/01/30/ed-reed-junior-seau -knew-what-he-was-signing-up-for/; Brayton et al., "Exploring the Missing Link."

33. Aaron Bower, "Leeds' Stevie Ward 'Haunted' by Future as Concussion Forces Retirement at 27," *Guardian*, January 6, 2021, https://www.theguardian.com/sport/2021/jan/05 /leeds-rhinos-captain-stevie-ward-retires-at-27-due-to-concussions-rugby-league; Tom Lutz, "The Brilliant Luke Kuechly Gave Us a Searing Image of Brain Trauma," *Guardian*, January 16, 2020, https://www.theguardian.com/sport/2020/jan/15/luke-kuechly-retirement -concussions; Adam Pengilly, "'New Age of Rugby League is Here': Cordner Hailed for Retirement Decision," *Sydney Morning Herald*, June 14, 2021, https://www.smh.com.au /sport/nrl/roosters-skipper-cordner-to-retire-over-concussion-issues-20210613-p580p8 .html; Greg Wyshynski, "Rick Nash, Third among Active Players in Goals, Retires," ESPN, January 12, 2019, https://www.espn.com/nhl/story/_/id/25736241/rick-nash-retires-due -concussion-related-symptoms.

34. David Cassilo and Jimmy Sanderson "'I Don't Think It's Worth the Risk': Media Framing of the Chris Borland Retirement in Digital and Print," *Communication & Sport* 6, no. 1 (2018): 86–110.

35. Brayton et al., "Exploring the Missing Link."

36. Jack Browne, "Colts' Varga Opens Up about His Concussion," The Score, 2016, https://www.thescore.com/nfl/news/1024199.

37. Nate Jackson, *Slow Getting Up: A Story of NFL Survival from the Bottom of the Pile* (HarperCollins, 2014).

38. Michael Atkinson and Kevin Young, *Deviance and Social Control in Sport* (Human Kinetics, 2008); Gruneau and Whitson, *Hockey Night in Canada*; Michael Russo and Chip Scoggins, "Deaths of NHL 'Enforcers' Raise Questions," *Star Tribune*, September 29, 2011, accessed November 14, 2021, https://video.startribune.com/deaths-of-nhl-enforcers-raise -questions/129560398/.

39. Adrian Dater, "Former Avalanche Enforcer Scott Parker Battling Effects of Concussions," *Denver Post*, November 30, 2013, https://www.denverpost.com/2013/11/30/former -avalanche-enforcer-scott-parker-battling-effects-of-concussions/.

40. Brayton et al., "Exploring the Missing Link."

41. Richard Sherman, "They're Gonna Use Us Up," *Players' Tribune*, November 2, 2018, https://www.theplayerstribune.com/videos/theyre-gonna-use-us-up-by-richard-sherman.

42. Rachel Allison, Adriene Davis, and Raymond Barranco, "A Comparison of Hometown Socioeconomics and Demographics for Black and White Elite Football Players in the U.S.," *International Review for the Sociology of Sport* 53, no. 5 (2018): 615–29; Harry Edwards, *The Revolt of the Black Athlete* (Free Press, 1970); Billy Hawkins, *The New Plantation: Black Athletes, College Sports, and Predominantly White NCAA Institutions* (Palgrave Macmillan, 2010).

43. Alana Semuels, "The White Flight from Football," *Atlantic*, February 2, 2019, https:// www.theatlantic.com/health/archive/2019/02/football-white-flight-racial-divide/581623/.

44. Semuels, "The White Flight," paragraph 7.

45. Rob Ruck, *Tropic of Football: The Long and Perilous Journey of Samoans to the NFL* (New Press, 2018); Fa'anofo Lisaclaire (Lisa) Uperesa, "Fabled Futures: Migration and Mobility for Samoans in American Football," *Contemporary Pacific* 26, no. 2 (2014): 281–301.

46. David Lakisa, Daryl Adair, and Tracy Taylor, "Pasifika Diaspora and the Changing Face of Australian Rugby League," *Contemporary Pacific* 26, no. 2 (2014): 347–67; Brent McDonald and Lena Rodriguez, "'It's Our Meal Ticket': Pacific Bodies, Labor, and Mobility in Australia," *Asia Pacific Journal of Sport and Social Science* 3, no. 3 (2014): 236–49.

47. Brendan Hokowhitu, "Māori Rugby and Subversion: Creativity, Domestication, Oppression and Decolonization," *International Journal of the History of Sport* 26, no. 16 (2009): 2314–34; Brent McDonald and Lena Rodriguez, "'It's Our Meal Ticket.'"

48. Hokowhitu, "Māori Rugby and Subversion."

49. Uperesa, "Fabled Futures," 294–295.

50. Charles Curtis, "What Exactly are the NFL's New Targeting Rules about Hitting Helmet First?" *USA Today*, August 3, 2018, https://ftw.usatoday.com/2018/08/nfl-new-targeting-rule-helmet-hitting-penalty-nfl-rulebook-wording-why-explanation; NFL Football Operations, "Defenseless Player." NFL.com, 2022, https://operations.nfl.com/the-rules/nfl-video-rulebook/defenseless-player/.

51. Greg Johnson, "More Stringent Targeting Rules Go into Effect," NCAA.org, August 27, 2013, https://www.ncaa.org/news/2013/8/27/more-stringent-targeting-rules-go-into-effect.aspx.

52. NHL Department of Player Safety, "The NHL DOPS explains Rule 48," NHL.com, April 20, 2018, accessed November 15, 2021, https://www.nhl.com/video/the-nhl-dops-explains-rule-48/t-277440360/c-60017103; Greg Wyshynski, "The First Decade of the NHL's Rule 48: How It Completely Changed the League's Trajectory," ESPN, November 1, 2021, https://www.espn.com/nhl/story/_/id/32503171/the-first-decade-nhl-rule-48-how-completely-changed-league-trajectory/.

53. "Law Application Guidelines: Head Contact Process," World Rugby, 2021, https://www.world.rugby/the-game/laws/guidelines/17.

54. Jimmy Sanderson and David Cassilo, "'I'm Glad I Played When the Country Still Had Gonads': Pop Warner's Kickoff Policy Change and the Framing of Health and Safety Initiatives in Football," *Journal of Sports Media* 14, no. 1–2 (2019): 1–22; Daniel Sailofsky and Madeleine Orr, "One Step Forward, Two Tweets Back: Exploring Cultural Backlash and Hockey Masculinity on Twitter," *Sociology of Sport Journal* 38, no. 1 (2021): 67–77.

55. Matt Ventresca and Mary G. McDonald, "Forces of Impact: Critically Examining Sport's 'Concussion Crises,'" in *Sociocultural Examinations of Sports Concussions*, ed. Matt Ventresca and Mary G. McDonald (Routledge, 2020), 4.

56. For example, Janie Cournoyer and T. Blaine Hoshizaki, "Head Dynamic Response and Brain Tissue Deformation for Boxing Punches with and without Loss of Consciousness," *Clinical Biomechanics* 67 (2019): 96–101; Marshall Kendall et al., "Accident Reconstructions of Falls, Collisions, and Punches in Sports," *Journal of Concussion* 4 (2020): doi: https://doi.org/10.1177/2059700220936957.

57. Laura Donaldson, Mark Asbridge, and Michael D. Cusimano, "Bodychecking Rules and Concussion in Elite Hockey," *PLoS ONE* 8, no. 7 (2013): 3–8; Suril B. Sheth et al., "Orthopedic and Brain Injuries over Last 10 Seasons in the National Football League (NFL): Number and Effect on Missed Playing Time," *BMJ Open Sport and Exercise Medicine* 6, no. 1 (2020): 1–8; Keith A. Stokes et al., "Does Reducing the Height of the Tackle through Law Change in Elite Men's Rugby Union (The Championship, England) Reduce the Incidence of Concussion? A Controlled Study in 126 Games," *British Journal of Sports Medicine* 55, no. 4 (2021): 220–25.

58. Kathleen E. Bachynski and Daniel S. Goldberg, "Youth Sports & Public Health: Framing Risks of Mild Traumatic Brain Injury in American Football and Ice Hockey," *Journal of Law, Medicine & Ethics* 42, no. 3 (2014): 323–33.

59. Weinberg, *Consensual Violence*, 23

60. "Sport Allowed to 'Mark Its Own Homework' on Reducing Concussion Risks," UK Parliament Committees, July 22, 2021, https://committees.parliament.uk/work/977 /concussion-in-sport/news/156748/sport-allowed-to-mark-its-own-homework-on-reducing -concussion-risks/.

61. Bachynski and Goldberg, "Time Out"; Peter Benson, "Big Football: Corporate Social Responsibility and the Culture and Color of Injury in America's Most Popular Sport," *Journal of Sport and Social Issues* 41, no. 4 (2017): 307–34; Fainaru-Wada and Fainaru, "League of Denial."

62. Goldberg, "What Does the Precautionary Principle Demand of Us?"

63. Peter Benson, "Big Football"; Michael J. McNamee, Bradley Partridge, and Lynley Anderson, "Concussion Ethics and Sports Medicine," *Clinics in Sports Medicine* 35, no. 2 (2016): 257–67.

64. "NFL Announces Play Smart. Play Safe., a New Commitment to Improve Player Health and Safety," NFL.com, 2016, accessed February 27, 2025, https://www.nfl.com /playerhealthandsafety/resources/press-releases/nfl-announces-play-smart-play-safe-new -commitment-improve-player-health-safety.

65. Gruneau and Whitson, *Hockey Night in Canada*.

66. Branch, *Boy on Ice*; Ken Dryden, *Game Change: The Life and Death of Steve Montador, and the Future of Hockey* (Signal, 2017).

67. Allingham, *Major Misconduct*; Nick Boynton, "Everything's Not OK", *Players' Tribune*, June 13, 2018, https://www.theplayerstribune.com/articles/nick-boynton-every things-not-ok; Gaetz, "Understanding Post-Career Adjustment."

68. Branch, *Boy on Ice*.

69. Greg Wyshynski. "'The New Normal': Why Fighting in the NHL Has Dropped to Historic Lows," ESPN, July 30, 2019, https://www.espn.com/nhl/story/_/id/27283018/the -new-normal-why-fighting-nhl-dropped-historic-lows.

70. Stephen Whyno, "20 Years Since NHL's Record-setting Brawl, Fighting is Sown but Not Going Anywhere," *LA Times*, February 28, 2024, https://www.latimes.com/sports /story/2024-02-28/20-years-since-nhl-record-setting-brawl.

71. See, for example, Aynsley Smith et al., "Eliminating Fighting and Head Hits from Hockey: Opportunities and Barriers," *Current Sports Medicine Reports* 18, no. 1 (2019): 35–40; "Sports-Related Concussions in Canada," House of Commons Canada—Subcommittee on Sports-Related Concussions in Canada of the Standing Committee on Health, September 11, 2019, https://www.ourcommons.ca/Committees/en/SCSC/StudyActivity ?studyActivityId=10295616.

72. Sean Gordon, "When Helmets Come Off Prior to a Fight, Officials Will Step In," *Globe and Mail*, October 23, 2013, https://www.theglobeandmail.com/sports/hockey/globe -on-hockey/gordon-linesmen-prevent-fight-in-the-name-of-player-safety/article15016053/.

73. Kennedy and Silva, "Knuckle-Dragging Thugs"; Sailofsky and Orr, "One Step Forward."

74. Gruneau and Whitson, *Hockey Night in Canada*.

75. Donaldson, Asbridge, and Cusimano, "Bodychecking Rules," 3–8.

76. Jonas Siegel, "NHL Fight Numbers Continue to Decline," Canadian Broadcasting Corporation, April 6, 2016, https://www.cbc.ca/sports/hockey/nhl/nhl-fighting-1.3523172.

77. Gary Bettman, "Bettman Responds to CTE Concerns," *New York Times*, July 26, 2016, https://www.nytimes.com/interactive/2016/07/26/sports/hockey/27hockey-doc.html; House of Commons Canada, "Sports-related Concussions in Canada."

78. Dryden, *Game Change*, 323.

79. In 2024, the Professional Women's Hockey League began allowing some bodychecks but still prohibits open-ice hits and fighting. See Karissa Donkin, "PWHL Showcases Physicality of Women's Game, with Full Approval from Players," CBC, January 6, 2024, https://www.cbc.ca/sports/hockey/pwhl/pwhl-physicality-officiating-2024-1.7076009.

2. CTE AND THE BRAINS BEHIND THE CONCUSSION CRISIS

1. Rick Westhead, "Researcher Sheds Light on Exam of Former NHL Player Todd Ewen's Brain," *TSN*, February 10, 2016, https://www.tsn.ca/researcher-sheds-light-on-exam-of-former-nhl-player-todd-ewen-s-brain-1.436245.

2. Alex Prewitt, "U.S. Senator Appalled by Gary Bettman's Stance on Concussions," *Sports Illustrated*, July 28, 2016, https://www.si.com/nhl/2016/07/28/nhl-concussions-cte-gary-bettman-us-senator-richard-blumenthal.

3. Andrew W. Kuhn et al., "Sports Concussion Research, Chronic Traumatic Encephalopathy and the Media: Repairing the Disconnect," *British Journal of Sports Medicine* 51, no. 24 (2017): 1732–33.

4. Rick Westhead, "BU Finds Former NHL Player Ewen had CTE, Contradicting Earlier Findings," TSN, November 30, 2018, https://www.tsn.ca/bu-finds-former-nhl-player-ewen-had-cte-contradicting-earlier-findings-1.1218836.

5. Stephen T. Casper et al., "First Report the Findings: Genuine Balance when Reporting CTE," *Lancet Neurology* 18, no. 6 (2019): 522–23; Adam M. Finkel et al., "First Report the Findings: Genuine Balance when Reporting CTE," *Lancet Neurology* 18, no. 6 (2019): 521–22.

6. Rick Westhead, "Her Fight with NHL Over, Kelli Ewen Wants to Help Partners of Struggling Players," TSN, July 5, 2021, https://www.tsn.ca/her-fight-with-nhl-over-kelli-ewen-wants-to-help-partners-of-struggling-players-1.1664030.

7. Kevin F. Bieniek, et al., "The Second NINDS/NIBIB Consensus Meeting to Define Neuropathological Criteria for the Diagnosis of Chronic Traumatic Encephalopathy," *Journal of Neuropathology & Experimental Neurology* 80, no. 3 (2021): 210–19.

8. For an accessible summary of this process, see, "The Science of CTE," Concussion Legacy Foundation, accessed August 8, 2023, https://concussionfoundation.org/CTE-resources/science-of-CTE.

9. Daniel H. Daneshvar et al., "Leveraging Football Accelerometer Data to Quantify Associations Between Repetitive Head Impacts and Chronic Traumatic Encephalopathy in Males," *Nature Communications* 14, no. 3470 (2023), doi: https://doi.org/10.1038/s41467-023-39183-0.

10. Megan Mariani et al., "Clinical Presentation of Chronic Traumatic Encephalopathy," *Seminars in Neurology* 40, no. 4 (2020): 370–83.

11. Grant L. Iverson et al., "The Need to Separate Chronic Traumatic Encephalopathy Neuropathology from Clinical Features," *Journal of Alzheimer's Disease* 61, no. 1 (2018): 17–28; Edward B. Lee et al., "Chronic Traumatic Encephalopathy is a Common Co-Morbidity, But Less Frequent Primary Dementia in Former Soccer and Rugby Players," *Acta Neuropathologica* 138, no. 3 (2019): 389–99.

12. Kevin Pierre et al., "Chronic Traumatic Encephalopathy: Diagnostic Updates and Advances," *AIMS Neuroscience* 9, no. 4 (2022): 519–35.

13. Stephen T. Casper, "Concussion: A History of Science and Medicine, 1870–2005," *Headache* 58, no. 6 (2018): 795–810; Emily A. Harrison, "The First Concussion Crisis: Head Injury and Evidence in Early American Football," *American Journal of Public Health* 104, no. 5 (2014): 822–33; Philip H. Montenigro et al., "Chronic Traumatic Encephalopathy: Historical Origins and Current Perspective," *Annual Review of Clinical Psychology* 11, no. 1 (2015): 309–30.

14. Bote Qi et al., "Bibliometric Analysis of Chronic Traumatic Encephalopathy Research from 1999 to 2019," *International Journal of Environmental Research and Public Health* 17, no. 15 (2020): 5411.

15. *Concussion*, directed by Peter Landesman (Columbia Pictures, 2015).

16. Mark Fainaru-Wada and Steve Fainaru, *League of Denial: The NFL, Concussions, and the Battle for Truth* (Three Rivers Press, 2013).

17. Ann C. McKee et al., "The Neuropathology of Chronic Traumatic Encephalopathy," *Brain Pathology* 25, no. 3 (2015): 350–64.

18. Catherine M. Suter et al., "Chronic Traumatic Encephalopathy in Australia: The First Three Years of the Australian Sports Brain Bank," *Medical Journal of Australia* 216, no. 10 (2022): 530–31.

19. Daniel F. Mackay et al., "Neurodegenerative Disease Mortality among Former Professional Soccer Players," *New England Journal of Medicine* 381, no. 19 (2019): 1801–08.

20. Zachary O. Binney and Kathleen E. Bachynski, "Estimating the Prevalence at Death of CTE Neuropathology among Professional Football Players," *Neurology* 92, no. 1 (2019): 43–45; Adam M. Finkel and Kevin F. Bieniek, "A Quantitative Risk Assessment for Chronic Traumatic Encephalopathy in Football: How Public Health Science Evaluates Evidence," *Human and Ecological Risk Assessment* 25, no. 3 (2019): 564–89.

21. Jesse Mez et al., "Duration of American Football Play and Chronic Traumatic Encephalopathy," *Annals of Neurology* 87, no. 1 (2020): 116–31; Emma R. Russell et al., "Association of Field Position and Career Length with Risk of Neurodegenerative Disease in Male Former Professional Soccer Players," *JAMA Neurology* 78, no. 9 (2021): 1058–63.

22. Bobak Abdolmohammadi et al., "Genetics of Chronic Traumatic Encephalopathy," *Seminars in Neurology* 40, no. 4 (2020): 420–29.

23. Catherine M. Suter et al., "Chronic Traumatic Encephalopathy in a Female Ex-Professional Australian Rules Footballer," *Acta Neuropathologica* 146 (2023): 547–49.

24. Philip H. Montenigro et al., "Clinical Subtypes of Chronic Traumatic Encephalopathy: Literature Review and Proposed Research Diagnostic Criteria for Traumatic Encephalopathy Syndrome," *Alzheimer's Research & Therapy* 6, no. 5 (2014): 1–17.

25. Michael L. Alosco et al., "Developing Methods to Detect and Diagnose Chronic Traumatic Encephalopathy During Life: Rationale, Design, and Methodology for the DIAGNOSE CTE Research Project," *Alzheimer's Research & Therapy* 13, no. 136 (2021): 1–23; Breton M. Asken and Gil D. Rabinovici, "Identifying Degenerative Effects of Repetitive

Head Trauma with Neuroimaging: A Clinically-Oriented Review," *Acta Neuropathologica Communications* 9, no. 1 (2021): 96.

26. Aryn Martin and Alasdair McMillan, "Concussion Killjoys: CTE, Violence and the Brain's Becoming," *BioSocieties* 17, no. 2 (2022): 229–50.

27. Martin and McMillan, 235.

28. Fainaru-Wada and Fainaru, *League of Denial.*

29. Alex Mitchell, "Senate Inquiry to Examine Sport Concussion," *Financial Review,* December 1, 2022, https://www.afr.com/companies/healthcare-and-fitness/senate-inquiry -to-examine-sport-concussion-20221201-p5c2t6.

30. "Graham 'Polly' Farmer is the First Australian Rules Player Diagnosed with Chronic Traumatic Encephalopathy," ABC News, February 27, 2020, https://www.abc .net.au/news/2020-02-27/australian-rules-great-graham-polly-farmer-diagnosed-with -cte/12005508; Michael E. Buckland et al., "Chronic Traumatic Encephalopathy in Two Former Australian National Rugby League Players," *Acta Neuropathologica Communica-tions* 7 (2019): 97.

31. Ruth Richardson, *Death, Dissection and the Destitute,* 2nd ed. (University of Chicago Press, 2001).

32. Richard Ian Kimball, *Legends Never Die: Athletes and their Afterlives in Modern America* (Syracuse University Press, 2017).

33. Matt Ventresca, "The Curious Case of CTE: Mediating Materialities of Traumatic Brain Injury," *Communication & Sport* 7, no. 2 (2018): 135–56; Martin and McMillan, "Concussion Killjoys."

34. Ryan Phillips, "Junior Seau's Passing Deprives San Diego of Its Finest Citizen," Bleacher Report, May 3, 2012, https://bleacherreport.com/articles/1170270.

35. David Shoalts and Allan Maki, "Rypien Death Sparks Closer Look at Enforcers," *Globe and Mail,* August 18, 2011, https://www.theglobeandmail.com/sports/hockey/rypien -death-sparks-closer-look-at-enforcers/article4182859/; Randy Starkman, Mark Zwolin-ski, and Kevin McGran, "'The Sweetest, Most Gentle Guy Ever,' Former Leaf Belak Com-mits Suicide," *Toronto Star,* September 1, 2011, https://www.thestar.com/sports/hockey/the -sweetest-most-gentle-guy-ever-former-leaf-belak-commits-suicide/article_f3d0496f -af49-5c8b-ad1e-fd00f69832de.html.

36. Virginia Smart and Lisa Ellenwood, "Pain, Agony and 'Years of Duress': How Hockey Wives Are Fighting Back Over Players' Chronic Brain Injuries," CBC News, November 24, 2019, https://www.cbc.ca/news/canada/hockey-players-enforcers-brain-injuries-1.5370444.

37. Kristy Williams, "AFL Legend Greg Williams Reveals He Can't Even Remember His Wedding, the Birth of His Kids or Winning the 1995 Grand Final as He Battles Devas-tating Effects of Concussions," *Daily Mail,* July 6, 2023, https://www.dailymail.co.uk/sport /afl/article-12269057/AFL-great-Greg-Williams-remember-wedding-kids-births-concuss ions-thinks-CTE.html.

38. Dominic Malcolm, "Soccer, CTE, and the Cultural Representation of Dementia," *Sociology of Sport Journal* 38, no. 1 (2020): 1–10.

39. Engber, "Inflategate," Slate, July 26, 2017, https://slate.com/culture/2017/07/the -press-is-overhyping-the-latest-study-on-cte-in-the-nfl.html; Kuhn et al., "Sports Concus-sion Research"; Stewart et al., "Primum non nocere."

40. Matt Ventresca, "Mixed Feelings: Understanding Emotion in Media Coverage of Sport-Related Traumatic Brain Injuries," in *Head in the Game: Critical Sociocultural*

Analyses of Sports Concussion, ed. Stephen Townsend, Rebecca Olive, Murray Phillips, and Gary Osmond (University of Manchester Press, forthcoming).

41. Kuhn et al., "Sports Concussion Research": 1732; Scott L. Zuckerman, "Benefits of Team Sport Participation versus Concerns of Chronic Traumatic Encephalopathy: Prioritizing the Health of Our Youth," *Future Medicine* 5, no. 2 (2020): doi: https://doi.org/10.2217/cnc-2020–0006.

42. Interview, January 13, 2020.

43. Kay Anderson and Susan J. Smith, "Editorial: Emotional Geographies," *Transactions of the Institute of British Geographers* 26, no. 1 (2001): 7–10; Evelyn Fox Keller, *Reflections on Gender and Science* (Yale University Press, 1985).

44. For example, Associated Press, "Judge: NFL Concussion Victims Hit with 'Deceptive Practices,'" *ESPN*, September 19, 2017, https://www.espn.com.au/nfl/story/_/id/20749340/judge-says-nfl-concussion-victims-hit-deceptive-practices; Steve Fainaru and Mark Fainaru-Wada, "Congressional Report Says NFL Waged Improper Campaign to Influence Government Study," ESPN, May 22, 2016, https://www.espn.com/espn/otl/story/_/id/15667689/congressional-report-finds-nfl-improperly-intervened-brain-research-cost-taxpayers-16-million.

45. Rick Westhead, "NHL Called the 'New League of Denial' in Concussion Case Hearing," TSN, March 28, 2018, https://www.tsn.ca/nhl-called-the-new-league-of-denial-in-concussion-case-hearing-1.1040918.

46. Emma Kemp, Melissa Davey, and Stephanie Convery, "Pain, Glory, Concussion: Former AFL Players and Their Families Speak Out about League Inaction," *Guardian*, April 10, 2022, https://www.theguardian.com/sport/2022/apr/10/pain-glory-concussion-former-afl-players-and-their-families-speak-out-about-league-inaction.

47. William B. Barr, "Believers versus Deniers: The Radicalization of Sports Concussion and Chronic Traumatic Encephalopathy Science," *Canadian Psychology* 61, no. 2 (2020): 151–62; Fainaru-Wada and Fainaru, *League of Denial*; Frédéric Gilbert, "State of the Concussion Debate: From Sceptical to Alarmist Claims," *Neuroethics* 8, no. 1 (2015): 47–53.

48. Richard S. Cowles, "Concussion: Hollywood Spotlights Neuroscience," Neurology Live, January 19, 2016, https://www.neurologylive.com/view/concussion-hollywood-spotlights-neuroscience.

49. Daniel S. Goldberg, "Mild Traumatic Brain Injury, the National Football League, and the Manufacture of Doubt: An Ethical, Legal, and Historical Analysis," *Journal of Legal Medicine*, 34, no. 2 (2013): 160.

50. Goldberg, "Mild Traumatic Brain Injury"; David Michaels, *The Triumph of Doubt: Dark Money and the Science of Deception* (Oxford University Press, 2020).

51. Goldberg, "Mild Traumatic Brain Injury;" Naomi Oreskes and Erik M. Conway, *Merchants of Doubt: How a Handful of Scientists Obscured the Truth on Issues from Tobacco Smoke to Climate Change* (Bloomsbury Press, 2011).

52. Stephanie Convery, "Australian Sport Looks at Concussion Like Big Tobacco Sees Smoking, Inquiry Told," *Guardian*, February 22, 2023, https://www.theguardian.com/australia-news/2023/feb/22/australian-sport-looks-at-concussion-like-big-tobacco-sees-smoking-inquiry-told; Fainaru-Wada and Fainaru, *League of Denial*; Jeffrey Kluger, "The NHL and Cigarette Companies Have Something Dangerous in Common," *TIME*, June 29, 2016, https://time.com/4385311/hockey-concussions-bettman-blumenthal/; Alan Schwarz,

Walt Bogdanich, and Jacqueline Williams, "N.F.L.'s Flawed Concussion Research and Ties to Tobacco Industry," *New York Times*, March 24, 2016, https://www.nytimes.com/2016/03/25/sports/football/nfl-concussion-research-tobacco.html.

53. Kathleen E. Bachynski and Daniel S. Goldberg, "Time Out: NFL Conflicts of Interest with Public Health Efforts to Prevent TBI," *Injury Prevention* 24, no. 3 (2018): 180–84; Melissa Davey, Stephanie Convery, and Emma Kemp, "The AFL, the Concussion Doctor and the Groundbreaking Brain Study that Never Appeared," *Guardian*, March 25, 2022, https://www.theguardian.com/sport/2022/mar/25/the-afl-the-concussion-doctor-and-the-groundbreaking-brain-study-that-never-appeared.

54. Michael J. McNamee, Bradley Partridge, and Lynley Anderson, "Concussion Ethics and Sports Medicine," *Clinics in Sports Medicine* 35, no. 2 (2016): 257–67; Stephen T. Casper et al., "Toward Complete, Candid, and Unbiased International Consensus Statements on Concussion in Sport," *Journal of Law, Medicine & Ethics* 49, no. 3 (2021): 372–77.

55. Mark Aubry et al., "Summary and Agreement Statement of the First International Conference on Concussion in Sport, Vienna 2001," *British Journal of Sports Medicine* 36 (2002): 6–10.

56. Jeremy Allingham, "Brain Trust: Big Questions Surround the Most Influential Concussion Research on the Planet," CBC, March 2, 2020, https://newsinteractives.cbc.ca/longform/brain-trust/.

57. See, for example, Paul McCrory, "Sports Concussion and the Risk of Chronic Neurological Impairment," *Clinical Journal of Sport Medicine* 21, no. 1 (2011): 6–12.

58. Angus Fontaine, "Concussion Kingpin Resigns from Global Post over Plagiarism Scandal," *Guardian*, March 5, 2022, https://www.theguardian.com/sport/2022/mar/05/concussion-kingpin-resigns-global-post-over-plagiarism-scandal; Helen Macdonald, "Update on the Investigation into the Publication Record of Former BJSM Editor-in-Chief Paul McCrory," *British Journal of Sports Medicine* 56, no. 23 (2022): doi: https://doi.org/10.1136/bjsports-2022–106408.

59. Emma Kemp and Melissa Davey, "New Investigation into Allegations of Plagiarism Against Concussion Expert Paul McCrory," *Guardian*, April 28, 2022, https://www.theguardian.com/sport/2022/apr/28/new-investigation-into-allegations-of-plagiarism-against-concussion-expert-paul-mccrory.

60. Melissa Davey, Stephanie Convery, and Emma Kemp, "AFL to Launch Review of Concussion Expert Paul McCrory's Work Following Plagiarism Claims," *Guardian*, March 24, 2022, https://www.theguardian.com/sport/2022/mar/24/afl-to-launch-review-of-concussion-expert-paul-mccrorys-work-following-plagarism-claims; Melissa Davey, Stephanie Convery, and Emma Kemp, "Concussion Researcher Claims AFL Hindered Two-Year Research Project into Players' Health," *Guardian*, April 5, 2022, https://www.theguardian.com/sport/2022/apr/05/concussion-researcher-claims-afl-hindered-two-year-research-project-into-players-health.

61. Paul McCrory et al., "Consensus Statement on Concussion in Sport: The 4th International Conference on Concussion in Sport, Zurich, November 2012," *Journal of Athletic Training* 48, no. 4 (2013): 554–75.

62. Ian Kennedy, "Growing the Game: NHL Commissioner Denies Link between Hockey and CTE," *Hockey News*, April 20, 2023, https://thehockeynews.com/news/growing-the-game-nhl-commissioner-denies-link-between-hockey-and-cte.

63. Bill Chappell, "In a First, NFL Executive Admits Football is Linked to Brain Damage," NPR, March 15, 2016, https://www.npr.org/sections/thetwo-way/2016/03/15/470513922/in-a-first-nfl-executive-admits-football-is-linked-to-brain-damage.

64. Dylan Cleaver, "Rugby Research Caught in the Breakdown," *NZ Herald*, June 18, 2016, https://www.nzherald.co.nz/sport/rugby-research-caught-in-the-breakdown/CLXARATH4RJJ6NDWD7QGVO3COQ/; Jeff Z. Klein, "In Debate about Fighting in Hockey, Medical Experts Weigh In," *New York Times*, December 12, 2011, https://www.nytimes.com/2011/12/13/sports/hockey/in-debate-about-fighting-in-hockey-medical-experts-weigh-in.html; Samantha Lane, "NFL Concussion Problem Overblown: AFL Expert Paul McCrory," *Age*, April 7, 2016, https://www.theage.com.au/sport/afl/nfl-concussion-problem-overblown-afl-expert-paul-mccrory-20160407-gooctx.html; Jill Martin, "NFL Acknowledges CTE Link with Football. Now What?," CNN Health, March 16, 2016, https://www.cnn.com/2016/03/15/health/nfl-cte-link/index.html.

65. Casper et al., "Toward Complete, Candid."

66. Brad Partridge, "Addressing Conflicts of Interest in the Consensus Statement on Concussion in Sport: A Proposal to Increase Transparency by Requiring Authors to Provide a Reflexive Explanation, Not Simply a Declaration, of Their Competing Interests," *Sport, Ethics, and Philosophy* (2024): 1–15; Mike Weed, "Informing Evidence-Based Policy for Sport-Related Concussion: Are the Consensus Statements of the Concussion in Sport Group Fit for This Purpose?" *Sport, Ethics, and Philosophy* (2024): 1–16.

67. Gilbert, "State of the Concussion Debate"; Christopher J. Nowinski et al., "Applying the Bradford Hill Criteria for Causation to Repetitive Head Impacts and Chronic Traumatic Encephalopathy," *Frontiers in Neurology* 13 (2022): 938163; Ventresca, "Tangled Multiplicities."

68. Adam M. Finkel and Kevin F. Bieniek, "A Quantitative Risk Assessment for CTE in Football: How Public Health Science Evaluates Evidence," *Human and Ecological Risk Assessment* 25, no. 3 (2019): 564–89.

69. Finkel and Bieniek, "A Quantitative Risk Assessment;" Nowinski et al., "Applying the Bradford Hill."

70. Lauren V. Fortington et al., "Epidemiological Principles in Claims of Causality: An Enquiry into Repetitive Head Impacts and CTE, *Sports Medicine* (2024): 1–20.

71. Grant L. Iverson et al., "Mild Chronic Traumatic Encephalopathy Neuropathology in People with No Known Participation in Contact Sports or History of Repetitive Neurotrauma," *Journal of Neuropathology and Experimental Neurology* 78, no. 7 (2019): 615–25.

72. Gain Davis, Rudolph Castellani, and Paul McCrory, "Neurodegeneration and Sport," *Neurosurgery* 76, no. 6 (2015): 643–56; Gary Solomon, "Chronic Traumatic Encephalopathy in Sports: A Historical and Narrative Review," *Developmental Neuropsychology* 43, no. 4 (2018): 279–311.

73. Iverson et al., "Mild Chronic Traumatic Encephalopathy;" Grant L. Iverson et al., "Chronic Traumatic Encephalopathy Neuropathology Might Not Be Inexorably Progressive or Unique to Repetitive Neurotrauma," *Brain* 142, no, 12 (2019): 3672–93.

74. See, for example, Ann C. McKee et al., "Practical Considerations in the Diagnosis of Mild Chronic Traumatic Encephalopathy and Distinction from Age-Related Tau Astrogliopathy," *Journal of Neuropathology and Experimental Neurology* 79, no. 8 (2020): 921–24; Lee et al., "Chronic Traumatic Encephalopathy." These rebuttals have also been summarized elsewhere. See Michael E. Buckland et al., "Chronic Traumatic Encephalopathy as a

Preventable Environmental Disease," *Frontiers in Neurology* 13 (2022): 880905; Nowinski et al., "Applying the Bradford Hill."

75. "OCEMB Levels of Evidence," Centre for Evidence-Based Medicine, accessed August 8, 2023, https://www.cebm.ox.ac.uk/resources/levels-of-evidence/ocebm-levels-of-evidence.

76. Daniel Goldberg, "What Does the Precautionary Principle Demand of Us? Ethics, Population Health Policy, and Sports-Related TBI," in *Sociocultural Examinations of Sports Concussions*, ed. Matt Ventresca and Mary G. McDonald (Routledge, 2020), 82.

77. Finkel and Bieniek, "A Quantitative Risk Assessment."

78. Goldberg, "What Does the Precautionary Principle Demand of Us?"

79. Brand and Finkel, "Decision-Analytic Approach"; Gilbert, "State of the Concussion Debate"; Alexander W. Gilbert, Jesse M. Bering, and Lynley C. Anderson, "Addressing Head Injury Risk in Youth Football: Are Heading Guidelines the Answer?," *Science and Medicine in Football* 6, no. 3 (2022): 340–46; Stewart, "Sport Associated Dementia"; Finkel and Bieniek, "Quantitative Risk Assessment."

80. Dominic Malcolm and Gareth Wiltshire, "Concussion, Causation and Interdisciplinary Research," *European Journal for Sport and Society* (2024): 1–10.

81. Helen Crowther, Wendy Lipworth, and Ian Kerridge, "Evidence-Based Medicine and Epistemological Imperialism: Narrowing the Divide between Evidence and Illness," *Journal of Evaluation in Clinical Practice* 17, no. 5 (2011): 868–72.

82. "NFL-LONG Study: Improving Life Beyond the Game," Boston Children's Hospital, accessed February 3, 2025, https://www.childrenshospital.org/nfl-long-study.

83. Interview, April 24, 2020.

84. Nowinski et al., "Applying the Bradford Hill," 14 (italics in the original).

85. "Focus on Traumatic Brain Injury Research," National Institute of Neurological Disorders and Stroke, accessed August 8, 2023, https://www.ninds.nih.gov/current-research/focus-disorders/focus-traumatic-brain-injury-research.

86. Jon Pierik, "'It Is Just Ridiculous': International Concussion Group, AFL at Odds over CTE Link," *Age*, June 16, 2023, https://www.theage.com.au/sport/afl/it-is-just-ridiculous-international-concussion-group-afl-at-odds-over-cte-link-20230616-p5dh4t.html.

87. Jon Pierik, "Tuck Inquest Hears AFL Considering Mandatory Helmets for Players," *Age*, July 28, 2023, https://www.theage.com.au/sport/afl/tuck-inquest-hears-afl-considering-mandatory-helmets-for-players-20230728-p5drx9.html.

88. Jon S. Patricios et al., "Consensus Statement on Concussion in Sport: The 6th International Conference on Concussion in Sport—Amsterdam, October 2022," *British Journal of Sports Medicine* 57, no. 11 (2023): 695–711.

89. Fainaru-Wada and Fainaru, *League of Denial*, 191.

90. Davis, Castellani, and McCrory, "Neurodegeneration and Sport."

91. For example, American football players, such as Tom McHale and Tyler Sash, and ice hockey players, including Derek Boogaard and Marek Svatos.

92. Nowinski et al., "Applying the Bradford Hill."

93. Nick Boyton, "Everything's Not O.K.," *The Players' Tribune*, June 13, 2018, https://www.theplayerstribune.com/articles/nick-boynton-everythings-not-ok; CBC Sports, "Jim McMahon, Ex-NFL QB, Opens Up about Health Problems," CBC Sports, June 18, 2014, https://www.cbc.ca/sports/football/nfl/jim-mcmahon-ex-nfl-qb-opens-up-about-health-problems-1.2679213; Eugene Monroe, "My Body Remembers," *The Players' Tribune*, August 4,

2017, https://www.theplayerstribune.com/articles/eugene-monroe-nfl-opioids-cannabis -my-body-remembers; Ryan Rowe, "DRUG TORMENT I'm a Scottish Sports Star Who Retired Early after an Addiction to Sleeping Pills and Painkillers—I Feel Dele Alli's Pain," *Scottish Sun*, June 26, 2023, https://www.thescottishsun.co.uk/sport/11005441/scottish -rugby-kieran-low-retired-early-sleeping-pills-painkillers/.

3. PROTECTING THE CHILDREN

1. Linda Carroll and David Rosner, *The Concussion Crisis* (Simon & Schuster, 2011), xii.

2. Carroll and Rosner, xii.

3. Robert Cantu and Mark Hyman, *Concussion and Our Kids: America's Leading Expert on How to Protect Young Athletes and Keep Sports Safe* (Houghton Mifflin Harcourt, 2012), 11–13.

4. Jason Laurendeau and Dan Konecny, "Where is Childhood? In Conversation with Messner and Musto," *Sociology of Sport Journal* 32, no. 3 (2015): 332–44; Michael A. Messner and Michela Musto, "Where Are the Kids?" *Sociology of Sport Journal* 31, no. 1 (2014): 102–22.

5. Davi Johnson Thornton, *Brain Culture: Neuroscience and Popular Media* (Rutgers University Press, 2011); André Turmel, *A Historical Sociology of Childhood: Developmental Thinking, Categorization and Graphic Visualization* (Cambridge University Press, 2008); Jan Mason, "Child Protection Policy and the Construction of Childhood," in *Children Taken Seriously: In Theory, Policy and Practice*, ed. Jan Mason and Toby Fattore (Jessica Kinsley, 2005), 91–97.

6. Mason, "Child Protection."

7. Barbara Baird, "Child Politics, Feminist Analyses," *Australian Feminist Studies* 23, no. 57 (2008): 291–305.

8. Mary G. McDonald, "Mapping Whiteness and Sport: An Introduction," *Sociology of Sport Journal* 22, no. 3 (2005): 247.

9. Kelsey Logan et al., "Organized Sports for Children, Preadolescents, and Adolescents," *Pediatrics* 143, no. 6 (2019): e20190997; Scott L. Zuckerman et al., "Benefits of Team Sport Participation Versus Concerns of Chronic Traumatic Encephalopathy: Prioritizing the Health of Our Youth," *Concussion* 5, no. 2 (2020): CNC75.

10. Tim Crabbe, "A Sporting Chance?: Using Sport to Tackle Drug Use and Crime," *Drugs: Education, Prevention and Policy* 7, no. 4 (2000): 381–91; Nicholas L. Holt et al., "Benefits and Challenges Associated with Sport Participation by Children and Parents from Low-Income Families," *Psychology of Sport and Exercise* 12, no. 5 (2011): 490–99.

11. Jay Coakley, "Youth Sports: What Counts as 'Positive Development?'" *Journal of Sport and Social Issues* 35, no. 3 (2011): 306–24; Michael Messner and Michela Musto, *Child's Play* (Rutgers University Press, 2016).

12. Mersine A. Bryan et al., "Sports- and Recreation-Related Concussions in U.S. Youth," *Pediatrics* 138, no. 1 (2016): e20154635.

13. William P. Meehan III, Alex M. Taylor, and Mark Proctor, "The Pediatric Athlete: Younger Athletes with Sport-Related Concussion," *Clinics in Sports Medicine* 30, no. 1 (2011): 133–44.

14. Sergio R. Russo Buzzini and Kevin M. Guskiewicz, "Sport-Related Concussion in the Young Athlete," *Current Opinion in Pediatrics* 18, no. 4 (2006): 376–82.

15. Christopher C. Giza and David A. Hovda, "The Neurometabolic Cascade of Concussion," *Journal of Athletic Training* 36, no. 3 (2001): 228–35; Julie M. Stamm, *The Brain on Youth Sports: The Science, the Myths, and the Future* (Rowman & Littlefield, 2021).

16. Silvia Manzanero et al., "Post-Concussion Recovery in Children and Adolescents: A Narrative Review," *Journal of Concussion* 1 (2017): doi: https://doi.org/10.1177/20597002 17726874.

17. Charles Tator et al., "Fatal Second Impact Syndrome in Rowan Stringer, a 17-Year-Old Rugby Player," *Canadian Journal of Neurological Sciences* 46, no. 3 (2019): 351–54; Virginia K. Terwilliger et al., "Additional Post-Concussion Impact Exposure May Affect Recovery in Adolescent Athletes," *Journal of Neurotrauma* 33, no. 8 (2016): 761–65.

18. Mark E. Halstead et al. "Sport-Related Concussion in Children and Adolescents," *Pediatrics* 142, no. 6 (2018): e20183074.

19. Scott L. Zuckerman et al., "Prognostic Factors in Pediatric Sport-Related Concussion," *Current Neurology and Neuroscience Reports* 18, no. 104 (2018): 1–8.

20. Vicki Anderson, Megan Spencer-Smith, and Amanda Wood, "Do Children Really Recover Better? Neurobehavioural Plasticity After Early Brain Insult," *Brain* 134, no. 8 (2011): 2197.

21. Joshua Kamins and Christopher C. Giza, "Concussion—Mild TBI: Recoverable Injury with Potential for Serious Sequelae," *Neurosurgery Clinics of North America* 27, no. 4 (2016): 441–52; R. Davis Moore, Jacob J. Kay, and Dave Ellemberg, "The Long-Term Outcomes of Sport-Related Concussion in Pediatric Populations," *International Journal of Psychophysiology* 132 (2018): 14–24.

22. Naeim Bahrami et al., "Subconcussive Head Impact Exposure and White Matter Tract Changes over a Single Season of Youth Football," *Radiology* 281, no. 3 (2016): 919–26;

23. Michael L. Alosco et al., "Age of First Exposure to Tackle Football and Chronic Traumatic Encephalopathy," *Annals of Neurology* 83, no. 5 (2018): 886–901; Ann C. McKee et al., "Neuropathologic and Clinical Findings in Young Contact Sport Athletes Exposed to Repetitive Head Impacts," *JAMA Neurology* 80, no. 10 (2023): 1037–50.

24. Landon B. Lempke et al., "Relating American Football Age of First Exposure to Patient-Reported Outcomes and Medical Diagnoses Among Former National Football League Players: An NFL-LONG study," *Sports Medicine* 53 (2023): 1073–84.

25. Katie Mah et al., "Re-Producing the Pediatric Concussion Discourse in Clinical Rehabilitation Practice," *Disability and Rehabilitation* 44, no. 24 (2022): 7464–74.

26. Laurendeau and Konecny, "Where is Childhood?"

27. Mah et al. "Re-Producing the Pediatric Concussion Discourse."

28. "Youth Football Helmet Ratings 2023 Edition," Virginia Tech Helmet Ratings, accessed December 5, 2023, https://www.helmet.beam.vt.edu/youth-football-helmet-rat ings.html#.

29. "Helmet Safety," Centers for Disease Control and Prevention, accessed December 5, 2023, https://www.cdc.gov/heads-up/safety/?CDC_AAref_Val=https://www.cdc.gov/head sup/helmets/index.html.

30. Michael Goutnik et al., "Neurotrauma Prevention Review: Improving Helmet Design and Implementation," *Biomechanics* 2, no. 4 (2022): 500–512; Clara Karton and T. Blaine Hoshizaki, "Concussive and Subconcussive Brain Trauma: The Complexity of Impact Biomechanics and Injury Risk in Contact Sport," in *Handbook of Clinical Neurology* 158, ed. Brian Hainline and Robert A. Stern (Elsevier, 2018).

31. Kianoosh Ghazi et al., "American Football Helmet Effectiveness Against a Strain-Based Concussion Mechanism," *Annals of Biomedical Engineering* 50, no. 11 (2022): 1498–1509.

32. Kerry Gillespie, "Birchmount Students Can't Play Football Without New Helmets, and Can't Afford Them. Now What?" *Toronto Star*, June 2, 2023, https://www.thestar.com/sports/amateur/birchmount-students-can-t-play-football-without-new-helmets-and-can-t-afford-them-now/article_23cf36cd-aef2-5882-8a27-985f0ac282de.html.

33. Travis R. Bell and Janelle Applequist, "'Do the Things You're Gonna Do on Game Day, Just Don't Get Hurt': A Narrative Analysis of the NFL's 'Future of Football' Advertising Campaign," *Journal of Broadcasting & Electronic Media* 66, no. 1 (2022): 110–28; Morrison, "Football Helmet Safety and the Veil of Standards."

34. Kathleen Bachynski, *No Game for Boys to Play: The History of Youth Football and the Origins of a Public Health Crisis* (University of North Carolina Press, 2019).

35. Kathleen E. Bachynski and Daniel S. Goldberg, "Youth Sports and Public Health: Framing Risks of Mild Traumatic Brain Injury in American Football and Ice Hockey," *Journal of Law, Medicine & Ethics* 42, no. 3 (2014): 323–33.

36. USA Football, "Teaching Tackling—Heads Up Tackling," YouTube, June 3, 2014, https://www.youtube.com/watch?v=cXx3f9AO9Uw.

37. Zachary Y. Kerr et al., "Comparison of Indiana High School Football Injury Rates by Inclusion of the USA Football 'Heads Up Football' Player Safety Coach," *Orthopaedic Journal of Sports Medicine* 4, no. 5 (2016): doi: https://doi.org/10.1177/2325967116648441; Elizabeth Sandel, *Shaken Brain: The Science, Care, and Treatment of Concussion* (Harvard University Press, 2020); Alan Schwarz, "N.F.L.-Backed Youth Program Says It Reduced Concussions. The Data Disagrees," *New York Times*, July 27, 2016, https://www.nytimes.com/2016/07/28/sports/football/nfl-concussions-youth-program-heads-up-football.html; Ellen Shanley et al., "Heads Up Football Training Decreases Concussion Rates in High School Football Players," *Clinical Journal of Sport Medicine* 31, no. 2 (2021): 120–26.

38. "Lower Tackle Height at the Heart of Plans to Enhance Community Rugby Experience," World Rugby, https://www.world.rugby/news/790960/lower-tackle-height-at-the-heart-of-plans-to-enhance-community-rugby-experience.

39. Bachynski, *No Game for Boys to Play*.

40. "Rowan's Law: Concussion Safety," Ontario Government, accessed December 5, 2023, https://www.ontario.ca/page/rowans-law-concussion-safety.

41. Dominic Malcolm, *The Concussion Crisis in Sport* (Routledge, 2020), 101.

42. Viviana Bompadre et al., "Washington State's Lystedt Law."

43. Tator et al., "Fatal Second Impact Syndrome."

44. Laura Armstrong, "Rugby Parents Hope Rowan's Law Might Change How Concussions Are Managed," *Toronto Star*, November 25, 2015. https://www.thestar.com/sports/rugby-parents-hope-rowan-s-law-might-change-how-concussions-are-managed/article_90956ddf-3af2-53b8-8d98-f42d6e67b02c.html.

45. Malcolm, *The Concussion Crisis in Sport*, 101.

46. Jennifer K. Wood, "In Whose Name? Crime Victim Policy and the Punishing Power of Protection," *National Women's Studies Association Journal* 17, no. 3 (2005): 1–17; Jonathan Simon, *Governing through Crime: How the War on Crime Transformed American Democracy* (Oxford University Press, 2007).

47. Simon, *Governing through Crime*, 109–10.

48. Teresa C. Kulig and Francis T. Cullen, "Where is Latisha's Law? Black Invisibility in the Social Construction of Victimhood," *Justice Quarterly* 34, no. 6 (2017): 978–1013.

49. Nathaniel Bryan, "Remembering Tamir Rice and Other Black Boy Victims: Imagining *Black PlayCrit Literacies* Inside and Outside Urban Literacy Education," *Urban Education* 56, no. 5 (2020): 744–71; Amir A. Gilmore and Pamela J. Bettis, "Antiblackness and the Adultification of Black Children in a U.S. Prison Nation," *Oxford Research Encyclopedia of Education* (2021): doi: https://doi.org/10.1093/acrefore/9780190264093.013.1293.

50. Aaron Trammel, *Repairing Play: A Black Phenomenology* (Massachussetts Institute of Technology Press: 2023), 26.

51. Bachynski, *No Game for Boys to Play*.

52. Roger Goodell, H. Hunt Batjer, and Richard G. Ellenbogen, "Accelerating Progress on the Road to Safer Sports: Based on Remarks of NFL Commissioner Roger Goodell in the Neurosurgical Society of America Medal Lecture," *Neurosurgery* 75, no. 4 (2014): S119–21.

53. "Roger Goodell, Jon Butler Announce NFL-Pop Warner Partnership," NFL News, August 1, 2023, https://www.nfl.com/news/roger-goodell-jon-butler-announce-nfl-pop-warner-partnership-0ap1000000224857.

54. Mary Brophy Marcus, "U.S. Soccer Federation Bans Headers for Young Kids," CBS News, November 10, 2015, https://www.cbsnews.com/news/u-s-soccer-bans-younger-kids-from-headers/; Ben Strauss, "U.S. Soccer, Resolving Lawsuit, Will Limit Headers for Youth Players," *New York Times*, November 9, 2015, https://www.nytimes.com/2015/11/10/sports/soccer/us-soccer-resolving-lawsuit-will-limit-headers-for-youth-players.html.

55. Caitlin Fitzsimmons, "'Using Your Head is Probably Not a Good Thing': Safety Concerns for Soccer Kids," *Sydney Morning Herald*, May 16, 2021, https://www.smh.com.au/sport/soccer/using-your-head-is-probably-not-a-good-thing-safety-concerns-for-soccer-kids-20210513-p57rre.html; "A Ban on Children Heading in Football (Soccer), Not the Best Approach," Sports Medicine Australia, August 24, 2023, https://sma.org.au/a-ban-on-children-heading-in-football-soccer-not-the-best-approach/.

56. "Rule 7.3—Body-Checking," Hockey Canada, accessed December 6, 2023, http://rulebook.hockeycanada.ca/english/part-ii-gameplay-fouls/section-7/rule-7-3/.

57. Amanda M. Black et al., "The Risk of Injury Associated with Body Checking Among Pee Wee Ice Hockey Players: An Evaluation of Hockey Canada's National Body Checking Policy Change," *British Journal of Sports Medicine* 51, no. 24 (2017): 1767–72.

58. Carolyn A. Emery et al., "Body Checking in Non-Elite Adolescent Ice Hockey Leagues: It is Never Too Late for Policy Change Aiming to Protect the Health of Adolescents," *British Journal of Sports Medicine* 56, no. 1 (2022): 12–17.

59. Jason P. Mihalik et al., "Head Impact Biomechanics Differ between Girls and Boys Youth Ice Hockey Players," *Annals of Biomedical Engineering* 48, no.1 (2020): 104–11.

60. Kristian Goulet and Suzanne Beno, "Sport-Related Concussion and Bodychecking in Children and Youth: Evaluation, Management, and Policy Implications," *Pediatrics & Child Health* 28, no. 4 (2023): 252–58.

61. Tator, Blanchet, and Ma, "Persisting Concussion Symptoms from Bodychecking."

62. Joel S. Brenner et al., "Tackling in Youth Football," *Pediatrics* 136, no. 5 (2015): e1419–30.

63. Ben Quinn, "UK Health Experts Call for Ban on Tackling in School Rugby," *Guardian*, March 2, 2016, https://www.theguardian.com/education/2016/mar/02/uk-health-experts-call-for-ban-on-tackling-in-school-rugby.

64. Adam John White et al., "Imposing Compulsory Rugby Union on Schoolchildren: An Analysis of English State-Funded Secondary Schools," *Frontiers on Sports and Active Living* 4 (2022): 784103.

65. Matthew Cross et al., "Professional Rugby Union Players Have a 60% Greater Risk of Time Loss Injury After Concussion: A 2-Season Prospective Study of Clinical Outcomes," *British Journal of Sports Medicine* 50, no. 15 (2016): 926–31.

66. Adam John White et al., "Tackling in Physical Education Rugby: An Unnecessary Risk?" *Injury Prevention* 24, no. 2 (2018): 114–15; White et al., "Imposing Compulsory Rugby Union."

67. Mark Dunphy, "Here's What Happened in the Five Other States that Tried to Ban Youth Tackle Football," Boston.com, March 3, 2019, https://www.boston.com/sports/parenting/2019/03/03/massachusetts-proposed-law-ban-youth-tackle-football/; Vicente Vera, "California Youth Tackle Football on the Line as Lawmakers, Makers Debate Sport," ABC News, March 6, 2023, https://www.abc10.com/article/sports/california-youth-tackle-football-on-the-line-parents-lawmakers-debate-sport/103-8a33f580-2c21-4306-a246-69b97b7f5bbb.

68. "Ready for Impact? Why Age 14 Matters," Concussion Legacy Foundation, accessed December 6, 2023, https://concussionfoundation.org/wp-content/uploads/2024/08/Why_Age_14_Infographic.pdf.

69. "Provocative New PSA 'Tackle Can Wait' Urges Parents to Wait to Enroll Their Children in Tackle Football Until Age 14," Concussion Legacy Foundation, October 10, 2019, accessed December 7, 2023, https://concussionfoundation.org/news/press-release/provocative-psa-tackle-can-wait-urges-parents-to-wait-until-14-to-enroll-kids-in-tackle-football.

70. Jesse Mez et al., "Duration of American Football Play and Chronic Traumatic Encephalopathy," *Annals of Neurology* 87, no. 1 (2020): 116–31.

71. Jimmy Golden, "Concussion PSA Compares Youth Football Dangers to Smoking," AP News, October 11, 2019, https://apnews.com/article/57832eb788b740eb88e36f8167cce976; Kelly Woo, "Kids Shown Smoking Cigarettes in Shocking New PSA," Yahoo!, October 11, 2019, https://www.yahoo.com/lifestyle/new-concussion-psa-tackle-can-wait-compares-youth-football-to-smoking-211057292.html.

72. "Professor Broglio Responds to Concussion Legacy Foundation PSA," Concussion Center, University of Michigan, accessed December 6, 2023, https://concussion.umich.edu/news/archive/professor-broglio-responds-to-concussion-legacy-foundation-psa/.

73. Jason Chung, Peter Cummings, and Uzma Samadani, "Does CTE Call for an End to Youth Tackle Football," *Star Tribune*, February 10, 2018, https://www.startribune.com/does-cte-call-for-an-end-to-youth-tackle-football/473655913; James MacDonald and Gregory D. Myer, "'Don't Let Kids Play Football': A Killer Idea," *British Journal of Sports Medicine* 51, no. 20 (2017): 1448–49; Rebekah Mannix, William P. Meehan III, and Alvaro Pascual-Leone, "Sports-Related Concussions—Media, Science and Policy," *Nature Reviews Neurology* 12, no. 8 (2016): 486–90; Zuckerman et al., "Benefits of Team Sport Participation."

74. Catherine Calderwood, Andrew Duncan Murray, and William Stewart, "Turning People into Couch Potatoes is not the Cure for Sports Concussion," *British Journal of Sports Medicine* 50, no. 4 (2016): 200–201; Chung, Cummings, and Samadani, "Does CTE Call for an End"; Christopher C. Giza, William Stewart, and Mayumi L. Prins, "Building Good Policy From Good Science—The Case for Concussion and Chronic Traumatic

Encephalopathy," *JAMA Pediatrics* 172, no. 9 (2018): 803–04; LaBella and Myer, "Youth Sports Injury Prevention"; MacDonald and Myer, "'Don't Let Kids Play Football'"; Zuckerman et al., "Benefits of Team Sport Participation."

75. Giza, Stewart, and Prins, "Building Good Policy from Good Science," 804.

76. MacDonald and Myer, "'Don't Let Kids Play Football'," 1448.

77. MacDonald and Myer, 1448.

78. Chung, Cummings, and Samadani, "Does CTE Call for an End"; MacDonald and Myer, "'Don't Let Kids Play Football'"; Mannix, Meehan, and Pascual-Leone, "Sports-Related Concussions"; Kenneth Lincoln Quarrie et al., "Facts and Values: On the Acceptability of Risks in Children's Sport Using the Example of Rugby—A Narrative Review," *British Journal of Sports Medicine* 51, no. 15 (2017): 1134–39.

79. Nancy T. Browne et al., "Childhood Obesity within the Lens of Racism," *Pediatric Obesity* 17, no. 5 (2022): e12878; Claudia Chaufan et al., "You Can't Walk or Bike Yourself Out of the Health Effects of Poverty: Active School Transport, Child Obesity, and Blind Spots in the Public Health Literature," *Critical Public Health* 25, no. 1 (2015): 32–47.

80. Lisa McDermott, "A Governmental Analysis of Children 'At Risk' in a World of Physical Inactivity and Obesity Epidemics," *Sociology of Sport Journal* 24, no. 3 (2007): 302–24; Shannon Jette, Krishna Bhagat, and David L. Andrews, "Governing the Child-Citizen: 'Let's Move!' as a National Biopedagogy," *Sport, Education and Society* 21, no. 8 (2016): 1109–26.

81. E. Cassandra Dame-Griff, "'He's Not Heavy, He's an Anchor Baby': Fat Children, Failed Futures, and the Threat of Latina/o Excess," *Fat Studies* 5, no. 2 (2016): 156–71; Rachel Sanders, "The Color of Fat: Racializing Obesity, Recuperating Whiteness, and Reproducing Injustice," *Politics, Groups, and Identities* 7, no. 2 (2019): 287–304.

82. Chung, Cummings, and Samadani, "Does CTE Call for an End"; Giza, Stewart, and Prins, "Building Good Policy from Good Science"; LaBella and Myer, "Youth Sports Injury Prevention"; MacDonald and Myer, "'Don't Let Kids Play Football'"; Mannix, Meehan III, and Pascual-Leone, "Sports-Related Concussions"; Quarrie et al., "Facts and Values"; Zuckerman et al., "Benefits of Team Sport Participation."

83. Je Yeong Sone et al., "High Prevalence of Prior Contact Sports Play and Concussion among Orthopedic and Neurosurgical Department Chairs," *Journal of Neurosurgery* 22, no. 1 (2018): 1–8.

84. Scott L. Zuckerman, "Benefits of Team Sport Participation"; Chung, Cummings, and Samadani, "Does CTE Call for an End."

85. Rebecca Mannix, William P. Meehan III, and Alvaro Pascual-Leone, "Sports-Related Concussions—Media, Science and Policy," *Nature Reviews Neurology* 12, (August 2016): 488.

86. Mannix, Meehan III, and Pascual-Leone, "Sports-Related Concussions," 488.

87. Zuckerman et al., "Benefits of Team Sport Participation."

88. Lerner and Frost, "Informed Consent," 3.

89. "The Benefits of Youth Tackle Football," Play Football, accessed February 3, 2025, https://playfootball.nfl.com/parents/benefits-of-youth-tackle-football/.

90. Vin Sehgal, "7 Reasons in Favor of Kids Playing Tackle Football," *USA Football* (blog), October 6, 2016, https://blogs.usafootball.com/blog/1374/7-reasons-in-favor-of-kids-playing-tackle-football.

91. Bachynski, *No Game for Boys to Play*; Richard Light and David Kirk, "High School Rugby, the Body, and the Reproduction of Hegemonic Masculinity," *Sport, Education and*

Society 5, no. 2 (2000): 163–76; Richard Gruneau and David Whitson, *Hockey Night in Canada: Sport, Identities, and Cultural Politics* (University of Toronto Press, 1994).

92. Mariah K. Warner and Chris Knoester, "When Kids Hitting Each Other Is Okay: Examining U.S. Adult Support for Youth Tackle Football," *Social Currents* 9, no. 3 (2022): 286–307; Jimmy Sanderson and David Cassilo, "'I'm Glad I Played When the Country Still Had Gonads': Pop Warner's Kickoff Policy Change and the Framing of Health and Safety Initiatives in Football," *Journal of Sports Media* 14, no. 1–2 (2019): 1–22.

93. Ryan A. Todd et al., "Understanding the Resistance to Creating Safer Ice Hockey: Essential Points for Injury Prevention," *Injury Prevention* 25, no. 3 (2019): 211–216.

94. Rebecca D Boneau, Brian K Richardson, and Joseph McGlynn, "'We Are a Football Family': Making Sense of Parents' Decisions to Allow Their Children to Play Tackle Football," *Communication & Sport* 8, no. 1 (2020): 26–49.

95. Sarah Nicola Harding, "'Boys, When They Do Dance, They Have to Do Football as Well, for Balance': Young Men's Construction of a Sporting Masculinity," *International Review for the Sociology of Sport* 57, no. 1 (2022): 19–33; Michael A Messner, *Power at Play: Sports and the Problem of Masculinity* (Beacon Press, 1995).

96. "Majority of Americans Say Tackle Football is Unsafe for Young Kids," University of Massachusetts-Lowell, August 21, 2017, https://www.uml.edu/research/public-opinion/polls/2017/youth-football.aspx.

97. Asher Clissold and Kathleen Bachynski, "NFL's Dangerous Strategies of Marketing Football to Youth: Shades of Big Tobacco," *Sport, Ethics and Philosophy* (2024): doi: https://doi.org/10.1080/17511321.2024.2365400; Adam Rugg, "Working Out Their Future: The NFL's Play 60 Campaign and the Production of Adolescent Fans and Players," *Journal of Sport and Social Issues* 43, no. 1 (2019): 69–88.

98. Joe Drape and Ken Belson, "The Future of Football Has Flags," *New York Times*, November 10, 2018, https://www.nytimes.com/2018/11/20/sports/football/flag-football-nfl.html; Jamal Murphy, "Flag Football Is a Safer, More Inclusive Pipeline for the NFL. Can It Be More?" Global Sports Matters, May 10, 2023, https://globalsportmatters.com/business/2023/05/10/flag-football-safer-inclusive-pipeline-nfl-can-it-be-more/.

99. Murphy, "Flag Football"; "Flag Football for All," NFL Football Operations, accessed February 3, 2025, https://operations.nfl.com/learn-the-game/flag-football/flag-football-for-all/.

100. Tim Nudd, "Inside the NFL's Fun, Frenetic Flag Football Campaign for the Super Bowl 2023," AdAge, February 12, 2023, https://adage.com/article/special-report-super-bowl/inside-nfls-flag-football-campaign-super-bowl-2023/2471501; Jon Springer, "How the NFL Grew Flag Football into an Olympic Sport Attracting Major Brands and Gen Z," AdAge, November 20, 2023, https://adage.com/article/marketing-news-strategy/how-nfl-turned-flag-football-olympic-sport-attracting-gen-z-and-brands/2529766.

101. Murphy, "Flag Football"; "The Future of Football," Aspen Institute, January 25, 2018, https://www.aspeninstitute.org/events/future-football-reimagining-games-pipeline/; Adam Rugg, "Working Out Their Future: The NFL's Play 60 Campaign and the Production of Adolescent Fans and Players," *Journal of Sport and Social Issues* 43, no. 1 (2019): 69–88.

102. Rugg, "Working Out Their Future."

103. Noah Cohan, "Red Tackles, Blue Flags," Slate, January 24, 2023, https://slate.com/human-interest/2024/01/tackle-football-youth-sports-bans.html.

104. Noah Cohan, "Red Tackles, Blue Flags"; Frankie de la Cretaz, "The Complicated Case for Gender Equality in Football," *In These Times*, May 1, 2023, https://inthesetimes.com/article/wfa-nfl-womens-football-gender-equality.

105. Dave Sheinen and Emily Giambalvo, "The Changing Face of America's Favorite Sport," *Washington Post*, December 18, 2023, https://www.washingtonpost.com/sports/interactive/2023/football-participation-decline-politics-demographics/; Emily Kroshus et al., "Association between Community Socioeconomic Characteristics and Access to Youth Flag Football," *Injury Prevention* 25, no. 4 (2019): 278–82.

106. Sheinen and Giambalvo, "The Changing Face"

107. "The Benefits of Youth Tackle Football," NFL Play Football, 2024, accessed February 3, 2025, https://playfootball.nfl.com/parents/benefits-of-youth-tackle-football/.

108. Emily Kroshus et al., "Association Between Community Socioeconomic Characteristics and Access to Youth Flag Football."

109. Sheinen and Giambalvo, "The Changing Face"; Sanderson and Cassilo, "I'm Glad I Played When the Country Still Had Gonads," 1–2; Joshua J. Dyck, John Cluverius, and Jeffrey N. Gerson, "Sports, Science, and Partisanship in the United States: Chronic Traumatic Encephalopathy and the Polarization of an Apolitical Issue," *International Journal of Sport Policy and Politics* 11, no. 1 (2019): 133–52.

110. Sheinen and Giambalvo, "The Changing Face," paragraph 80.

4. THE SPORT-MILITARY RESEARCH COMPLEX

1. Joseph Maroon, "Concussion, CTE and TES," Vanderbilt Talks About Sports Concussion Quarterly Lecture Series, filmed April 2022, YouTube, https://www.youtube.com/watch?v=6s6MLIqUYUI.

2. Scott A. Clark, "Upon the Fields of Friendly Strife: An 'Athletic Charter' to Reform the Army's Sports Culture and Build Better Leaders," *Military Review*, May–June 2023: 133–46.

3. Kathleen Bachynski, *No Game for Boys to Play: The History of Youth Football and the Origins of a Public Health Crisis* (University of North Carolina Press, 2019); Steve W. Pope, "An Army of Athletes: Playing Fields, Battlefields, and the American Military Sporting Experience, 1890–1920," *Journal of Military History* 59, no. 3 (1995): 435–56.

4. John Maker, "Hand Grenades and Hockey Sticks: The Positive Influence of the Military on Physical Education and Sport in Canada, 1900–1945," *Physical & Health Education Journal* 75, no. 1 (2009): 16–19; Daryl Adair, John Nauright, and Murray Phillips. "Playing fields through to battle fields: The development of Australian sporting manhood in its imperial context, c. 1850–1918." *Journal of Australian Studies* 22, no. 56 (1998): 51–67.

5. "Sport and Australian Military Life," Anzac Portal, Australian Government Department of Veterans' Affairs, https://anzacportal.dva.gov.au/resources/sport-and-australian-military-life.

6. Varda Burstyn, *The Rites of Men: Manhood, Politics, and the Culture of Sport* (University of Toronto Press, 1999), 67.

7. Michael L. Butterworth, ed., *Sport and Militarism: Contemporary Global Perspectives* (Routledge, 2017).

8. Michael L. Butterworth, "Everybody's All-Americans: High School Football and the U.S. Military," in *Football, Culture and Power*, eds. David J. Leonard, Kimberly B. George

and Wade Davis (Routledge, 2016): 139–55; Paul A. Reimann, "The G.I. Bill and Collegiate Football Recruiting after World War II," *International Sports Journal* 8, no. 2 (2004): 126–33.

9. SGT M, "Building a Stronger Australian Army—Recruitment," The Cove, accessed February 3, 2025, https://cove.army.gov.au/article/building-stronger-australian-army-recruitment; Mishall Rehman, "CAF Sports Strategy Aims to Support Retention, Recruitment and Culture Change," *Canadian Military Family Magazine*, accessed February 3, 2025, https://www.cmfmag.ca/policy/caf-sports-strategy-aims-to-support-retention-recruitment-and-culture-change/.

10. Samantha King, "Offensive Lines: Sport-State Synergy in an Era of Perpetual War," *Cultural Studies ↔ Critical Methodologies* 8, no. 4 (2008): 527–39.

11. King, "Offensive Lines"; Adam Rugg, "America's Game: The NFL's 'Salute to Service' Campaign, the Diffused Military Presence, and Corporate Social Responsibility," *Popular Communication* 14, no. 1 (2016): 21–29.

12. King, "Offensive Lines," 538.

13. Michael L. Butterworth, "Public Memorializing in the Stadium: Mediated Sport, the Tenth Anniversary of 9/11, and the Illusion of Democracy," *Communication & Sport* 2 (2014): 203–24; Kyle W. Kusz, "Trumpism, Tom Brady, and the Reassertion of White Supremacy in Militarized Post-9/11 America," in *Sport and Militarism: Contemporary Global Perspectives*, ed. Michael L. Butterworth (Routledge, 2017): 229–44.

14. Jay Scherer and Jordan Koch, "Living With War: Sport, Citizenship, and the Cultural Politics of Post-9/11 Canadian Identity," *Sociology of Sport Journal* 27, no. 1 (2010): 1–29.

15. Jennifer Terry, *Attachments to War: Biomedical Logics and Violence in Twenty-First-Century America* (Duke University Press, 2015), 12.

16. Edgar Jones, Nicola T. Fear, and Simon Wessely, "Shell Shock and Mild Traumatic Brain Injury: A Historical Review," *American Journal of Psychiatry* 164, no. 11 (2007): 1641–45.

17. Peter Hayward, "Traumatic Brain Injury: The Signature of Modern Conflicts," *Lancet Neurology* 7, no. 3 (2008): 200–01.

18. Ann C. McKee and Meghan E. Robinson, "Military-Related Traumatic Brain Injury and Neurodegeneration," *Alzheimer's & Dementia* 10, no. 35 (2014): S242–53.

19. Morgan S. Hardy, Jan E. Kennedy, and Douglas B. Cooper, "Patient Attribution of Posttraumatic Symptoms to Brain Injury Versus PTSD in Military-Related Mild TBI," *Journal of Neuropsychiatry and Clinical Neurosciences* 32, no. 3 (2020): 252–58; Judy C. Kelly, Efland H. Amerson, and Jeffrey T. Barth, "Mild Traumatic Brain Injury: Lessons Learned from Clinical, Sports, and Combat Concussions," *Rehabilitation Research and Practice* (2012): 371970.

20. Pink Concussions (@PinkConcussions) "Do we have to put all our military suffering with TBI in NFL jerseys to get the attention this issue deserves," X, October 18, 2022, https://twitter.com/PinkConcussions/status/1582350059106373632?s=20.

21. Frank Larkin, "Outrage Over NFL Brain Injuries; Silence Over Military Brain Injuries," *Military Times*, October 26, 2022, https://www.militarytimes.com/opinion/commentary/2022/10/25/outrage-over-nfl-brain-injuries-silence-over-military-brain-injuries/.

22. Hayward, "Traumatic Brain Injury."

23. Terri Tanielian and Lisa H. Jaycox, eds., *Invisible Wounds of War: Psychological and Cognitive Injuries, Their Consequences, and Services to Assist Recovery* (RAND Corporation,

2008), https://www.rand.org/content/dam/rand/pubs/monographs/2008/RAND_MG720
.sum.pdf; Heidi Terrio et al., "Traumatic Brain Injury Screening: Preliminary Findings in a
U.S. Army Brigade Combat Team," *Journal of Head Trauma Rehabilitation* 24, no. 1 (2009): 14–23.

24. Kalyn C. Jannace et al., "Lifetime Traumatic Brain Injury and Risk of Post-Concussive Symptoms in the Millennium Cohort Study," *Journal of Neurotrauma* 41, no. 5–6 (2024): 613–22.

25. Brian G. Garber, Corneliu Rusu, and Mark A. Zamorski, "Deployment-Related Mild Traumatic Brain Injury, Mental Health Problems, and Post-Concussive Symptoms in Canadian Armed Forces Personnel," *BMC Psychiatry* 14 (2014): 325; Duncan Wallace, "Improvised Explosive Devices and Traumatic Brain Injury: The Military Experience in Iraq and Afghanistan," *Australasian Psychiatry* 17, no. 3 (2009): 218–24.

26. "Thousands of Soldiers Live with 'Silent Epidemic,'" NBC News, September 10, 2007, https://www.nbcnews.com/health/health-news/thousands-soldiers-live-silent-epidemic
-flna1c9468034; Hayward, "Traumatic Brain Injury"; RAND, *Invisible Wounds of War*.

27. "Thousands of Soldiers Live with 'Silent Epidemic.'"

28. Traumatic Brain Injury Center of Excellence, "DoD Numbers for Traumatic Brain Injury—Worldwide Totals," Health.mil, accessed February 3, 2025, https://health.mil
/Military-Health-Topics/Centers-of-Excellence/Traumatic-Brain-Injury-Center-of
-Excellence/DOD-TBI-Worldwide-Numbers.

29. Josh L. Duckworth, Jamie Grimes, and Geoffrey S.F. Ling, "Pathophysiology of Battlefield Traumatic Brain Injury," *Pathophysiology* 20, no. 1 (2013): 22–30.

30. Duckworth et al., "Pathophysiology of Battlefield Traumatic Brain Injury."

31. Lauren Fish and Paul Scharre, "Protecting Warfighters from Blast Injury," Center for a New American Security, April 29, 2018, https://www.cnas.org/publications/reports
/protecting-warfighters-from-blast-injury.

32. Dave Philips, "Senators Seek Answers from Pentagon on Troops' Blast Exposure," *New York Times*, January 19, 2024, https://www.nytimes.com/2024/01/19/us/senators
-letter-defense-department-blast-exposure.html; Daniel Zwerdling and Joaquin Sapien, "Before Reaching War Zones, Troops Risk Concussions," NPR, https://www.npr.org/2012
/08/24/158873690/before-reaching-war-zones-troops-risk-concussions.

33. Lisa A. Brenner et al., "Associations of Military-Related Traumatic Brain Injury with New-Onset Mental Health Conditions and Suicide Risk," *JAMA Network Open* 6, no. 7 (2023): e2326296; Jannace et al., "Lifetime Traumatic Brain Injury and Risk of Post-Concussive Symptoms in the Millennium Cohort Study."

34. Deborah E. Barnes et al., "Association of Mild Traumatic Brain Injury with and without Loss of Consciousness with Dementia in U.S. Military Veterans," *JAMA Neurology* 75, no. 9 (2018): 1055–61.

35. Jannace et al., "Lifetime Traumatic Brain Injury and Risk of Post-Concussive Symptoms in the Millennium Cohort Study"; Anthony P. Kontos et al., "Residual Effects of Combat-Related Mild Traumatic Brain Injury," *Journal of Neurotrauma* 30, no. 8 (2013): doi: https://doi.org/10.1089/neu.2012.2506.

36. McKee and Robinson, "Military-Related Traumatic Brain Injury and Neuro-degeneration."

37. "Project Enlist," Research for Military, Concussion Legacy Foundation, accessed February 3, 2025, https://concussionfoundation.org/programs/project-enlist.

38. "Polytrauma/TBI System of Care," U.S. Department of Veterans Affairs, accessed February 3, 2025, https://www.polytrauma.va.gov/.

39. Katherine E. Porter et al. "Postconcussive Symptoms Following Combat-Related Traumatic Brain Injury in Veterans with Posttraumatic Stress Disorder: Influence of TBI, PTSD, and Depression on symptoms measured by the Neurobehavioral Symptom Inventory (NSI)," *Journal of Psychiatric Research* 102, (2018): 8–13.

40. Lisa A. Brenner et al., "Soldiers Returning from Deployment: A Qualitative Study Regarding Exposure, Coping, and Reintegration," *Rehabilitation Psychology* 60, no. 3 (2015): 277–85.

41. Murray B. Stein and Thomas W. McCallister, "Exploring the Convergence of Post-traumatic Stress Disorder and Mild Traumatic Brain Injury," *American Journal of Psychiatry* 166, no. 7 (2009): 768–76.

42. Hardy et al., "Patient Attribution of Posttraumatic Symptoms to Brain Injury Versus PTSD in Military-Related Mild TBI"; Jones et al., "Shell Shock and Mild Traumatic Brain Injury"; Stein and McCallister, "Exploring the Convergence of Posttraumatic Stress Disorder."

43. Alexandra Loignon, Marie-Christine Ouellet, and Geneviève Belleville, "A Systematic Review and Meta-analysis on PTSD Following TBI Among Military/Veteran and Civilian Populations," *Journal of Head Trauma Rehabilitation* 35, no. 1 (2020): E21–35.

44. Heather G. Belanger et al., "Symptom complaints Following Combat-Related Traumatic Brain Injury: Relationship to Traumatic Brain Injury Severity and Posttraumatic Stress Disorder," *Journal of the International Neuropsychological Society* 16, no. 1 (2010): 194–99.

45. Charles W. Hoge et al., "Mild Traumatic Brain Injury in U.S. Soldiers Returning from Iraq," *New England Journal of Medicine* 358, no. 5, (2008): 453–63; Jones et al., "Shell Shock and Mild Traumatic Brain Injury"; Wallace, "Improvised Explosive Devices and Traumatic Brain Injury."

46. Barbara Sigford et al., "Care of War Veterans with Mild Traumatic Brain Injury," *New England Journal of Medicine* 361, no. 5 (2009): 536–38.

47. Brenner et al., "Soldiers Returning from Deployment"; Stein and McCallister, "Exploring the Convergence of Posttraumatic Stress Disorder."

48. Brenner et al., "Soldiers Returning from Deployment."

49. Melissa N. Anderson et al., "Concussion Reporting Intentions for Incoming Military Athletes and Cadets," *Brain Injury* 36, no. 3 (2022): 332–38; Alison M. Cogan, Christine E. Haines, and Maria D. Devore, "Intersections of U.S. Military Culture, Hegemonic Masculinity, and Health Care among Injured Male Service Members," *Men and Masculinities* 24, no. 3 (2021): 468–82.

50. Anderson et al., "Concussion Reporting Intentions for Incoming Military Athletes and Cadets"; Michelle L. Weber Rawlins et al., "United States Air Force Academy Cadets' Perceived Costs of Concussion Disclosure," *Military Medicine* 185, no. 1–2 (2020): e269–75.

51. Sandra Whitworth, *Men, Militarism and UN Peacekeeping: A Gendered Analysis* (Lynne Rienner, 2004).

52. Cogan et al., "Intersections of U.S. Military Culture, Hegemonic Masculinity, and Health Care among Injured Male Service Members."

53. Anderson et al., "Concussion Reporting Intentions for Incoming Military Athletes and Cadets"; Christine M. Baugh et al., "Pluralistic Ignorance as a Contributing Factor to Concussion Underreporting," *Health Education and Behavior* 49 no. 2 (2022): 340–46.

54. Burstyn, *The Rites of Men*.

55. "Traumatic Brain Injury Center of Excellence," Health.mil, accessed February 3, 2025, https://www.health.mil/Military-Health-Topics/Centers-of-Excellence/Traumatic -Brain-Injury-Center-of-Excellence.

56. LIMBIC-CENC, accessed February 3, 2024, https://www.limbic-cenc.org/.

57. "Warfighter Brain Health Hub," Traumatic Brain Injury Center of Excellence, accessed February 3, 2025, https://www.health.mil/Military-Health-Topics/Warfighter -Brain-Health?type=Articles; "H.R.9532—Warfighter Brain Health Act of 2022," Congress .Gov, last modified December 14, 2022, https://www.congress.gov/bill/117th-congress /house-bill/9532.

58. Steven P. Broglio et al., "A National Study on the Effects of Concussion in Collegiate Athletes and U.S. Military Service Academy Members," *Sports Medicine* 47 (2017): 1437–45.

59. Broglio et al., 1438.

60. Cernak Ibolja and Farid A. Ahmed, "A Comparative Analysis of Blast-Induced Neurotrauma and Blunt Traumatic Brain Injury Reveals Significant Differences in Injury Mechanisms," *Medical Data* 2, no. 4 (2010): 297–304; Peskind et al., "Military- and Sports-Related Mild Traumatic Brain Injury".

61. Kelly et al., "Mild Traumatic Brain Injury."

62. Kelly et al., "Mild Traumatic Brain Injury"; Mark Lovell, Micky Collins, and Jamie E. Pardini, "Management of Cerebral Concussion in Military Personnel: Lessons Learned From Sports Medicine," *Operative Techniques in Sports Medicine* 13, no. 4 (2005): 212–21.

63. Dena S. Davis, "Medical Research with College Athletes: Some Ethical Issues," *IRB: Ethics & Human Research* 20, no. 4 (1998): 10–11.

64. Kelly et al., "Mild Traumatic Brain Injury; Louis French, Michael McCrea, and Mark Baggett, "The Military Acute Concussion Evaluation (MACE)," ResearchGate, last modified January 16, 2014, https://www.researchgate.net/profile/Louis-French/publi cation/232729375_The_Military_Acute_Concussion_Evaluation_MACE/links/0dee c52d7e8d26842d000000/The-Military-Acute-Concussion-Evaluation-MACE.pdf; Lovell et al., "Management of Cerebral Concussion in Military Personnel."

65. Louis French, Michael McCrea, and Mark Baggett, "The Military Acute Concussion Evaluation (MACE)."

66. "NFL, Military Partner to Reduce Concussions," ABC News, last modified June 15, 2012, https://abcnews.go.com/US/nfl-military-partner-reduce-concussions/story ?id=16571549.

67. Joyce P. Brayboy, "Army Team Continues Collaboration with NFL, Under Armour, GE for Head Health Challenge II," US Army, last modified December 21, 2015, https://www .army.mil/article/160239/army_team_continues_collaboration_with_nfl_under_armour _ge_for_head_health_challenge_ii.

68. "NFL Making $40 Million Available for Medical Research," NFL, last modified August 29, 2017, https://www.nfl.com/news/nfl-making-40-million-available-for-medical -research-0ap3000000836554.

69. "NFL Making $40 Million Available for Medical Research,", paragraph 1.

70. "NFL Making $40 Million Available for Medical Research,", paragraph 8.

71. Kimberly S. Schimmel, "Not an 'Extraordinary Event': NFL Games and Militarized Civic Ritual," *Sociology of Sport Journal* 34, no. 1 (2017): 79–89; Kimberly S. Schimmel,

"From 'Violence-Complacent' to 'Terrorist-Ready': Post-9/11 Framing of the U.S. Super Bowl," *Urban Studies* 48, no. 15 (2011): 3277–91.

72. Kathleen E. Bachynski and Daniel S. Goldberg, "Time Out: NFL Conflicts of Interest with Public Health Efforts to Prevent TBI," *Injury Prevention* 24, no. 3 (2018): 180.

73. Michael L. Butterworth and Stormi D. Moskal, "American Football, Flags, and 'Fun': The Bell Helicopter Armed Forces Bowl and the Rhetorical Production of Militarism," *Communication, Culture & Critique* 2, no. 4 (2009): 411–433; Michael L. Butterworth, "Everybody's All-Americans."

74. Butterworth and Moskal, "American Football, Flags, and 'Fun,'" 417.

75. Henry A. Giroux, *University in Chains: Confronting the Military-Industrial-Academic Complex* (Routledge, 2015).

76. Henry A. Giroux, *Neoliberalism's War on Higher Education* (Haymarket, 2014), 78.

77. David L. Andrews, Ross H. Miller, and Stephanie Cork, "Weaponizing Kinesiology: Illuminating the Militarization of the Sport Sciences," in *Sport and Militarism: Contemporary Global Perspectives*, ed. Michael L. Butterworth (Routledge, 2017), 31–47.

78. Terry, *Attachments to War*, 187.

79. Jasbir K. Puar, *The Right to Maim: Debility, Capacity, Disability* (Duke University Press, 2017).

80. Matt Ventresca and Samantha King, "'Anesthetized Gladiators': Painkilling and Racial Capitalism in the NFL," *Sociology of Sport Journal* 40, no. 1 (2023): 21–22.

81. Ken MacLeish, "Churn: Mobilization–Demobilization and the Fungibility of American Military Life," *Security Dialogue, 51*, nos. 2–3 (2020): 196.

82. MacLeish, 196.

83. Robert Burns, "Pentagon: 34 Troops Suffered Brain Injuries in Iran Strike," *AP News*, January 25, 2020, https://apnews.com/article/donald-trump-ap-top-news-traumatic-brain-injuries-trauma-iraq-5aba061e7f7c2632a618d491a0a15c87.

84. Jill Colvin, "Trump Minimizes Severity of Head Injuries in Iran attacks," *AP News*, January 23, 2020, https://apnews.com/trump-minimizes-severity-of-head-injuries-in-iran-attacks-1a542a36d35c4491555e458c53bf7288.

85. Luis Martinez and Karen Travers, "President Trump Minimizes Concussion-Like Injuries in Iraq Attack as Merely 'Headaches,'" *ABC News*, January 23, 2020, https://abcnews.go.com/Politics/president-trump-minimizes-concussion-injuries-iraq-attack-headaches/story?id=68448853.

86. Callie Batts and David L. Andrews, "'Tactical Athletes': The United States Paralympic Military Program and the Mobilization of the Disabled Soldier/Athlete," *Sport in Society* 14, no.5 (2011): 557.

87. "BIAA Responds to Trump's Statement About Service Members with Traumatic Brain Injury," Brain Injury Association of America, last modified January 22,2020, https://www.biausa.org/public-affairs/public-awareness/news/biaa-responds-to-trumps-disregard-for-service-members-with-traumatic-brain-injury; "Trump Downplays U.S. Soldiers' Head Injuries, But Combat Brain Trauma Can Be Serious," NPR, last modified January 22, 2020, https://www.npr.org/2020/01/22/798644728/trump-downplays-u-s-soldiers-head-injuries-but-combat-brain-trauma-can-be-seriou.

88. Amanda Macias, "Trump signs $738 Billion Defense Bill. Here's What the Pentagon is Poised to Get," CNBC News, December 20, 2019, https://www.cnbc.com/2019/12/21/trump-signs-738-billion-defense-bill.html.

89. Terry, *Attachments to War*, 7.

90. Field notes, December 18, 2017

91. Sean Cowlishaw et al., "Health Service Interventions for Intimate Partner Violence among Military Personnel and Veterans: A Framework and Scoping Review," *International Journal of Environmental Research and Public Health* 19, no. 6 (2022): 3551; Kylee Trevillion et al., "A Systematic Review of Mental Disorders and Perpetration of Domestic Violence among Military Populations," *Social Psychiatry and Psychiatric Epidemiology* 50 (2015): 1329–46.

92. Fieldnotes, December 18, 2017.

93. "Invisible Veteran," PBS, aired January 5, 2024, video, 2:3, https://www.pbs.org/video/invisible-veteran-iy5jr6/.

94. "Invisible Veteran."

95. "Invisible Veteran."

96. Field notes, June 5, 2024.

97. Terry, *Attachments to War*, 28.

98. Sofya Aptekar, *Green Card Soldier: Between Model Immigrant and Security Threat* (Massachussetts Institute of Technology Press, 2023); Wendy R. Christensen, "The Black Citizen-Subject: Black Single Mothers in U.S. Military Recruitment Materials," *Ethnic and Racial Studies* 39, no. 14 (2016): 2508–26.

99. Butterworth, "Everybody's All-Americans."

100. Lisa Uperesa, *Gridiron Capital: How Football Became a Samoan Game* (Duke University Press, 2022), 15.

101. Tim Kane, "Who Bears the Burden? Demographic Characteristics of U.S. Military Recruits Before and After 9/11," Heritage Foundation, November 7, 2005, https://www.heritage.org/defense/report/who-bears-the-burden-demographic-characteristics-us-military-recruits-and-after-911; Uperesa presents data that indicates this overrepresentation is even higher in the NFL.

102. Clara E. Dismuke-Greer et al., "Geographic Disparities in Mortality Risk Within a Racially Diverse Sample of U.S. Veterans with Traumatic Brain Injury," *Health Equity* 2, no. 1 (2018): 304–12.

103. Alex S. Aguirre, Kenny Rojas, and Alcy R. Torres, "Pediatric Traumatic Brain Injuries in War Zones: A Systematic Literature Review," *Frontiers in Neurology* 14 (2023): doi: https://doi.org/10.3389/fneur.2023.1253515; Ibrahem Hanafi et al., "War-Related Traumatic Brain Injuries during the Syrian Armed conflict in Damascus 2014–2017: A Cohort Study and a Literature Review," *BMC Emergency Medicine* 23, 35 (2023): doi: https://doi.org/10.1186/s12873-023-00799-6; Rafif Younis et al., "Causes of Traumatic Brain Injury in Patients Admitted to Rafidia, Al-Ittihad and the Specialized Arab Hospitals, Palestine, 2006–2007," *Brain Injury* 25, no. 3 (2011): 282–91.

104. Z. Chemali et al., "A Perspective From the Middle East on the Topic of Concussion," *Global Journal of Health Science* 12, no. 6 (2020): doi: https://doi.org/10.5539/gjhs.v12n6p30; Omar Dewachi, "Revealed in the Wound: Medical Care and the Ecologies of War in Post-Occupation Iraq," in *Vulnerability and the Politics of Care: Transdisciplinary Dialogues*, ed. Victoria Browne, Jason Danely, and Doerthe Rosenow (Oxford University Press, 2021), 126–40; Catherine Lutz and Andreas Mazzarino, eds., *War and Health: The Medical Consequences of the Wars in Iraq and Afghanistan* (New York University Press, 2019).

105. Nirmala Everelles, *Disability and Difference in Global Contexts: Enabling a Transformative Body Politic* (Springer, 2011); Sona Kazemi, "Disabling Power of Class and Ideology: Analyzing War Injury through the Transnational Disability Theory and Praxis," Disability Studies Quarterly 39, no. 3 (2019): doi: https://doi.org/10.18061/dsq.v39i3.6496; Sona Kazemi, "Whose Disability (Studies)? Defetishizing Disablement of the Iranian Survivors of the Iran-Iraq War by (Re)Telling their Resilient Narratives of Survival," *Canadian Journal of Disability Studies* 8, no. 4 (2019): 195–226.

106. Kazemi, "Whose Disability Studies?" 196.

107. Puar, *The Right to Maim*, xvii.

5. ADVOCATING FOR WOMEN

1. "VA's National PTSD Brain Bank Collaborates with PINK Concussions Group," *VAntage Point* (blog), January 24, 2018, https://blogs.va.gov/VAntage/44641/vas-national-ptsd-brain-bank-collaborates-pink-concussions-group/.

2. Terry Gross, "A Brain Injury Cut Short Briana Scurry's Soccer Career. It Didn't End Her Story," NPR, July 27, 2022, https://www.npr.org/2022/07/27/1112731819/soccer-briana-scurry-my-greatest-save-brain-injury.

3. Rachel Allison, "Privileging Difference: Negotiating Gender Essentialism in U.S. Women's Professional Soccer," *Sociology of Sport Journal* 38, no. 2 (2020): 158–66.

4. Eileen Narcotta-Welp, "A Black Fly in White Milk: The 1999 Women's World Cup, Briana Scurry, and the Politics of Inclusion," *Journal of Sport History* 42, no. 3 (2015): 382–93.

5. Jayne Caudwell, "Gender, Feminism, and Football Studies," *Soccer & Society* 12, no. 3 (2011): 330–42.

6. "Concussion Awareness: From Athlete to Advocate," Brianna Scurry, accessed February 3, 2025, https://www.briscurry.com/advocacy; Jane McManus, "Brandi Chastain Pledges to Donate Brain to Concussion Research," ESPN, March 3, 2016, https://www.espn.com/espnw/sports/story/_/id/14891507/brandi-chastain-donates-brain-concussion-research.

7. Rene Almeling, *GUYnecology: The Missing Science of Men's Reproductive Health* (University of California Press, 2020).

8. Joanne L. Parsons, Stephanie E. Coen, and Sheree Bekker, "Anterior Cruciate Ligament Injury: Towards a Gendered Environment Approach," *British Journal of Sports Medicine* 55 (2021): 988; Victoria Pitts-Taylor, *The Brain's Body: Neuroscience and Corporeal Politics* (Duke University Press, 2016), 9.

9. Stephen T. Casper and Kelly O'Donnell, "The Punch-Drunk Boxer and the Battered Wife: Gender and Brain Injury Research," *Social Science & Medicine* 245 (2020): e112688.

10. Tracey Covassin, Ryan Moran, and R. J. Elbin, "Sex Differences in Reported Concussion Injury Rates and Time Loss from Participation: An Update of the National Collegiate Athletic Association Injury Surveillance Program From 2004–2005 through 2008–2009," *Journal of Athletic Training* 51, no. 3 (2016): 189–94; Jennifer M. Hootman, Randall Dick, and Julie Agel, "Epidemiology of Collegiate Injuries for 15 Sports: Summary and Recommendations for Injury Prevention Initiatives," *Journal of Athletic Training* 42, no. 2 (2007): 311–19; Andrew E. Lincoln et al., "Trends in Concussion Incidence in High School Sports: A Prospective 11-Year Study," *American Journal of Sports Medicine* 39, no. 5 (2011): 958–63.

11. Peter Keating, "Why Does It Seem like Nobody Cares about Female Concussions?" ESPN, June 30, 2017, https://www.espn.com/espnw/story/_/id/19775123/why-does-seem-cares-female-concussions.

12. Cameron French, "Science Playing Catch Up in Women's Concussion Research," CTV News, May 31, 2021, https://www.ctvnews.ca/health/science-playing-catch-up-in-women-s-concussion-research-1.5449924.

13. Christie Aschwanden, "Women Get Sports Concussions at Higher Rates than Men," fivethirtyeight, May 17, 2016, https://fivethirtyeight.com/features/women-get-sports-concussions-at-higher-rates-than-men/; John Baldock, "Women and Girls Face a Greater Risk of Brain Condition CTE, Caused by Repeated Blows to the Head," SBS, September 13, 2020, https://www.sbs.com.au/news/article/women-and-girls-face-a-greater-risk-of-brain-condition-cte-caused-by-repeated-blows-to-the-head/7onm75760; Stephanie Convery, "Damage Found after Late AFLW Player Jacinda Barclay's Brain Donated for Concussion Research," *Guardian*, April 30, 2021, https://www.theguardian.com/sport/2021/apr/30/damage-found-after-late-aflw-player-jacinda-barclay-donates-brain-for-concussion-research.

14. Raeesa P. Gupte et al., "Sex Differences in Traumatic Brain Injury: What We Know and What We Should Know," *Journal of Neurotrauma* 36, no. 22 (2019): 3063.

15. Field notes, December 19, 2017.

16. Gupte et al., "Sex Differences," 3064.

17. Eve M. Valera et al., "Understanding Traumatic Brain Injury in Females: A State-of-the-Art Summary and Future Directions," *Journal of Head Trauma Rehabilitation* 36, no. 1 (2021): e1.

18. Rick Maese, "Soccer Star Brandi Chastain Pledges to Donate her Brain to CTE Research for Women," *Washington Post*, March 3, 2016, https://www.washingtonpost.com/sports/dcunited/brandi-chastain-pledges-to-donate-brain-to-concussion-research/2016/03/02/a17affac-e0d3–11e5–8c00–8aa03741dced_story.html.

19. Anne Fausto-Sterling, *Sexing the Body: Gender Politics and the Construction of Sexuality* (Basic, 2000).

20. "Sex as a Biological Variable," NIH, accessed February 28, 2025, https://orwh.od.nih.gov/sex-as-biological-variable. See also Virginia Gewin, "Trump Executive Order Puts STEM Diversity Efforts on Hold," Science, January 28, 2025, https://www.science.org/content/article/trump-executive-order-puts-stem-diversity-efforts-hold.

21. This approach is specific to the United States. The Canadian Institutes of Health Research (CIHR) outline expectations "that *all research applicants will integrate gender and sex into their research designs when appropriate* . . . to make health research more just, more rigorous, and more useful." See "How to Integrate Sex and Gender into Research," CIHR, last modified August 21, 2017, http://www.cihr-irsc.gc.ca/e/32019.html.

22. Sebra L. Klein et al., "Sex Inclusion in Basic Research Drives Discovery," *Proceedings of the National Academy of Sciences of the United States of America* 112, no. 17 (2015): 5257–58; Sarah S. Richardson et al., "Focus on Preclinical Sex Differences Will Not Address Women's and Men's Health Disparities," *Proceedings of the National Academy of Sciences of the United States of America* 112, no. 44 (2015): 13419–20.

23. Valera et al., "Traumatic Brain Injury in Females," e1.

24. Workshop presentations about gender were relatively limited, with one dedicated to explaining how gender is distinct from sex and another addressing social inequities.

25. Field notes, December 18, 2017.

26. Ashley Shew and Keith Johnson, "Companion Animals as Technologies in Biomedical Research," *Perspectives on Science* 26, no. 3 (2018): 400–417; Sarah Wolfensohn and P. Honess, "Laboratory Animal, Pet Animal, Farm Animal, Wild Animal: Which Gets the Best Deal?" *Animal Welfare* 16, no. S1 (2007): 117–23. While Shew and Johnson acknowledge these norms, their analysis complicates claims animals are seen merely as technologies.

27. Isabelle Dussauge and Anelis Kaiser, "Neuroscience and Sex/Gender," *Neuroethics* 5, no. 1 (2012): 211–15; Fausto-Sterling, *Sexing the Body*.

28. Kathryn Henne, "The 'Science' of Fair Play in Sport: Gender and the Politics of Testing," *Signs* 39, no. 3 (2014): 767–812.

29. Pitts-Taylor, *Brain's Body*, 10.

30. Pitts-Taylor, *Brain's Body*, 119. Recognizing this challenge, Mollayeva and colleagues identify the "consistent consideration of the interrelated constructs of sex and gender in TBI research" as an important avenue for study. See Tatyana Mollayeva, Shirin Mollayeva, and Angela Colantonio, "Traumatic Brain Injury: Sex, Gender, and Intersecting Vulnerabilities," *Nature Reviews Neurology* 14 (2018): 712.

31. Field notes, December 18, 2017.

32. For further discussion, see Lynda Birke, "Telling the Rat What to Do: Laboratory Animals, Science, and Gender," in *Gender and the Science of Difference: Cultural Politics of Contemporary Science and Medicine*, ed. Jill A. Fisher (Rutgers University Press, 2011): 91–107.

33. Workshop participants did acknowledge that categories used "in humans do not easily translate into the mouse or rat model," with some proposing using large animal models, such as pigs, as subjects.

34. Henne, "The 'Science' of Fair Play."

35. Pitts-Taylor, *Brain's Body*, 119.

36. Covassin, Moran, and Elbin, "Sex Differences in Reported Concussion Injury Rates and Time Loss from Participation."

37. Raeesa P. Gupte et al., "Sex Differences in Traumatic Brain Injury: What We Know and What We Should Know," *Journal of Neurotrauma* 36, no. 22 (2019): 3063–91; Harvey S. Levin et al., "Association of Sex and Age with Mild Traumatic Brain Injury-Related Symptoms: A TRACK-TBI Study," *JAMA Network Open* 4, no. 4 (2021): e213046.

38. Kathryn Wunderle et al., "Menstrual Phase as Predictor of Outcome after Mild Traumatic Brain Injury in Women," *Journal of Head Trauma Rehabilitation* 29, no. 5 (2014): e1–e8; Virginia Gallagher et al., "The Effects of Sex Differences and Hormonal Contraception on Outcomes after Collegiate Sports-Related Concussion," *Journal of Neurotrauma* 35, no. 11 (2018): 1242–47.

39. Christina L. Master et al., "Differences in Sport-Related Concussion for Female and Male Athletes in Comparable Collegiate Sports: A Study from the NCAA-DoD Concussion Assessment, Research and Education Consortium," *British Journal of Sports Medicine* 55, no. 24 (2021): 1387–94.

40. Christy L. Collins et al., "Neck Strength: A Protective Factor Reducing Risk for Concussion in High School Sports," *Journal of Primary Prevention* 35, no. 5 (2014): 309–19; Jacob E. Resch et al., "Sport Concussion and the Female Athlete," *Clinics in Sport Medicine* 36, no. 4 (2017): 717–39.

41. Christian Chavarro-Nieto et al., "Neck Strength in Rugby Union Players: A Systematic Review of the Literature," *The Physician and Sports Medicine*, 49, no. 4 (2021): 392–409.

42. Elisabeth M. P. Williams et al., "Sex Differences in Neck Strength and Head Impact Kinematics in University Rugby Union Players," *European Journal of Sport Science* 22, no. 11 (2021): 1649–58; see also Ed Daly, Alan J. Pearce, and Lisa Ryan, "A Systematic Review of Strength and Conditioning Protocols for Improving Neck Strength and Reducing Concussion Incidence and Impact Injury Risk in Collision Sports; Is There Evidence?" *Journal of Function Morphology and Kinesiology* 6, no. 1 (2021): doi: https://doi.org/10.3390/jfmk6010008.

43. Parsons, Coen, and Bekker, "Anterior Cruciate Ligament Injury."

44. Nancy Theberge, "Studying Gender and Injuries: A Comparative Analysis of the Literature on Women's Injuries in Sport and Work," *Ergonomics* 55, no. 2 (2012): 187.

45. Patricia Vertinsky, "Exercise, Physical Capability, and the Eternally Wounded Woman in Late Nineteenth Century North America," *Journal of Sport History* 14, no. 1 (1987): 8.

46. Annemarie Mol, *The Body Multiple: Ontology in Medical Practice* (Duke University Press, 2003).

47. Field notes, December 19, 2017.

48. Field notes, December 19, 2017.

49. Kimberly G. Harmon et al., "American Medical Society for Sports Medicine Position Statement: Concussion in Sport," *British Journal of Sports Medicine* 47 (2013): 15–26; Resch et al., "Sport Concussion"; Field notes December 19, 2017.

50. Covassin, Moran, and Elbin, "Sex Differences in Reported Concussion Injury Rates"; Theresa L. Miyashita, Eleni Diakogeorgiou, and Christina Vander Vegt, "Gender Differences in Concussion Reporting among High School Athletes," *Sports Health* 8 (2016): 359–63.

51. Will Courtenay, *Dying to Be Men: Psychosocial, Environmental, and Biobehavioral Directions in Promoting the Health of Men and Boys* (Taylor & Francis, 2011).

52. R. W. Dick, "Is There a Gender Difference in Concussion Incidence and Outcomes?" *British Journal of Sports Medicine* 43 (2009): i4–50.

53. Emily Kroshus et al., "Concussion Reporting, Sex, and Conformity to Traditional Gender Norms in Young Adults," *Journal of Adolescence*, 54 (2017): 110–19.

54. Margaret Carlisle Duncan, "Gender Warriors in Sport: Women and the Media," in *Handbook of Sports and Media*, ed. Arthur A. Raney and Jennings Bryan (Routledge, 2006), 231–52; Vikki Krane, "We Can Be Athletic and Feminine, but Do We Want to? Challenging Hegemonic Femininity in Women's Sport," *Quest* 53, no. 1 (2001): 115–33.

55. Mary G. McDonald, "Queering Whiteness: The Peculiar Case of the Women's National Basketball Association," *Sociological Perspectives* 45, no. 4 (2002): 379–96.

56. Field notes, December 19, 2017.

57. Jaclyn B. Caccese et al., "Sex Differences in Recovery Trajectories of Assessments for Sport-Related Concussion Among NCAA Athletes: A CARE Consortium Study," *Sports Medicine*, (December 2023): doi: https://doi.org/10.1007/s40279-023-01982-2.

58. Emily Caldwell, "No Sex Difference in Concussion Recovery among College Athletes," *Ohio State News*, January 23, 2024, https://news.osu.edu/no-sex-difference-in-concussion-recovery-among-college-athletes/.

59. "Katherine Price Snedaker, Executive Director," PINK Concussions, accessed April 1, 2019, https://www.pinkconcussions.com/about.

60. "Female Brain Injury," PINK Concussions, accessed April 1, 2019, https://www.pinkconcussions.com/new-page-1.

61. "About Us," PINK Concussions, April 11, 2022, https://www.pinkconcussions.com/pageus.

62. "Concussions and the Female Athlete," Twin Cities Public Broadcasting Services, August 4, 2017, https://video.tpt.org/video/tpt-documentaries-concussions-and-female-athletes/.

63. Field notes, December 18, 2017.

64. Parsons, Coen, and Bekker, "Anterior Cruciate Ligament Injury," 988.

65. Howard L. Nixon, "A Social Network Analysis of Influences on Athletes to Play with Pain and Injuries," *Journal of Sport & Social Issues* 16, no. 2 (1992): 127–35; Howard L. Nixon, "Explaining Pain and Injury Attitudes and Experiences in Sport in Terms of Gender, Race, and Sport Status," *Journal of Sport & Social Issues* 20, no. 2 (1996): 33–44.

66. Sarah M. Peitzmeier et al., "Intimate Partner Violence in Transgender Populations: Systematic Review and Meta-analysis of Prevalence and Correlates," *American Journal of Public Health* 110 (2020): e1–14.

67. Henne, "The 'Science' of Fair Play."

68. Pitts-Taylor, *Brain's Body*, 59.

69. Steven Epstein, *Inclusion: The Politics of Difference in Medical Research* (University of Chicago Press, 2007).

70. Mollayeva et al., "Traumatic Brain Injury."

71. Samira Omar, Stephanie Nixon, and Angela Colantonio, "Integrated Care Pathways for Black Persons with Traumatic Brain Injury: A Critical Transdisciplinary Scoping Review of the Clinic Care Journey," *Trauma, Violence, & Abuse* (2021): doi: https://doi.org/10.1177/15248380211062221.

72. Brendan Hokowhitu, "Tackling Māori Masculinity: A Colonial Genealogy of Savagery and Sport," *Contemporary Pacific* 16, no. 2 (2004): 259–84; Antonio Moore, "Football's War on the Minds of Black Men," Vice Sports, December 24, 2015, https://sports.vice.com/en_us/article/eze4gj/footballs-war-on-the-minds-of-black-men; Kyle Siler, "Pipelines on the Gridiron: Player Backgrounds, Opportunity Structures and Racial Stratification in American College Football," *Sociology of Sport Journal* 36, no. 1 (2019): 57–76.

73. David R. Williams and Selina A. Mohammed, "Discrimination and Racial Disparities in Health: Evidence and Needed Research," *Journal of Behavioral Medicine* 32, no. 1 (2009): 31.

74. Arline T. Geronimus et al., "'Weathering' and Age Patterns of Allostatic Load Scores among Blacks and Whites in the United States," *American Journal of Public Health* 96, no. 5 (2006): 826–33.

75. Joe Fagin and Zinobia Bennefield, "Systemic Racism and U.S. Health Care," *Social Science & Medicine* 103, no. 1 (2014): 7–14.

76. Williams and Mohammed, "Discrimination and Racial Disparities," 31.

77. Kimberlé W. Crenshaw, "Mapping the Margins: Intersectionality, Identity Politics, and Violence against Women of Color," *Stanford Law Review* 43, no. 6 (1991): 1241–99.

78. Amanda St. Ivany et al., "Living in Fear and Prioritizing Safety: Exploring Women's Lives after Traumatic Brain Injury from Intimate Partner Violence," *Qualitative Health Research* 28, no. 11 (2018): 1708–18.

79. Field notes, March 7, 2020.

80. Michael Marmot et al., "Closing the Gap in a Generation: Health Equity Through Action on the Social Determinants of Health," *Lancet* 372, no. 9650 (2008): 1661–69.

81. Ruqaiijah Yearby, "Structural Racism and Health Disparities: Reconfiguring the Social Determinants of Health Framework to Include the Root Cause," *Journal of Law, Medicine & Ethics* 48, no. 3 (2020): 518–26.

6. A HIDDEN EPIDEMIC AT HOME

1. We use terms that the various ways our participants refer to domestic violence, including domestic and family violence, gender-based violence, intimate partner violence, partner-inflicted violence, and violence against women. Although some experts working on TBI-related concerns prefer not to use "domestic violence" on grounds that it is not precise, we use this language because of its centrality in many feminist social movements.

2. Christa Hillstrom, "The Hidden Epidemic of Brain Injuries from Domestic Violence," *New York Times Magazine*, March 1, 2022, https://www.nytimes.com/2022/03/01/magazine/brain-trauma-domestic-violence.html.

3. Brain Injury Research Center (BIRC) of Mount Sinai, "This #BrainAwarenessWeek, we are raising awareness for the intersection of #IntimatePartnerViolence (IPV) and #TBI . . . The number of women who have experienced TBI from domestic violence is 11-12X MORE than the number of TBIs experienced by military personnel AND athletes COMBINED," X, March 17, 2023, https://twitter.com/SinaiTBI/status/1636775850312974364; Hayley Gleeson, "Shaken Brains, Shattered Lives," Australian Broadcasting News, August 6, 2023; Theresa Currier Thomas, Caitlin E. Bromberg, and Gokul Krishna, "Female Sex in Experimental Traumatic Brain Injury Research: Forging a Path Forward," Neural Regeneration Research 17, no. 3 (2020): 550–52.

4. Nicole F. Roberts, "A Global Public Health Epidemic Going Completely Untreated: Intimate Partner Violence," *Forbes*, April 19, 2019, https://www.forbes.com/sites/nicolefisher/2019/04/08/a-global-public-health-epidemic-going-completely-untreated-intimate-partner-violence/?sh=7f8611781701.

5. Research illustrates the blurred distinctions regarding how people who experience violence self-identify. We use "victim-survivor" here (except in cases where other language has been used), recognizing that "survivor" and "victim" are rarely adequate and can reflect a false binary. See Kaitlin M. Boyle and Kimberly B. Rogers, "Beyond the Rape 'Victim'– 'Survivor' Binary: How Race, Gender, and Identity Processes Interact to Shape Distress," *Sociological Forum* 35, no. 2 (2020): 323–45.

6. Field notes, March 7, 2020.

7. Jonathan Simon, *Governing through Crime: How the War on Crime Changed American Democracy and Created a Culture of Fear* (Oxford University Press, 2007).

8. Renee Shelby, "Technology, Sexual Violence, and Power-Evasive Politics: Mapping the Anti-violence Sociotechnical Imaginary," *Science, Technology, & Human Values* 48, no. 3 (2023): 552–81.

9. Shelby, "Technology, Sexual Violence, and Power-Evasive Politics," 552–53.

10. Mimi Kim, "The Carceral Creep: Gender-based Violence, Race, and the Expansion of the Punitive State, 1973–1983," *Social Problems* 67, no. 2 (2020): 251–69.

11. Kim, "The Carceral Creep," 254.

12. Kellianne Costello and Brian D. Greenwald, "Update on Domestic Violence and Traumatic Brain Injury: A Narrative Review," *Brain Sciences* 12, no. 1 (2022): doi: https://doi .org/10.3390/brainsci12010122.

13. Stephen T. Casper and Kelly O'Donnell, "The Punch-Drunk Boxer and the Battered Wife: Gender and Brain Injury Research," *Social Science & Medicine* 245 (2020): 112688.

14. Casper and O'Donnell, "The Punch-Drunk Boxer and the Battered Wife."

15. Haley Gleeson, "Why Isn't the Brain Injury Crisis in Our Homes Causing as Much Concern as Concussion in Sport?" *ABC News*, August 19, 2023, https://www.abc.net .au/news/2023-08-19/brain-injury-domestic-violence-crisis-concussion-sports /102740930.

16. Jonathan Lifshitz, "Brain Injury in the NFL is Miniscule Compared to those from Intimate Partner Violence," LinkedIn, October 10, 2023, https://www.linkedin.com/pulse /brain-injury-nfl-miniscule-compared-those-from-partner-lifshitz/.

17. Gleeson, "Why Isn't the Brain Injury Crisis in Our Homes Causing as Much Concern as Concussion in Sport?"

18. Eve Valera et al., "Understanding Traumatic Brain Injury in Females: A State-of-the-Art Summary and Future Directions," *Journal of Head Trauma Rehabilitation* 36, no. 1 (2021): E1–17.

19. Molly Hayes, "How Does Intimate Partner Violence Affect Women's Brains? Scientists, Social Workers Advocate for More Research," *Globe and Mail*, December 28, 2002, https:// www.theglobeandmail.com/canada/article-intimate-partner-violence-brain-injuries/.

20. Standing Courageous, Inc, https://standingcourageous.com/.

21. Amy Lehrner and Nicole E. Allen, "Still a Movement After All These Years? Current Tensions in the Domestic Violence Movement," *Violence Against Women* 15, no. 6 (2009): 656–77.

22. Lehrner and Allen, "Still a Movement After All These Years? Current Tensions in the Domestic Violence Movement"; Beth Richie, "A Black Feminist Reflection on the Anti-Violence Movement," *Signs* 25, no. 4 (2000): 1133–7.

23. Kristin Bumiller, *In an Abusive State: How Neoliberalism Appropriated the Feminist Movement against Sexual Violence* (Duke University Press, 2008); Gita R. Mehrotra, Ericka Kimball, and Stéphanie Wehab, "The Braid That Binds Us: The Impact of Neoliberalism, Criminalization, and Professionalization on Domestic Violence Work," *Affilia* 31, no. 2 (2016): 153–63.

24. Kim, "The Carceral Creep," 256.

25. Kim, "The Carceral Creep," 257.

26. Field notes, March 7, 2020.

27. See, for example, "PINK Concussions Annual Report 2023," PINK Concussions, https://www.canva.com/design/DAF2-dOZiPo/xbCoKGLHkR4fB3YNeTErUA/view.

28. This trend became clear through interviews and observations conducted over time (e.g., December 18–19, 2017, Washington, DC; August 11–16, 2018, Toronto, Ontario; March 7, 2020, Phoenix, Arizona).

29. For more on sports TBI and structural violence, see Daniel S. Goldberg, *Tackle Football and Traumatic Brain Injuries: Law, Ethics, and Public Health* (Johns Hopkins University Press, 2024).

30. Catherine Tunney, "Trudeau says Deaths and Disappearances of Indigenous Women and Girls Amount to 'Genocide,'" CBC News, June 4, 2019, https://www.cbc.ca/news/poli tics/trudeau-mmiwg-genocide-1.5161681.

31. Michelle S. Fitts, Jennifer Cullen, and Karen Soldatic, "First Nations Women are 69 Times More Likely to Have a Head Injury after Being Assaulted. We Show How Hard It Is to Get Help," The Conversation, November 22, 2022, https://theconversation.com/first -nations-women-are-69-times-more-likely-to-have-a-head-injury-after-being-assaulted -we-show-how-hard-it-is-to-get-help-194249; Michelle S. Fitts et al., "'I Don't Think It's on Anyone's Radar': The Workforce and System Barriers to Healthcare for Indigenous Women Following a Traumatic Brain Injury Acquired through Violence in Remote Australia," *International Journal of Environmental Research and Public Health* 19, no. 22 (2022): 14744.

32. Fitts et al., "'I Don't Think It's on Anyone's Radar.'".

33. Rebecca M. Jordan-Young, *Brain Storm: The Flaws in the Science of Sex Differences* (Harvard University Press, 2011); Victoria Pitts-Taylor, *The Brain's Body: Neuroscience and Corporeal Politics* (Duke University Press, 2016); Oliver Rollins, *Conviction: The Making and Unmaking of the Violent Brain* (Stanford University Press, 2021).

34. Yvonne Roberts, "'I Got a Brain Injury and a Life Sentence': The Hidden Legacy of Male Violence Against Women," *Guardian*, April 2, 2023, https://www.theguardian.com /society/2023/apr/02/i-got-a-brain-injury-and-a-life-sentence-the-hidden-legacy-of-male -violence-against-women.

35. Julia K. Campbell et al., "The Prevalence of Brain Injury Among Survivors and Perpetrators of Intimate Partner Violence and the Prevalence of Violence Victimization and Perpetration Among People With Brain Injury: A Scoping Review," *Injury Epidemiology* 9 (2022): 290–315.

36. Roberts, "'I Got a Brain Injury and a Life Sentence.'"

37. Roberts, "'I Got a Brain Injury and a Life Sentence.'"

38. "NIH Policy on Sex as a Biological Variable," National Institutes of Health, accessed February 16, 2025, https://orwh.od.nih.gov/sex-as-biological-variable. Due to the Trump administration's mandates, this document has been labeled a "historic document" published prior to January 20, 2025.

39. Anastasia Teterina et al., "Gender Versus Sex in Predicting Outcomes of Traumatic Brain Injury: A Cohort Study Utilizing Large Administrative Databases," *Scientific Reports* 13 (2023): 18453.

40. Isabelle Dussauge and Anelis Kaiser, "Neuroscience and Sex/Gender," *Neuroethics* 5, no. 1 (2012): 212.

41. See Leigh Goodmark, *A Troubled Marriage: Domestic Violence and the Legal System* (New York University Press, 2013); Beth E. Richie, *Arrested Justice: Black Women, Violence, and America's Prison Nation* (New York University Press, 2012).

42. Kim, "The Carceral Creep," 254.

43. "PINK Concussions Annual Report 2023," PINK Concussions, 3.

44. For example, from 2020, its Partner-Inflicted TBI Task Force meetings explicitly discussed these issues and invited experts who worked in these areas or studied these interlocking considerations in depth.

45. Michael W. Kraus, Brittany Torrez, and LaStarr Hollie, "How Narratives of Racial Progress Create Barriers to Diversity, Equity, and Inclusion in Organizations," Current Opinion in Psychology, 43 (2022): 108–13.

46. Field notes, October 26, 2018.

47. Field notes, March 7, 2020.

48. Kellianne Costello and Brian D. Greenwald, "Update on Domestic Violence and Traumatic Brain Injury; Gwen Hunnicutt et al., "The Intersection of Intimate Partner

Violence and Traumatic Brain Injury: A Call for Interdisciplinary Research," *Journal of Family Violence* 32 (2017): 471–80; Halina (Lin) Haag et al., "Battered and Brain Injured: Assessing Knowledge of Traumatic Brain Injury Among Intimate Partner Violence Service Providers," *Journal of Women's Health* 28, no. 7 (2019): 990–96.

49. Anne P. Deprince and Kim Gorgens, "The Invisible Victims of Traumatic Brain Injury," *Scientific American* (blog), November 13, 2019, https://blogs.scientificamerican.com/voices/the-invisible-victims-of-traumatic-brain-injury/

50. Field notes, December 18, 2017.

51. "Domestic Violence: Improved Data Needed to Identify the Prevalence of Brain Injuries among Victims," GAO, last modified June 12, 2020, https://www.gao.gov/products/gao-20-534.

52. Gleeson, "Why Isn't the Brain Injury Crisis in Our Homes Causing as Much Concern as Concussion in Sport?"

53. Field notes, March 7, 2020.

54. Gleeson, "Why Isn't the Brain Injury Crisis in Our Homes Causing as Much Concern as Concussion in Sport?"

55. Roberts, "'I Got a Brain Injury and a Life Sentence.'"

56. Field notes, March 7, 2020; see also Mark Higbee et al., "Involving Police Departments in Early Awareness of Concussion Symptoms during Domestic Violence Calls," *Journal of Aggression, Maltreatment & Trauma* 28, no. 7 (2019): 826–37.

57. Hilary Gleeson, "Domestic Violence Victims Who Suffer Repetitive Head Injury Should Be Screened for CTE, Australian Experts Say," ABC News, August 18, 2023, https://www.abc.net.au/news/2023-08-10/domestic-violence-repetitive-head-injury-cte-routine-screening/102682870.

58. Denise A. Donnelly et al., "White Privilege, Color Blindness, and Services to Battered Women," *Violence Against Women* 11, no. 1 (2005): 6–37; Sarah R. Leat et al., "Do I Belong Here? Experiences of Transgender Survivors of Intimate Partner Violence in Domestic Violence Shelters," Families in Society, accessed February 3, 2025, doi: https://doi.org/10.1177/10443894231196929; Nkiru A. Nnawulezi and Cris M. Sullivan, "Oppression Within Safe Spaces: Exploring Racial Microaggressions Within Domestic Violence Shelters," *Journal of Black Psychology* 40, no. 6 (2024): 563–91; Mikel L. Walters, *Invisible at Every Turn: An Examination of Lesbian Intimate Partner Violence* (Georgia State University, 2009).

59. Mary Iliadis et al., "How Police Body-Worn Cameras Can Facilitate Misidentification in Domestic and family Violence Responses," *Trends & Issues in Crime and Criminal Justice* 684 (2024): doi: https://doi.org/10.52922/ti77277.

60. Michelle Fitts, Jennifer Cullen, and Jody Barney, "Barriers Preventing Indigenous Women with Violence-related Head Injuries from Accessing Services in Australia," *Australian Social Work* 76, no. 3 (2023): 411.

61. National Network to End Domestic Violence, *Funding Challenges for Domestic Violence Programs: The Impact on Victims*, July 2019, accessed December 5, 2023. https://nnedv.org/resources-library/library_public_policy_fundingchallenges/.

62. "How Does Intimate Partner Violence Affect Women's Brains? Scientists, Social Workers Advocate for More Research," *Globe and Mail*, last modified September 15, 2023, https://www.theglobeandmail.com/canada/article-intimate-partner-violence-brain-injuries/.

63. Gleeson, "Why Isn't the Brain Injury Crisis in Our Homes Causing as Much Concern as Concussion in Sport?"

64. Vivienne Elizabeth, Nicola Gavey, and Julia Tolmie, ". . . He's Just Swapped his Fists for the System: The Governance of Gender through Custody Law," *Gender & Society* 26, no. 2 (2012): 239–60; Echo A. Rivera, Cris M. Sullivan, and April M. Zeoli, "Secondary Victimization of Abused Mothers by Family Court Mediators," *Feminist Criminology* 7, no. 3 (July 2012): 234–52; Richie, *Arrested Justice*.

65. Carol Smart, *Feminism and the Power of Law* (Routledge, 1989).

66. Liat Ben-Moshe, *Decarcerating Disability: Deinstitutionalization and Prison Abolition* (University of Minnesota Press, 2020); Linda Steele, *Disability, Criminal Justice, and the Law: Reconsidering Court Diversion* (Routledge, 2020).

67. For example, an interviewee whose insights were an outlier during this research discussed a more targeted use of law to support disability recognition, service support, and trauma-informed approaches to working with victim-survivors (August 2018).

68. Field notes, August 15, 2018.

69. Molly Hayes, "How Does Intimate Partner Violence Affect Women's Brains? Scientists, Social Workers Advocate for More Research."

70. Sam Levin, "'I Didn't Think I'd Survive': Women Tell of Hidden Sexual Abuse by Phoenix Police," *Guardian*, August 10, 2020, https://www.theguardian.com/us-news/2020/aug/10/phoenix-police-officers-rape-sexual-assault.

71. Hayley Gleeson, "Abusers in the Ranks," ABC News, October 19, 2020, https://www.abc.net.au/news/2020-10-19/police-in-australia-are-failing-to-take-action-against-domestic/12757914; Julie Ireton, "'Blue Wall of Silence' Protects Police Officers Accused of Gender-based Violence, Victims Say," CBC News, April 24, 2024, https://www.cbc.ca/news/canada/ottawa/paid-to-stay-home-one-third-officers-accused-gender-based-violence-1.7181385.

72. Richie, *Arrested Justice*.

73. Field notes, December 18, 2017. Additional testimonials are available via the PINK Concussions YouTube channel: https://www.youtube.com/c/PINKConcussions.

74. Louise Robinson and Karen Spilsbury, "Systematic Review of the Perceptions and Experiences of Accessing Health Services by Adult Victims of Domestic Violence," *Health and Social Care in the Community* 16, no. 1 (2008): 16–31; June Keeling and Coleen Fisher, "Health Professionals' Responses to Women's Disclosure of Domestic Violence," *Journal of Interpersonal Violence* 30, no. 13 (2015): 2363–78.

75. For example, Walter S. DeKeseredy, "Bringing Feminist Sociological Analyses of Patriarchy Back to the Forefront of the Study of Woman Abuse," *Violence Against Women* 27, no. 5 (2021): 621–38.

76. Dawn Moore and Rashmee Singh, "Seeing Crime, Feeling Crime: Visual Evidence, Emotions and the Persecution of Domestic Violence," *Theoretical Criminology* 22, no. 1 (2018): 116–32.

77. Elizabeth Bernstein, "The Sexual Politics of the 'New Abolitionism,'" *differences* 18, no. 3(2007): 128–51.

78. Field notes, March 7, 2020.

79. Natalie Sokoloff and Ida Dupont, "Domestic Violence: Examining the Intersections of Race, Class, and Gender," *Violence Against Women* 11, no. 1 (2005): 3–64.

80. Kimberlé Crenshaw, "Mapping the Margins: Intersectionality, Identity Politics, and Violence against Women of Color," *Stanford Law Review* 43, no. 6 (1991): 1241–99.

7. FROM CRIMINAL MINDS TO DEVIANT BRAINS

1. David J. Leonard, *Playing While White: Privilege and Power On and Off the Field* (University of Washington Press, 2017), 93.

2. Leonard, *Playing While White*, 93.

3. Adam Kilgore, "Aaron Hernandez Suffered from Most Severe CTE Ever Found in a Person His Age," *Washington Post*, November 9, 2017, https://www.washingtonpost.com/sports/aaron-hernandez-suffered-from-most-severe-cte-ever-found-in-a-person-his-age/2017/11/09/fa7cd204-c57b-11e7-afe9-4f60b5a6c4a0_story.html.

4. Nadia Kounang, "Aaron Hernandez Suffered from Worst CTE Seen in Someone His Age," CNN, November 10, 2017, https://www.cnn.com/2017/11/09/health/aaron-hernandez-brain-cte/index.html.

5. Kounang, "Aaron Hernandez Suffered from Worst CTE Seen."

6. The series includes speculation that protecting these elements of his personal life may have contributed to Hernandez murdering Lloyd. See Kathryn Henne and Matt Ventresca, "A Criminal Mind? A Damaged Brain? Narratives of Criminality and Culpability in the Celebrated Case of Aaron Hernandez," *Crime, Media, Culture* 16, no. 3 (2020): 392–413; Matt Ventresca and Kathryn Henne, "How Portrayals of the NFL Are Shaping Criminal Justice Reform," The Conversation, February 20, 2020, https://theconversation.com/how-portrayals-of-the-nfl-are-shaping-criminal-justice-reform-131766.

7. "Former NFL Player Accused of Killing Six People was Suffering from Severe CTE," *Guardian*, December 14, 2021, https://www.theguardian.com/sport/2021/dec/14/former-nfl-player-accused-of-killing-six-people-was-suffering-from-severe-cte.

8. Pamela K. Lattimore et al., "The Association of Traumatic Brain Injury, Post-Traumatic Stress Disorder, and Criminal Recidivism," *Health and Justice* 10, no. 7 (2022): 1–7.

9. E. Durand et al., "History of Traumatic Brain Injury in Prison Populations: A Systematic Review," *Annals of Physical and Rehabilitation Medicine* 60 (2017): 95–101.

10. Jacob L. Stubbs et al., "Traumatic Brain Injury in Homeless and Marginally Housed Individuals: A Systematic Review and Meta-Analysis," *Lancet Public Health* 5, no. 1 (2020): e19–e32; Cilia Mejia-Lancheros et al., "Effect of Housing First on Violence-Related Traumatic Brain Injury in Adults with Experiences of Homelessness and Mental Illness: Findings from the At Home/Chez Soi Randomized Trial, Toronto Site," *BMJ Open* 10 (2020): e038443.

11. Walter Benjamin, "Critique of Violence," in *Reflections: Essays, Aphorisms, Autobiographical Writings*, trans. Edmund Jephcott (Schocken Books, 1978), 277–300; Robert Cover, "Violence and the Word," in *Narrative, Violence, and the Law: The Essays of Robert Cover*, ed. Martha Minow, Michael Ryan, and Austin Sarat (University of Michigan Press, 1995), 208.

12. Oliver Rollins, *Conviction: The Making and Unmaking of the Violent Brain* (Palo Alto: Stanford University Press, 2021), 18 (italics in the original).

13. Jesse Mez et al., "Validity of the 2014 Traumatic Encephalopathy Syndrome Criteria for CTE Pathology," *Alzheimer's & Dementia* 17, no. 10 (2021): 1709–24.

14. Jose Baez, *Unnecessary Roughness: Inside the Trial and Final Days of Aaron Hernandez* (Hachette, 2018).

15. Amy J. Dillard and Lisa A. Tucker, "Is C.T.E. a Defense for Murder?" *New York Times*, September 22, 2017, https://www.nytimes.com/2017/09/22/opinion/aaron-hernandez-cte.html.

16. Michael McCann, "What Legal Impact Could the Potential Discovery of CTE in Aaron Hernandez's Brain Have?" *Sports Illustrated*, April 20, 2017, https://www.si.com/nfl/2017/04/20/aaron-hernandez-brain-cte-legal-impact.

17. Michael McCann, "Could Kellen Winslow Jr.'s Attorneys Use Football-Induced Brain Injury as Defense for Alleged Crimes?" *Sports Illustrated*, June 16, 2018, https://www.si.com/nfl/2018/06/17/kellen-winslow-rape-sexual-assault-charges-cte-defense; A. J. Perez, "Could Kellen Winslow Jr.'s Lawyers Use CTE as a Defense in Sex-Crimes Case?" *USA Today*, June 15, 2018, https://www.usatoday.com/story/sports/nfl/2018/06/15/kellen-winslow-cte-defense-rape-sexual-assault-charges/707277002/.

18. "Former NFL Player Accused of Killing Six People was Suffering from Severe CTE," *Guardian*, December 14, 2021, https://www.theguardian.com/sport/2021/dec/14/former-nfl-player-accused-of-killing-six-people-was-suffering-from-severe-cte.

19. "BU CTE Center: Ex-NFL Player Phillip Adams had Stage 2 CTE When He Killed Six People in April," Concussion Legacy Foundation, December 14, 2021, https://concussionfoundation.org/news/press-release/ex-nfl-player-phillip-adams-cte-killed-six-people.

20. "Former NFL Player Accused of Killing."

21. Mallory Fallin, Owen Whooley, and Kristin Kay Barker, "Criminalizing the Brain: Neurocriminology and the Production of Strategic Ignorance," *BioSocieties* 14, no. 3 (2019): 441.

22. Sean Gregory, "Aaron Hernandez Had CTE. How Much More Damage Can the NFL Take?" *TIME*, September 22, 2017, http://time.com/4952568/aaron-hernandez-cte-brain-trauma-nfl-football/.

23. Fallin, Whooley, and Barker, "Criminalizing the Brain," 439–40.

24. "Aaron Hernandez Suffered Head Trauma—Does it Explain his Behavior?" *Hartford Courant*, September 24, 2017, https://www.courant.com/sports/hc-aaron-hernandez-brain-scan-follow-0923-20170922-story.html.

25. Matt Ventresca, "The Curious Case of CTE: Mediating Materialities of Traumatic Brain Injury" *Communication & Sport* 7, no. 2 (2019): 135–56.

26. Jay D. Aronson and Simon A. Cole, "Science and the Death Penalty: DNA, Innocence, and the Debate over Capital Punishment in the United States," *Law & Social Inquiry* 34, no. 3 (2009): 606.

27. John McMullen, "Lost Lives at Westray: Official Discourse, Public Truth and Controversial Death," *Canadian Journal of Law and Society* 22, no. 1 (2007): 23, 26.

28. Estimated rates of TBI among incarcerated persons in the United States vary greatly due to differences in methodological approaches to measurement. See Pamela K. Lattimore et al., "The Association of Traumatic Brain Injury, Post-Traumatic Stress Disorder, and Criminal Recidivism, *Health & Justice* 10, no. 7 (2022): 1–7; Kristi Wall et al., "Violence-Related Traumatic Brain Injury in Justice-Involved Women," *Criminal Justice and Behavior* 45, no. 10 (2018): 1588–1605.

29. Bradley Ray and Nicholas J. Richardson, "Traumatic Brain Injury and Recidivism Among Returning Inmates," *Criminal Justice and Behavior* 44, no. 3 (2017): 472–86.

30. Aaron Roussell et al., "The Dark Footprint of State Violence: A Synthetic Approach to the American Crime Decline," *Theoretical Criminology* 26, no. 2 (2022): 328.

31. Roussell et al., 328 (italics in original).

32. Jillian M. Berkman, Joseph A. Rosenthal, and Altaf Saadi, "Carotid Physiology and Neck Restraints in Law Enforcement," *JAMA Neurology* 78, no. 3 (2021): 267–68.

33. Kimberly Kindy, Kevin Schaul, and Ted Mellnik, "Half of the Nation's Largest Police Departments Have Banned or Limited Neck Restraints Since June," *Washington Post*, September 6, 2023, https://www.washingtonpost.com/graphics/2020/national/police-use-of-force-chokehold-carotid-ban/; Mark Morales, "New York Supreme Court Ruling Reinstates Law Banning Police Officers from Using Chokeholds During Arrests," CNN, May 20, 2022, https://edition.cnn.com/2022/05/19/us/nypd-chokehold-diaphragm-ban-state-supreme-court-ruling/index.html.

34. Department of Justice, "Department of Justice Announces Department-Wide Policy on Chokeholds and 'No-Knock' Entries," *Justice News*, September 14, 2021, https://www.justice.gov/opa/pr/department-justice-announces-department-wide-policy-chokeholds-and-no-knock-entries; Catharine Tunney, "RCMP Not Banning Controversial Neck Hold Despite Instructions from Minister," CBC News, January 18, 2023, https://www.cbc.ca/news/politics/rcmp-neck-hold-1.6715536.

35. Devon W. Carbabo, "Blue-on-Black Violence: A Provisional Model of Some of the Causes," *Georgetown Law Journal* 104, no. 6 (2016): 1482.

36. Katheryn Russell-Brown, "Body Cameras, Police Violence and Racial Credibility," *Florida Law Review Forum* 67 (2016): 207–13.

37. Erin M. Kerrison, Jennifer Cobbina, and Kimberly Bender, "Stop-Gaps, Lip Service, and the Perceived Futility of Body-Worn Police Officer Cameras in Baltimore City," *Journal of Ethnic & Cultural Diversity in Social Work* 27, no. 3 (2018): 284.

38. Kerrison, Cobbina, and Bender, "Stop-Gaps, Lip Service," 284–85.

39. See Kathryn Henne, Krystle Shore, and Jenna Imad Harb, "Body-Worn Cameras, Police Violence and the Politics of Evidence: A Case of Ontological Gerrymandering," *Critical Social Policy* 42, no. 3 (2022): 388–407.

40. American Public Health Association, *Addressing Law Enforcement Violence as a Public Health Issue*, Policy Number 201811, November 13, 2018, https://www.apha.org/policies-and-advocacy/public-health-policy-statements/policy-database/2019/01/29/law-enforcement-violence.

41. The Yorta Yorta people are an Aboriginal people whose traditional lands span both sides of the Murray River in what is now known as northeastern Victoria and southern New South Wales in Australia.

42. Records of the commission are available through the National Archives of Australia: "Royal Commission into Aboriginal Deaths in Custody," National Archives of Australia, https://www.naa.gov.au/explore-collection/first-australians/royal-commission-aboriginal-deaths-custody.

43. "Tanya Day—Overview of the Coronial Inquest into Her Death," Human Rights Law Centre, accessed June 14, 2023, https://www.hrlc.org.au/tanya-day-overview.

44. Calla Wahlquist, "Tanya Day Died 17 Days after Falling Asleep on a Train. Now Her Family Want Answers," *Guardian*, August 24, 2019, https://www.theguardian.com/australia-news/2019/aug/24/tanya-day-death-custody-inquest-family-want-answers; "Tanya Day—Summary of Findings," Human Rights Law Centre, April 9, 2020, https://www.hrlc.org.au/human-rights-case-summaries/2020/9/8/tanya-day-inquest-summary-of-findings.

45. Human Rights Law Centre, "Tanya Day—Summary"; Calla Wahlquist, "Tanya Day Inquest: Coroner Refers Death in Custody of Aboriginal Woman for Possible Prosecution," *Guardian*, April 9, 2020, https://www.theguardian.com/australia-news/2020/apr/09/tanya-day-inquest-coroner-refers-death-custody-aboriginal-woman-public-prosecutor.

46. Wahlquist, "Tanya Day Inquest."

47. Wahlquist, "Tanya Day Inquest."

48. Wahlquist, "Tanya Day Inquest."

49. Steven Schubert, "Tanya Day's Family 'Devastated and Angry' No Police Officers Will be Charged Over the Indigenous Woman's Death," ABC News, August 27, 2020, https://www.abc.net.au/news/2020-08-27/victoria-police-officers-not-charged-over-tanya-day-death/12600798.

50. Latoya Aroha Rule and Larissa Behrendt, "The Families of Indigenous People Who Die in Custody Need a Say in What Happens Next," The Conversation, April 28, 2021, https://theconversation.com/the-families-of-indigenous-people-who-die-in-custody-need-a-say-in-what-happens-next-159127; "Public Intoxication Reform," Victoria Department of Health, reviewed March 2, 2023, https://www.health.vic.gov.au/alcohol-and-drugs/public-intoxication-reform-0.

51. Alison Whittaker, "Aboriginal Woman Tanya Day Died in Custody. Now an Inquest Is Investigating if Systemic Racism Played a Role," The Conversation, August 28, 2019, https://theconversation.com/aboriginal-woman-tanya-day-died-in-custody-now-an-inquest-is-investigating-if-systemic-racism-played-a-role-122471.

52. Merran McAlister and Samantha Bricknell, *Deaths in Custody in Australia 2021–22*, Statistical Report no. 41 (Canberra: Australian Institute of Criminology, 2022), https://www.aic.gov.au/publications/sr/sr41.

53. Edward Heffernan et al., "PTSD among Aboriginal and Torres Strait Islander People in Custody in Australia: Prevalence and Correlates," *Journal of Traumatic Stress* 28, no. 6 (2015): 523–30; Bronwyn Honorato, Nerina Caltabiano, and Alan R. Clough, "From Trauma to Incarceration: Exploring the Trajectory in a Qualitative Study in Male Prison Inmates from North Queensland, Australia," *Health & Justice* 4, no. 3 (2016): 1–10.

54. Tamara Walsh, "Women Who Die in Custody: What Australian Coroners' Reports Tell Us," *Howard Journal of Crime and Justice* 61, no. 4 (2022): 540–55.

55. Walsh, "Women Who Die in Custody," 550.

56. Sherene H. Razack, "Timely Deaths: Medicalizing the Deaths of Aboriginal People in Police Custody," *Law, Culture and the Humanities* 9, no. 2 (2011): 360.

57. Chelsea Watego, "Racism is a Public Health Crisis—But Black Death Tolls Aren't the Answer," The Conversation, February 15, 2022, https://theconversation.com/racism-is-a-public-health-crisis-but-black-death-tolls-arent-the-answer-176453.

58. Chelsea J. Bond et al., "Now We Say Black Lives Matter But . . . The Fact of the Matter Is, We Just Black Matter to Them," *Medical Journal of Australia* 213, no. 6 (2020): 248–50.

59. Michelle S. Fitts et al., "A Qualitative Study on the Transition Support Needs of Indigenous Australians Following Traumatic Brain Injury," *Brain Impairment* 20, no. 2 (2019): 137–59.

60. Field notes, June 30, 2022.

61. Marcia Langton and Kristen Smith, "The Role of Brain Injury in Family Violence for Aboriginal and Torres Strait Islander Peoples," paper presented at the Brain Injury Australia Conference, Sydney, NSW, June 30, 2022.

62. Stephanie Collett, "The Role of Brain Injury in Family Violence," ABC RN Breakfast, June 29, 2022, https://www.abc.net.au/radionational/programs/breakfast/the-role-of-brain-injury-in-family-violence/13951112.

63. Field notes, June 30, 2022.

64. Johan Galthug, "Cultural Violence," *Journal of Peace Research* no. 27 (1990): 291, 294.

65. Nakari Thorpe, "NSW Police to Review Incident Which Left 14yo Indigenous Teenager in Hospital," ABC News, September 15, 2022, https://www.abc.net.au/news/2022-09-15/nsw-police-review-incident-teen-boy-hospitalised-coraki/101446068.

66. Field notes, June 30, 2022; see also Collett, "The Role of Brain Injury in Family Violence."

67. Field notes, June 30, 2022.

68. Chelsea Watego et al., "Black to the Future: Making the Case for Indigenist Health Humanities," *International Journal of Environmental Research and Public Health* 18, no. 16 (2021): doi: https://doi.org/10.3390/ijerph18168704.

69. Ken Belson, "Black Former N.F.L. Players Say Racial Bias Skews Concussion Payouts," *New York Times*, August 25, 2020, https://www.nytimes.com/2020/08/25/sports/football/nfl-concussion-racial-bias.html.

70. *Henry and Davenport v. National Football League and NFL Properties, LLC.* Civil Action No. 20–4165, 2020, https://www.classaction.org/media/henry-et-al-v-national-football-league-et-al.pdf.

71. Maryclaire Dale, "Lawyers: NFL Concussion Awards Discriminate Against Blacks," AP News, August 25, 2020, https://apnews.com/article/sports-virus-outbreak-nfl-race-and-ethnicity-football-78a2408bfadac1a50ce8eff4d91337f4.

72. Henry and Davenport v. National Football League et al.

73. Maryclaire Dale and Michelle R. Smith, "Retired Black Players Say NFL Brain-Injury Payouts Show Bias," *AP News*, May 14, 2021, https://apnews.com/article/health-nfl-race-and-ethnicity-sports-066d9fd6bd85f5b5023207467701fde4.

74. Tracie Canada and Chelsea R. Carter, "The NFL's Racist 'Race Norming' is an Afterlife of Slavery," *Scientific American*, July 8, 2021, https://www.scientificamerican.com/article/the-nfls-racist-race-norming-is-an-afterlife-of-slavery/. See also Lucia Trimbur and Lundy Braun, "Race-ing the NFL: How Anti-Black Standards Are Built into the 2015 Concussion Settlement," *Tropics of Meta*, November 1, 2020, https://tropicsofmeta.com/2020/11/01/race-ing-the-nfl-how-anti-black-standards-are-built-into-the-2015-concussion-settlement//.

75. Trimbur and Braun, "Race-Ing the NFL."

76. Jennifer J. Manly, "Advantages and Disadvantages of Separate Norms for African Americans," *Clinical Neuropsychologist* 19, no. 2 (2005): 272.

77. Dale and Smith, "Retired Black Players Say."

78. Dale and Smith, "Retired Black Players Say."

79. "4 Members of Congress Question NFL on Concussion Payments," AP News, September 2, 2020, https://apnews.com/general-news-ce3318eb5ede5763d9e5d4651322cc3c.

80. Trimbur and Braun, "Race-Ing the NFL."

81. "Judge Dismisses Lawsuit Over 'Race-Norming' in NFL Dementia Tests," ESPN, March 8, 2021, https://www.espn.com.au/nfl/story/_/id/31027492/judge-dismisses-lawsuit-race-norming-nfl-dementia-tests.

82. Michael Yudell et al., "NFL Must Confront the Use of Race in Science," *Science* 369, no. 6509 (2020): 1313–14.

83. Victoria Pitts-Taylor, "Neurobiologically Poor? Brain Phenotypes, Inequality, and Biosocial Determinism," *Science, Technology, & Human Values* 44, no. 4 (2019): 660–85.

84. Pitts-Taylor, "Neurobiologically Poor?" 678.

85. Fallin, Whooley, and Barker, "Criminalizing the Brain," 439.

86. Watego et al., "Black to the Future: Making the Case for Indigenist Health Humanities."

EPILOGUE

1. "Maine Mass Shooter Maine Mass Shooter Who Killed 18 had Traumatic Brain Injury, Researchers Find: No Evidence of CTE," *Mercury News*, March 3, 2024, https://www.mer curynews.com/2024/03/08/maine-mass-shooter-robert-card-had-traumatic-brain-injury -boston-university-cte-researchers-find/.

2. Shwetha Surendran and Mark Fainaru-Wada, "How Fears Over CTE and Football Outpaced What Researchers Know," ESPN, February 1, 2024, https://www.espn.com/nfl /story/_/id/39417850/how-fears-cte-football-exceeded-scientific-certainty.

3. Mark Blackburn, "Family of Chris Simon Believes CTE Played a Role in His Death," *National News*, March 20, 2024, https://www.aptnnews.ca/national-news/family-of-chris -simon-strongly-believes-cte-played-a-role-in-his-death/.

4. Field notes, Jun 5, 2024, edited to protect the participant's identity.

5. Rene Almeling, *GUYnecology: The Missing Science of Men's Reproductive Health* (University of California Press, 2020).

6. Stewart Macaulay, "Presidential Address: Images of Law in Everyday Life: The Lessons of School, Entertainment, and Spectator Sports," *Law & Society Review* 21, no. 2 (1987): 185–218.

7. Daniel S. Goldberg, *Tackle Football and Traumatic Brain Injuries: Law, Ethics, and Public Health* (Johns Hopkins University Press, 2024).

8. Christopher J. Nowinski et al., "Applying the Bradford Hill Criteria for Causation to Repetitive Head Impacts and Chronic Traumatic Encephalopathy," *Frontiers in Neurology* 13 (2022): doi: https://doi.org/10.3389/fneur.2022.938163; Kevin Pierre et al., "Chronic Traumatic Encephalopathy: Update on Current Clinical Diagnosis and Management," *Biomedicines* 9, no. 4 (2021): 415.

9. Michael Marmot et al., "Closing the Gap in a Generation: Health Equity Through Action on the Social Determinants of Health," *Lancet* 372, no. 9650 (2008): 1661–69.

10. Ruqaiijah Yearby, "Structural Racism and Health Disparities: Reconfiguring the Social Determinants of Health Framework to Include the Root Cause," *Journal of Law, Medicine & Ethics* 48, no. 3 (2020): 518–26.

11. Michael C. Dewan et al., "Estimating the Global Incidence of Traumatic Brain Injury," *Journal of Neurosurgery* 130, no. 4 (2019): 1080–97; Maria Pia Tropeano et al., "A Comparison of Publication to TBI Burden Ratio of Low- and Middle-Income Countries Versus High-Income Countries: How Can We Improve Worldwide Care of TBI?" *Neurosurgical Focus* 47, no. 5 (2019): E5.

12. Sona Kazemi, "Disabling Power of Class and Ideology: Analyzing War Injury through the Transnational Disability Theory and Praxis," Disability Studies Quarterly 39, no. 3 (2019): doi: https://doi.org/10.18061/dsq.v39i3.6496.

13. Jennifer Terry, *Attachments to War: Biomedical Logics and Violence in Twenty-First-Century America* (Duke University Press, 2015).

AFL	Australian Football League
AFLW	AFL Women's
CCC	Canadian Concussion Center
CDC	Centers for Disease Control and Prevention
CISG	International Concussion in Sports Group
CLF	Concussion Legacy Foundation
CTE	Chronic traumatic encephalopathy
DoD	Department of Defense
EBM	Evidence-based medicine
FIFA	Fédération Internationale de Football Association
IPV	Intimate partner violence
LIMBIC	Long-Term Impact of Military-Related Brain Injury Consortium
NCAA	National Collegiate Athletic Association
NFL	National Football League
NHL	National Hockey League
NIH	National Institutes of Health
NRL	National Rugby League
PSA	Public service announcement
PTSD	Posttraumatic Stress Disorder
SABV	Sex as a biological variable
STS	Science and technology studies

RCT	Randomized controlled trial
TBI	Traumatic brain injury
US	United States
VA	Veterans Affairs
WWE	World Wrestling Entertainment

Abdolmohammadi, Bobak, Alicia Dupre, Laney Evers, and Jesse Mez. "Genetics of Chronic Traumatic Encephalopathy." *Seminars in Neurology* 40, no. 4 (2020): 420–29.

Adair, Darly, John Nauright, and Murray Phillips. "Playing Fields through to Battle fields: The Development of Australian Sporting Manhood in its Imperial Context, c. 1850–1918." *Journal of Australian Studies* 22, no. 56 (1998): 51–67.

Adams, Stephen, Courtney W. Mason, and Michael A. Robidoux. "'If You Don't Want to Get Hurt, Don't Play Hockey': The Uneasy Efforts of Hockey Injury Prevention in Canada." *Sociology of Sport Journal* 32, no. 3 (2015): 248–65.

Aguirre, Alex S., Kenny Rojas, and Alcy R. Torres. "Pediatric Traumatic Brain Injuries in War Zones: A Systematic Literature Review." *Frontiers in Neurology* 14 (2023): doi: https://doi.org/10.3389/fneur.2023.1253515.

Allison, Rachel. "Privileging Difference: Negotiating Gender Essentialism in U.S. Women's Professional Soccer." *Sociology of Sport Journal* 38, no. 2 (2020): 158–66.

Allison, Rachel, Adriene Davis, and Raymond Barranco. "A Comparison of Hometown Socioeconomics and Demographics for Black and White Elite Football Players in the U.S.," *International Review for the Sociology of Sport* 53, no. 5 (2018): 615–29.

Almeling, Rene. *GUYnecology: The Missing Science of Men's Reproductive Health*. University of California Press, 2020.

Alosco, Michael L., Megan L. Mariani, Charles H. Adler, et al. "Developing Methods to Detect and Diagnose Chronic Traumatic Encephalopathy During Life: Rationale, Design, and Methodology for the DIAGNOSE CTE Research Project." *Alzheimer's Research & Therapy* 13, no. 136 (2021): 1–23.

Alosco, Michael L., Jesse Mez, Yorghos Tripodis, et al. "Age of First Exposure to Tackle Football and Chronic Traumatic Encephalopathy." *Annals of Neurology* 83, no. 5 (2018): 886–901.

American Public Health Association, *Addressing Law Enforcement Violence as a Public Health Issue*, Policy Number 201811, November 13, 2018, https://www.apha.org/policies

-and-advocacy/public-health-policy-statements/policy-database/2019/01/29/law
-enforcement-violence.

Anderson, Ben, Matthew Kearnes, Colin McFarlane, and Dan Swanton. "On Assemblages and Geography." *Dialogues in Human Geography* 2, no. 2 (2012): 171–89.

Anderson, Kay, and Susan J. Smith. "Editorial: Emotional Geographies." *Transactions of the Institute of British Geographers* 26, no. 1 (2001): 7–10.

Anderson, Melissa N., Christopher D'Lauro, Brian R. Johnson, Craig A. Foster, and Julianne D. Schmidt. "Concussion Reporting Intentions for Incoming Military Athletes and Cadets." *Brain Injury* 36, no. 3 (2022): 332–38.

Anderson, Vicki, Megan Spencer-Smith, and Amanda Wood. "Do Children Really Recover Better? Neurobehavioural Plasticity After Early Brain Insult." *Brain* 134, no. 8 (2011): 2197.

Andrews, David L., Ross H. Miller, and Stephanie Cork. "Weaponizing Kinesiology: Illuminating the Militarization of the Sport Sciences." In *Sport and Militarism: Contemporary Global Perspectives*, edited by Michael L. Butterworth, 31–47. Routledge, 2017.

Aptekar, Sofya. *Green Card Soldier: Between Model Immigrant and Security Threat.* Massachussetts Institute of Technology Press, 2023.

Aronson, Jay D., and Simon A. Cole. "Science and the Death Penalty: DNA, Innocence, and the Debate over Capital Punishment in the United States." *Law & Social Inquiry* 34, no. 3 (2009): 603–33.

Asken, Breton M., and Gil D. Rabinovici. "Identifying Degenerative Effects of Repetitive Head Trauma with Neuroimaging: A Clinically-Oriented Review." *Acta Neuropathologica Communications* 9, no. 1 (2021): 96.

Atkinson, Michael, and Kevin Young, *Deviance and Social Control in Sport* (Champaign: Human Kinetics, 2008).

Aubry, Mark, Robert Cantu, Jiri Dvorak, et al. "Summary and Agreement Statement of the First International Conference on Concussion in Sport, Vienna 2001." *British Journal of Sports Medicine* 36 (2002): 6–10.

Bachynski, Kathleen. *No Game for Boys to Play: The History of Youth Football and the Origins of a Public Health Crisis.* University of North Carolina Press, 2019.

Bachynski, Kathleen E., and Daniel S. Goldberg. "Time Out: NFL Conflicts of Interest with Public Health Efforts to Prevent TBI." *Injury Prevention* 24, no. 3 (2018): 180–84.

Bachynski, Kathleen E., and Daniel S. Goldberg. "Youth Sports and Public Health: Framing Risks of Mild Traumatic Brain Injury in American Football and Ice Hockey." *Journal of Law, Medicine & Ethics* 42, no. 3 (2014): 323–33.

Baez, Jose. *Unnecessary Roughness: Inside the Trial and Final Days of Aaron Hernandez.* Hachette, 2018.

Bahrami, Naeim, Dev Sharma, Scott Rosenthal, et al. "Subconcussive Head Impact Exposure and White Matter Tract Changes over a Single Season of Youth Football." *Radiology* 281, no. 3 (2016): 919–26.

Bailes, Julian E., and Robert C. Cantu. "Head Injury in Athletes." *Neurosurgery* 48, no. 1 (2001): 26–46.

Baird, Barbara. "Child Politics, Feminist Analyses." *Australian Feminist Studies* 23, no. 57 (2008): 291–305.

Bal, Mieke. "Visual Essentialism and the Object of Visual Culture." *Journal of Visual Culture* 2, no. 1 (2003): 5–32.

Baldwin, Grant T., Matthew J. Breiding, and R. Dawn Comstock. "Epidemiology of Sports Concussion in the United States." In *Sports Neurology*, edited by Brian Hainline and Robert A. Stern, 63–74. Elsevier, 2018.

Barnes, Deborah E., Amy L. Byers, Raquel C. Gardner, Karen H. Seal, W. John Boscardin, and Kristine Yaffe. "Association of Mild Traumatic Brain Injury with and without Loss of Consciousness with Dementia in U.S. Military Veterans." *JAMA Neurology* 75, no. 9 (2018): 1055–61.

Barr, William B. "Believers versus Deniers: The Radicalization of Sports Concussion and Chronic Traumatic Encephalopathy (CTE) Science." *Canadian Psychology* 61, no. 2 (2020): 151–62.

Batts, Callie, and David L. Andrews. "'Tactical Athletes': The United States Paralympic Military Program and the Mobilization of the Disabled Soldier/Athlete." *Sport in Society* 14, no. 5 (2011): 553–68.

Baugh, Christine M., Craig A. Foster, Brian R. Johnson, and Christopher D'Lauro. "Pluralistic Ignorance as a Contributing Factor to Concussion Underreporting." *Health Education and Behavior* 49, no. 2 (2022): 340–46.

Belanger, Heather G., Tracy Kretzmer, Rodney D. Vanderploeg, and Louis M. French. "Symptom complaints Following Combat-Related Traumatic Brain Injury: Relationship to Traumatic Brain Injury Severity and Posttraumatic Stress Disorder." *Journal of the International Neuropsychological Society* 16, no. 1 (2010): 194–99.

Bell, Travis R., and Janelle Applequist. "'Do the Things You're Gonna Do on Game Day, Just Don't Get Hurt': A Narrative Analysis of the NFL's 'Future of Football' Advertising Campaign." *Journal of Broadcasting & Electronic Media* 66, no. 1 (2022): 110–28.

Benjamin, Walter. "Critique of Violence." In *Reflections: Essays, Aphorisms, Autobiographical Writings*, translated by Edmund Jephcott, 277–300. Schocken Books, 1978.

Ben-Moshe, Liat. *Decarcerating Disability: Deinstitutionalization and Prison Abolition* (Minneapolis: University of Minnesota Press, 2020).

Benson, Peter. "Big Football: Corporate Social Responsibility and the Culture and Color of Injury in America's Most Popular Sport." *Journal of Sport and Social Issues* 41, no. 4 (2017): 307–34.

Berger, Peter L., and Thomas Luckmann. *The Social Construction of Reality*. Penguin, 1967.

Berkman, Jillian M., Joseph A. Rosenthal, and Altaf Saadi. "Carotid Physiology and Neck Restraints in Law Enforcement." *JAMA Neurology* 78, no. 3 (2021): 267–68.

Bernstein, Elizabeth. "The Sexual Politics of the 'New Abolitionism.'" *differences* 18, no. 3(2007): 128–51.

Bieniek, Kevin F., Nigel J. Cairns, John F. Crary, et al. "The Second NINDS/NIBIB Consensus Meeting to Define Neuropathological Criteria for the Diagnosis of Chronic Traumatic Encephalopathy." *Journal of Neuropathology & Experimental Neurology* 80, no. 3 (2021): 210–19.

Binney, Zachary O., and Kathleen E. Bachynski. "Estimating the Prevalence at Death of CTE Neuropathology among Professional Football Players." *Neurology* 92, no. 1 (2019): 43–45.

Birke, Lynda. "Telling the Rat What to Do: Laboratory Animals, Science, and Gender." In *Gender and the Science of Difference: Cultural Politics of Contemporary Science and Medicine*, ed. Jill A. Fisher, 91–107. Rutgers University Press, 2011.

Black, Amanda M., Brent E. Hagel, Luz Palacios-Derflingher, Kathryn J. Schneider, and Carolyn A. Emery. "The Risk of Injury Associated with Body Checking Among Pee Wee Ice Hockey Players: An Evaluation of Hockey Canada's National Body Checking Policy Change." *British Journal of Sports Medicine* 51, no. 24 (2017): 1767–72.

Bond, Chelsea J., Lisa J. Whop, David Singh, and Helena Kajlich. "Now We Say Black Lives Matter But . . . The Fact of the Matter Is, We Just Black Matter to Them." *Medical Journal of Australia* 213, no. 6 (2020): 248–50.

Boneau, Rebecca D., Brian K. Richardson, and Joseph McGlynn. "'We Are a Football Family': Making Sense of Parents' Decisions to Allow Their Children to Play Tackle Football." *Communication & Sport* 8, no. 1 (2020): 26–49.

Boyle, Kaitlin M., and Kimberly B. Rogers. "Beyond the Rape 'Victim'-'Survivor' Binary: How Race, Gender, and Identity Processes Interact to Shape Distress." *Sociological Forum* 35, no. 2 (2020): 323–45.

Branch, John. *Boy on Ice: The Life and Death of Derek Boogaard*. HarperCollins, 2014.

Brayton, Sean, Michelle T. Helstein, Mike Ramsey, and Nicholas Rickards. "Exploring the Missing Link Between the Concussion 'Crisis' and Labor Politics in Professional Sports." *Communication & Sport* 7, no. 1 (2019): 110–31.

Brenner, Joel S., Cynthia R. LaBella, Margaret A. Brooks, et al. "Tackling in Youth Football." *Pediatrics* 136, no. 5 (2015): e1419–30.

Brenner, Lisa A., Jeri E. Forster, Jaimie L. Gradus, et al. "Associations of Military-Related Traumatic Brain Injury with New-Onset Mental Health Conditions and Suicide Risk." *JAMA Network Open* 6, no. 7 (2023): e2326296

Brenner, Lisa A., Lisa M. Betthauser, Nazanin Bahraini, et al. "Soldiers Returning from Deployment: A Qualitative Study Regarding Exposure, Coping, and Reintegration." *Rehabilitation Psychology* 60, no. 3 (2015): 277–85.

Broglio, Steven P., Michael McCrea, Thomas McAllister, et al. "A National Study on the Effects of Concussion in Collegiate Athletes and U.S. Military Service Academy Members." *Sports Medicine* 47 (2017): 1437–45.

Brown, Michelle. "Visual Criminology and Carceral Studies: Counter-Images in the Carceral Age." *Theoretical Criminology* 18, no. 2 (2014): 176–97.

Brown, Phil. "Naming and Framing: The Social Construction of Diagnosis and Illness." *Journal of Health and Social Behavior* 35 (1995): 34–52.

Browne, Nancy T., Eric A. Hodges, Leigh Small, et al. "Childhood Obesity within the Lens of Racism." *Pediatric Obesity* 17, no. 5 (2022): e12878.

Bryan, Mersine A., Ali Rowhani-Rahbar, R. Dawn Comstock, and Frederick Rivara. "Sports- and Recreation-Related Concussions in U.S. Youth." *Pediatrics* 138, no. 1 (2016): e20154635.

Bryan, Nathaniel. "Remembering Tamir Rice and Other Black Boy Victims: Imagining *Black PlayCrit Literacies* Inside and Outside Urban Literacy Education." *Urban Education* 56, no. 5 (2020): 744–71.

Buckland, Michael E., Andrew J. Affleck, Alan J. Pearce, and Catherine M. Suter. "Chronic Traumatic Encephalopathy as a Preventable Environmental Disease." *Frontiers in Neurology* 13 (2022): 880905.

Bumiller, Kristin. *In an Abusive State: How Neoliberalism Appropriated the Feminist Movement against Sexual Violence*. Duke University Press, 2008.

Burstyn, Varda. *The Rites of Men*. University of Toronto Press, 1999.

Butterworth, Michael L. "Everybody's All-Americans: High School Football and the U.S. Military." In *Football, Culture and Power*, edited by David J. Leaonard, Kimberly B. George, and Wade Davis, 139–55. Routledge, 2016.

Butterworth, Michael L. "Public Memorializing in the Stadium: Mediated Sport, the Tenth Anniversary of 9/11, and the Illusion of Democracy." *Communication & Sport* 2 (2014): 203–24.

Butterworth, Michael L., ed. *Sport and Militarism: Contemporary Global Perspectives*. Routledge, 2017.

Butterworth, Michael L., and Stormi D. Moskal. "American Football, Flags, and 'Fun': The Bell Helicopter Armed Forces Bowl and the Rhetorical Production of Militarism." *Communication, Culture & Critique* 2, no. 4 (2009): 411–33.

Buzzini, Sergio R. Russo, and Kevin M. Guskiewicz. "Sport-Related Concussion in the Young Athlete." *Current Opinion in Pediatrics* 18, no. 4 (2006): 376–82.

Caccese, Jaclyn B., Christina L. Master, Thomas A. Buckley, et al. "Sex Differences in Recovery Trajectories of Assessments for Sport-related Concussion Among NCAA Athletes: A CARE Consortium Study." *Sports Medicine*, (December 2023): doi: https://doi.org/10.1007/s40279-023-01982-2.

Calderwood, Catherine, Andrew Duncan Murray, and William Stewart. "Turning People into Couch Potatoes is not the Cure for Sports Concussion." *British Journal of Sports Medicine* 50, no. 4 (2016): 200–01.

Campbell, Julia K., Annie-Lori C. Joseph, Emily F. Rothman, and Eve M. Valera. "The Prevalence of Brain Injury Among Survivors and Perpetrators of Intimate Partner Violence and the Prevalence of Violence Victimization and Perpetration Among People With Brain Injury: A Scoping Review." *Injury Epidemiology* 9 (2022): 290–315.

Canada, Tracie, and Chelsea R. Carter. "The NFL's Racist 'Race Norming' is an Afterlife of Slavery." *Scientific American*. July 8, 2021. https://www.scientificamerican.com/article/the-nfls-racist-race-norming-is-an-afterlife-of-slavery/.

Cantu, Robert, and Mark Hyman. *Concussion and Our Kids: America's Leading Expert on How to Protect Young Athletes and Keep Sports Safe*. Houghton Mifflin Harcourt, 2012.

Carbado, Devon W. "Blue-on-Black Violence: A Provisional Model of Some of the Causes." *Georgetown Law Journal* 104, no. 6 (2016): 1479–1529.

Casper, Stephen. "Concussion: A History of Science and Medicine, 1870–2005." *Headache: The Journal of Head and Face Pain* 58, no. 6 (2018): 795–810.

Casper, Stephen. "How the 1950s Changed our Understanding of Traumatic Encephalopathy and its Sequelae." *Canadian Medical Association Journal* 190, no. 5 (2018): E140–42.

Casper, Stephen T., Janet Golden, Naomi Oreskes, et al. "First Report the Findings: Genuine Balance when Reporting CTE." *Lancet Neurology* 18, no. 6 (2019): 522–23.

Caudwell, Jayne. "Gender, Feminism, and Football Studies." *Soccer & Society* 12, no. 3 (2011): 330–42.

Centers for Disease Control and Prevention. *Surveillance Report of Traumatic Brain Injury-Related Emergency Department Visits, Hospitalizations, and Deaths—United States, 2014*. U.S. Department of Health and Human Services, 2014.

Centers for Disease Control and Prevention. *Traumatic Brain Injury in the United States: Epidemiology and Rehabilitation*. U.S. Department of Health and Human Services, 2015.

Chaufan, Claudia, Jarmin Yeh, Leslie Ross, and Patrick Fox. "You Can't Walk or Bike Your-self Out of the Health Effects of Poverty: Active School Transport, Child Obesity, and Blind Spots in the Public Health Literature." *Critical Public Health* 25, no. 1 (2015): 32–47.

Chavarro-Nieto, Christian, Martyn Beaven, Nicholas Gill, and Kim Hébert-Losier. "Neck Strength in Rugby Union Players: A Systematic Review of the Literature." *The Physician and Sports Medicine* 49, no. 4 (2021): 392–409.

Chemali, Zeina, Farrah Ezzeddine, R. Tcheroyan, and Diler Acar. "A Perspective from the Middle East on the Topic of Concussion." *Global Journal of Health Science* 12, no. 6 (2020): doi: https://doi.org/10.5539/gjhs.v12n6p30.

Chen, Stephen T., Prabha Siddarth, David A. Merrill, et al. "FDDNP-PET Tau Brain Protein Binding Patterns in Military Personnel with Suspected Chronic Traumatic Encepha-lopathy." *Journal of Alzheimer's Disease* 65, no. 1 (2018): 79–88.

Cho, Hyunkag. "Racial Differences in the Prevalence of Intimate Partner Violence against Women and Associated Factors." *Journal of Interpersonal Violence* 27, no. 2 (2012): 344–63.

Christensen. "Wendy R. The Black Citizen-Subject: Black Single Mothers in U.S. Military Recruitment Materials." *Ethnic and Racial Studies* 39, no. 14 (2016): 2508–26.

Clark, Scott A,. "Upon the Fields of Friendly Strife: An 'Athletic Charter' to Reform the Army's Sports Culture and Build Better Leaders." *Military Review*, May–June 2023: 133–46.

Clissold, Asher, and Kathleen Bachynski. "NFL's Dangerous Strategies of Marketing Foot-ball to Youth: Shades of Big Tobacco." *Sport, Ethics, and Philosophy* (2024): 1–18.

Coakley, Jay. "Youth Sports: What Counts as 'Positive Development?'" *Journal of Sport and Social Issues* 35, no. 3 (2011): 306–24.

Cogan, Alison M., Christine E. Haines, and Maria D. Devore. "Intersections of U.S. Military Culture, Hegemonic Masculinity, and Health Care among Injured Male Service Mem-bers." *Men and Masculinities* 24, no. 3 (2021): 468–82.

Cole, Wesley R., Amy S. Cecchini, Rosemay A. Remigio-Baker, et al. "'Return to Duty' as an Outcome Metric in Military Concussion Research: Problems, Pitfalls, and Potential Solutions." *Clinical Neuropsychologist* 34, no. 6 (2019): 1156–74.

Collins, Christy L., Erica N. Fletcher, Sarah K. Fields, et al. "Neck Strength: A Protective Factor Reducing Risk for Concussion in High School Sports." *Journal of Primary Preven-tion* 35, no. 5 (2014): 309–19.

Collins, Patricia Hill. *Black Feminist Thought: Knowledge, Consciousness, and the Politics of Empowerment.* Unwin Hyman, 1990.

Commonwealth of Australia. *Concussions and Repeated Head Trauma in Contact Sports.* Official Committee Hansard, Senate, Community Affairs References Committee. March 1, 2023. https://parlinfo.aph.gov.au/parlInfo/search/display/display.w3p;query =Id%3A%22committees%2Fcommsen%2F26589%2F0000%22.

"Concussions and the Female Athlete." Twin Cities Public Broadcasting Services. August 4, 2017. https://video.tpt.org/video/tpt-documentaries-concussions-and-female-athletes/.

Costello, Kellianne, and Brian D. Greenwald. "Update on Domestic Violence and Trau-matic Brain Injury: A Narrative Review." *Brain Sciences* 12, no. 1 (2022): doi: https://doi .org/10.3390/brainsci12010122.

Cournoyer, Janie, and T. Blaine Hoshizaki. "Head Dynamic Response and Brain Tissue Deformation for Boxing Punches with and without Loss of Consciousness." *Clinical Biomechanics* 67 (2019): 96–101.

Courtenay, Will. *Dying to Be Men: Psychosocial, Environmental, and Biobehavioral Directions in Promoting the Health of Men and Boys.* Taylor & Francis, 2011.

Covassin, Tracey, Ryan Moran, and R. J. Elbin. "Sex Differences in Reported Concussion Injury Rates and Time Loss from Participation: An Update of the National Collegiate Athletic Association Injury Surveillance Program From 2004–2005 through 2008–2009." *Journal of Athletic Training* 51, no. 3 (2016): 189–94.

Cover, Robert. "Violence and the Word." In *Narrative, Violence, and the Law,* edited by Martha Minow, Michael Ryan, and Austin Sarat, 203–38. University of Michigan Press, 1995.

Cowlishaw, Sean, Alyssa Sbisa, Isabella Freijah, Dzenana Kartal, Ashlee Mulligan, MaryAnn Notarianni, Katherine Iverson, Anne-Laure Couineau, David Forbes, Meaghan O'Donnell, Andrea Phelps, Patrick Smith, and Fardous Hosseiny. "Health Service Interventions for Intimate Partner Violence among Military Personnel and Veterans: A Framework and Scoping Review." *International Journal of Environmental Research and Public Health* 19, no. 6 (2022): 3551.

Crabbe, Tim. "A Sporting Chance?: Using Sport to Tackle Drug Use and Crime." *Drugs: Education, Prevention and Policy* 7, no. 4 (2000): 381–91.

Crenshaw, Kimberlé W. "Mapping the Margins: Intersectionality, Identity Politics, and Violence against Women of Color." *Stanford Law Review* 43, no. 6 (1991): 1241–99.

Cross, Matthew, Simon Kemp, Andrew Smith, Grant Trewartha, and Keith Stokes. "Professional Rugby Union Players Have a 60% Greater Risk of Time Loss Injury After Concussion: A 2-Season Prospective Study of Clinical Outcomes." *British Journal of Sports Medicine* 50, no. 15 (2016): 926–31.

Crowther, Helen, Wendy Lipworth, and Ian Kerridge. "Evidence-Based Medicine and Epistemological Imperialism: Narrowing the Divide between Evidence and Illness." *Journal of Evaluation in Clinical Practice* 17, no. 5 (2011): 868–72.

Currier Thomas, Theresa, Caitlin E. Bromberg, and Gokul Krishna. "Female Sex in Experimental Traumatic Brain Injury Research: Forging a Path Forward." *Neural Regeneration Research* 17, no. 3 (2020): 550–52.

Dame-Griff, E. Cassandra. "'He's Not Heavy, He's an Anchor Baby': Fat Children, Failed Futures, and the Threat of Latina/o Excess." *Fat Studies* 5, no. 2 (2016): 156–71.

Daly, Ed, Alan J. Pearce, and Lisa Ryan. "A Systematic Review of Strength and Conditioning Protocols for Improving Neck Strength and Reducing Concussion Incidence and Impact Injury Risk in Collision Sports; Is There Evidence?" *Journal of Function Morphology and Kinesiology* 6, no. 1 (2021): doi: https://doi.org/10.3390/jfmk6010008.

Daneshvar, Daniel H., Evan S. Nair, Zachary H. Baucom, et al. "Leveraging Football Accelerometer Data to Quantify Associations Between Repetitive Head Impacts and Chronic Traumatic Encephalopathy in Males." *Nature Communications* 14, no. 3470 (2023): doi: https://doi.org/10.1038/s41467-023-39183-0.

Davis, Dena S. "Medical Research with College Athletes: Some Ethical Issues." *IRB: Ethics & Human Research* 20, no. 4 (1998): 10–11.

Davis, Gain, Rudolph Castellani, and Paul McCrory. "Neurodegeneration and Sport." *Neurosurgery* 76, no. 6 (2015): 643–56.

Deaton, Augus, and Nancy Cartwright. "Understanding and Misunderstanding Randomized Controlled Trials." *Social Science & Medicine* 210 (2018, August): 2–21.

DeKeseredy, Walter S. "Bringing Feminist Sociological Analyses of Patriarchy Back to the Forefront of the Study of Woman Abuse." *Violence Against Women* 27, no. 5 (2021): 621–38.

Deleuze, Gilles, and Félix Guattari. *A Thousand Plateaus: Capitalism and Schizophrenia.* Athlone, 1988.

Dewachi, Omar. "Revealed in the Wound: Medical Care and the Ecologies of War in Post-Occupation Iraq." In *Vulnerability and the Politics of Care: Transdisciplinary Dialogues,* edited by Victoria Browne, Jason Danely, and Doerthe Rosenow, 126–40. Oxford University Press, 2021.

Dewan, Michael C., Abbas Rattani, Saksham Gupta, et al. "Estimating the Global Incidence of Traumatic Brain Injury." *Journal of Neurosurgery* 130, no. 4 (2019): 1080–97.

Dick, R. W. "Is There a Gender Difference in Concussion Incidence and Outcomes?" *British Journal of Sports Medicine* 43 (2009): i4–50.

DiMattia, Dominic. "How Much Brain Deterioration Do You Need to Get into Court: Analyzing the Issue of Statutes of Limitations for Athletes' Concussion-Related Injury Litigation through the Lens of Toxic Tort Law." *University of Baltimore Law Review* 48, no. 3 (2019): 435–52.

Dismuke-Greer, Clara E., Mulugeta Gebregziabher, Tiarney Ritchwood, Mary Jo Pugh, Rebekah J. Walker, Uch S. Uchendu, and Leonard E. Egede. "Geographic Disparities in Mortality Risk Within a Racially Diverse Sample of U.S. Veterans with Traumatic Brain Injury." *Health Equity* 2, no. 1 (2018): 304–12.

"Domestic Violence: Improved Data Needed to Identify the Prevalence of Brain Injuries among Victims." GAO. Last modified June 12, 2020, https://www.gao.gov/products/gao-20-534.

Donaldson, Laura, Mark Asbridge, and Michael D. Cusimano. "Bodychecking Rules and Concussion in Elite Hockey." *PLoS ONE* 8, no. 7 (2013): 3–8.

Donnelly, Denise A., Kimberly J. Cook, Debra van Ausdale, and Lara Foley. "White Privilege, Color Blindness, and Services to Battered Women." *Violence Against Women* 11, no. 1 (2005): 6–37.

Dryden, Ken. *Game Change: The Life and Death of Steve Montador, and the Future of Hockey.* Signal, 2017.

Duckworth, Josh L., Jamie Grimes, and Geoffrey S.F. Ling. "Pathophysiology of Battlefield Traumatic Brain Injury." *Pathophysiology* 20, no. 1 (2013): 22–30.

Dumit, Joseph. *Picturing Personhood: Brain Scans and Biomedical History.* Princeton University Press, 2004.

Durand, Eric, Mathilde P. Chevignard, Alexis Ruet, A. Dereix, Christel Jourdan, and P. Pradat-Diehl. "History of Traumatic Brain Injury in Prison Populations: A Systematic Review." *Annals of Physical and Rehabilitation Medicine* 60 (2017): 95–101.

Dussauge, Isabelle and Anelis Kaiser. "Neuroscience and Sex/Gender." *Neuroethics* 5, no. 1 (2012): 211–15.

Dyck, Joshua J., John Cluverius, and Jeffrey N. Gerson. "Sports, Science, and Partisanship in the United States: Chronic Traumatic Encephalopathy and the Polarization of an Apolitical Issue." *International Journal of Sport Policy and Politics* 11, no. 1 (2019): 133–52.

Edwards, Harry. *The Revolt of the Black Athlete.* Free Press, 1970.

Eime, Rochelle M., Janet A. Young, Jack T. Harvey, Melanie J. Charity, and Warren R. Payne. "A Systematic Review of the Psychological and Social Benefits of Participation in Sport for Children and Adolescents: Informing Development of a Conceptual Model of Health through Sport." *International Journal of Behavioral Nutrition and Physical Activity* 10, no. 98 (2013): doi: https://doi.org/10.1186/1479-5868-10-135.

Elizabeth, Vivienne, Nicola Gavey, and Julia Tolmie. ". . . He's Just Swapped his Fists for the System: The Governance of Gender through Custody Law." *Gender & Society*, 26, no. 2 (2012): 239–60.

Emery, Carolyn A., Paul Eliason, Vineetha Warriyar, et al. "Body Checking in Non-Elite Adolescent Ice Hockey Leagues: It is Never Too Late for Policy Change Aiming to Protect the Health of Adolescents." *British Journal of Sports Medicine* 56, no. 1 (2022): 12–17.

Epstein, Steven. *Impure Science: AIDS, Activism, and the Politics of Knowledge*. University of California Press, 1998.

Epstein, Steven. *Inclusion: The Politics of Difference in Medical Research*. University of Chicago Press, 2007.

Everelles, Nirmala, *Disability and Difference in Global Contexts: Enabling a Transformative Body Politic*. Springer, 2011.

Fagin, Joe and Zinobia Bennefield. "Systemic Racism and U.S. Health Care." *Social Science & Medicine* 103, no. 1 (2014): 7–14.

Fainaru-Wada, Mark, and Steve Fainaru. *League of Denial: The NFL, Concussions, and the Battle for Truth*. Three Rivers Press, 2013.

Fallin, Mallory, Owen Whooley, and Kristin Kay Barker. "Criminalizing the Brain: Neurocriminology and the Production of Strategic Ignorance." *BioSocieties* 14, no. 3 (2019): 438–62.

Fares, Youssef, Fouad Ayoub, Jawad Fares, Rabi Khazim, Mahmoud Khazim, and Souheil Gebeily. "Pain and Neurological Sequelae of Cluster Munitions on Children and Adolescents in South Lebanon." *Neurological Sciences* 34, no. 11 (2013): 1971–76.

Farmer, Paul E., Bruce Nizeye, Sara Stulac, and Salmaan Keshavjee. "Structural Violence and Clinical Medicine." *PLOS Medicine* 3, no. 10 (2006): e449.

Faul, Mark, Likang Xu, Marlena M. Wald, and Victor G. Coronado. *Traumatic Brain Injury in the United States: Emergency Department Visits, Hospitalizations, and Deaths*. Centers for Disease Control and Prevention, National Center for Injury Prevention and Control, 2010.

Fausto-Sterling, Anne. *Sexing the Body: Gender Politics and the Construction of Sexuality*. Basic, 2000.

Finkel, Adam M. and Kevin F. Bieniek. "A Quantitative Risk Assessment for Chronic Traumatic Encephalopathy in Football: How Public Health Science Evaluates Evidence." *Human and Ecological Risk Assessment: An International Journal* 25, no. 3 (2019): 564–89.

Finkel, Adam M., Kevin P. Brand, Arthur L. Caplan, John S. Evans, and Paul R Wolpe. "First Report the Findings: Genuine Balance when Reporting CTE." *Lancet Neurology* 18, no. 6 (2019): 521–22.

Fitts, Michelle S., Jennifer Cullen, and Karen Soldatic. "First Nations Women are 69 Times More Likely to Have a Head Injury after Being Assaulted. We Show How Hard It Is to Get Help." The Conversation. November 22, 2022. https://theconversation.com/first-nations-women-are-69-times-more-likely-to-have-a-head-injury-after-being-assaulted-we-show-how-hard-it-is-to-get-help-194249.

Fitts, Michelle S., Jennifer Cullen, Gail Kingston, Elaine Wills, and Karen Soldatic. "'I Don't Think It's on Anyone's Radar': The Workforce and System Barriers to Healthcare for Indigenous Women Following a Traumatic Brain Injury Acquired through Violence in Remote Australia." *International Journal of Environmental Research and Public Health* 19, no. 22 (2022): 14744.

Fitts, Michelle S., Katrina Bird, John Gilroy, Jennifer Fleming, Alan R. Clough, Adrian Esterman, Paul Maruff, Yaqoot Fatima, and India Bohanna. "A Qualitative Study on the Transition Support Needs of Indigenous Australians Following Traumatic Brain Injury." *Brain Impairment* 20, no. 2 (2019): 137–59.

Fitts, Michelle, Jennifer Cullen, and Jody Barney. "Barriers Preventing Indigenous Women with Violence-related Head Injuries from Accessing Services in Australia." *Australian Social Work* 76, no. 3 (2023): 406–19.

Fox Keller, Evelyn. *Reflections on Gender and Science.* Yale University Press, 1985.

French, Louis, Michael McCrea, and Mark Baggett. "The Military Acute Concussion Evaluation (MACE)." ResearchGate. Last modified January 16, 2014. https://www.researchgate .net/profile/Louis-French/publication/232729375_The_Military_Acute_Concussion _Evaluation_MACE/links/0deec52d7e8d26842d000000/The-Military-Acute-Concus sion-Evaluation-MACE.pdf.

Gallagher, Virginia, Natalie Kramer, Kristin Abbott, John Alexander, Hans Breiter, Amy Herrold, Tory Lindley, Jeffrey Mjaanes, and James Reilly. "The Effects of Sex Differences and Hormonal Contraception on Outcomes after Collegiate Sports-Related Concussion." *Journal of Neurotrauma* 35, no. 11 (2018): 1242–47.

Galthug, Johan. "Cultural Violence." *Journal of Peace Research* 27, no. 3 (1990): 291–305.

Garber, Brian G. Corneliu Rusu, and Mark A. Zamorski. "Deployment-Related Mild Traumatic Brain Injury, Mental Health Problems, and Post-Concussive Symptoms in Canadian Armed Forces Personnel." *BMC Psychiatry* 14 (2014): 325.

Geronimus, Arline T., Margaret Hicken, Danya Keene, and John Bound. "'Weathering' and Age Patterns of Allostatic Load Scores among Blacks and Whites in the United States." *American Journal of Public Health* 96, no. 5 (2006): 826–33.

Ghazi, Kianoosh, Mark Begonia, Steven Rowson, and Songbai Ji. "American Football Helmet Effectiveness Against a Strain-Based Concussion Mechanism." *Annals of Biomedical Engineering* 50, no. 11 (2022): 1498–1509.

Gilbert, Frédéric. "State of the Concussion Debate: From Sceptical to Alarmist Claims." *Neuroethics* 8, no. 1 (2015): 47–53.

Gilmore, Amir A. and Pamela J. Bettis. "Antiblackness and the Adultification of Black Children in a U.S. Prison Nation." *Oxford Research Encyclopedia of Education* (2021): doi: https://doi.org/10.1093/acrefore/9780190264093.013.1293.

Gilmore, Ruth Wilson. *Golden Gulag: Prisons, Surplus, Crisis, and Opposition in Globalizing California.* University of California Press, 2007.

Giroux, Henry A. *Neoliberalism's War on Higher Education.* Haymarket, 2014.

Giroux, Henry A. *University in Chains: Confronting the Military-Industrial-Academic Complex.* Routledge, 2015.

Giza, Christopher C. and David A. Hovda. "The Neurometabolic Cascade of Concussion." *Journal of Athletic Training* 36, no. 3 (2001): 228–35.

Giza, Christopher C., William Stewart, and Mayumi L. Prins. "Building Good Policy from Good Science—The Case for Concussion and Chronic Traumatic Encephalopathy." *JAMA Pediatrics* 172, no. 9 (2018): 803–04.

Goldberg, Daniel S. "Mild Traumatic Brain Injury, the National Football League, and the Manufacture of Doubt: An Ethical, Legal, and Historical Analysis." *Journal of Legal Medicine* 34, no. 2 (2013): 157–91.

Goldberg, Daniel S. *Tackle Football and Traumatic Brain Injuries: Law, Ethics, and Public Health*. Johns Hopkins University Press, 2024.

Goodell, Roger H., Hunt Batjer, and Richard G. Ellenbogen. "Accelerating Progress on the Road to Safer Sports: Based on Remarks of NFL Commissioner Roger Goodell in the Neurosurgical Society of America Medal Lecture." *Neurosurgery* 75, no. 4 (2014): S119–21.

Goodmark, Leigh. *A Troubled Marriage: Domestic Violence and the Legal System*. New York University Press, 2013.

Goulet, Kristian, and Suzanne Beno. "Sport-related Concussion and Bodychecking in Children and Youth: Evaluation, Management, and Policy Implications." *Pediatrics & Child Health* 28, no. 4 (2023): 252–58.

Goutnik, Michael, Joel Goeckeritz, Zackary Sabetta, Tala Curry, Matthew Willman, Jonathan Willman, Theresa Currier Thomas, and Brandon Lucke-Wold. "Neurotrauma Prevention Review: Improving Helmet Design and Implementation." *Biomechanics* 2, no. 4 (2022): 500–12.

Grano, Daniel A. "Football after Fragmentation: Brain Banking, Chronic Traumatic Encephalopathy, and Racial Biosociality in the NFL." *Communication and Critical/Cultural Studies* 17, no. 4 (2020): 339–59.

Gruneau, Richard, and David Whitson. *Hockey Night in Canada: Sport, Identities and Cultural Politics*. University of Toronto Press, 1993.

Gupte, Raeesa P., William Brooks, Rachel Vukas, Janet Pierce, and Janna Harris. "Sex Differences in Traumatic Brain Injury: What We Know and What We Should Know." *Journal of Neurotrauma* 36, no. 22 (2019): 3063–91.

Haag, Halina (Lin), Sandra Sokoloff, Nneka MacGregor, Shirley Broekstra, Nora Cullen, and Angela Colantonio. "Battered and Brain Injured: Assessing Knowledge of Traumatic Brain Injury Among Intimate Partner Violence Service Providers." *Journal of Women's Health* 28, no. 7 (2019): 990–96.

Halstead, Mark E., Kevin D. Walter, Kody Moffatt, et al. "Sport-Related Concussion in Children and Adolescents." *Pediatrics* 142, no. 6 (2018): e20183074.

Hanafi, Ibrahem, Eskander Munder, Sulafa Ahmad, Iman Arabhamo, Suzan Alziab, Noor Badin, Ahmad Omarain, Mhd Khaled Jawish, Muhannad Saleh, Vera Nickl, Tamara Wipplinger, Christoph Wipplinger, and Robert Nickl. "War-Related Traumatic Brain Injuries during the Syrian Armed conflict in Damascus 2014–2017: A Cohort Study and a Literature Review." *BMC Emergency Medicine* vol. 23, no. 35 (2023): doi: https://doi.org/10.1186/s12873-023-00799-6.

Haraway, Donna. "Situated Knowledges: The Science Question in Feminism and the Privilege of Partial Perspective." *Feminist Studies* 14, no. 3 (1988): 575–99.

Harding, Sarah Nicola. "'Boys, When They Do Dance, They Have to Do Football as Well, for Balance': Young Men's Construction of a Sporting Masculinity." *International Review for the Sociology of Sport* 57, no. 1 (2022): 19–33.

Hardy, Morgan S., Jan E. Kennedy, and Douglas B. Cooper. "Patient Attribution of Posttraumatic Symptoms to Brain Injury Versus PTSD in Military-Related Mild TBI." *Journal of Neuropsychiatry and Clinical Neurosciences* 32, no. 3 (2020): 252–58.

Harmon, Kimberly G., Jonathan A. Drezner, Matthew Gammons, Kevin M. Guskiewicz, Mark Halstead, Stanley A. Herring, Jeffrey S. Kutcher, Andrea Pana, Margot Putukian, and William O. Roberts. "American Medical Society for Sports Medicine Position Statement: Concussion in Sport." *British Journal of Sports Medicine* 47, no. 1 (2013): 15–26.

Harrison, Emily A. "The First Concussion Crisis: Head Injury and Evidence in Early American Football." *American Journal of Public Health* 104, no. 5 (2014) 822–33.

Hawkins, Billy. *The New Plantation: Black Athletes, College Sports, and Predominantly White NCAA Institutions.* Palgrave Macmillan, 2010.

Hayward, Peter, "Traumatic Brain Injury: The Signature of Modern Conflicts." *Lancet Neurology* 7, no. 3 (2008): 200–01.

Head Games: The Global Concussion Crisis, directed by Steve James (2012, Variance Films).

Hearn, Jeff, *The Violences of Men: How Men Talk About and How Agencies Respond to Men's Violence to Women* (Thousand Oaks: Sage, 1998).

Heffernan, Edward, Kimina Andersen, Fiona Davidson, and Stuart A. Kinner. "PTSD among Aboriginal and Torres Strait Islander People in Custody in Australia: Prevalence and Correlates." *Journal of Traumatic Stress* 28, no. 6 (2015): 523–30.

Helmick, Katherine M., Cynthia A. Spells, Saafan Z. Malik, Cathleen A. Davies, Donald W. Marion, and Sidney R. Hinds. "Traumatic Brain Injury in the U.S. Military: Epidemiology and Key Clinical and Research Programs." *Brain Imaging and Behavior* 9, no. 3 (2015): 358–66.

Henne, Kathryn. "Brain Politics: Gendered Difference and Traumatic Brain Injury in Sport." In *Sociocultural Examinations of Sports Concussions,* edited by Matt Ventresca and Mary G. McDonald, 151–69. Routledge, 2019.

Henne, Kathryn. "Multi-Sited Fieldwork in Regulatory Studies" In *Regulatory Theory: Foundations and Applications,* edited by Peter Drahos, 97–114. ANU Press, 2017.

Henne, Kathryn. "The 'Science' of Fair Play in Sport: Gender and the Politics of Testing." *Signs* 39, no. 3 (2014): 767–812.

Henne, Kathryn, and Rita Shah. "Feminist Criminology and the Visual." In *Oxford Research Encyclopedia of Crime, Media and Popular Culture,* edited by Michelle Brown. Oxford University Press, 2016. doi: https://doi.org/10.1093/acrefore/9780190264079.013.56.

Henne, Kathryn, Krystle Shore, and Jenna Imad Harb. "Body-Worn Cameras, Police Violence and the Politics of Evidence: A Case of Ontological Gerrymandering." *Critical Social Policy* 42, no. 3 (2022): 388–407.

Henne, Kathryn, and Matt Ventresca. "A Criminal Mind? A Damaged Brain? Narratives of Criminality and Culpability in the Celebrated Case of Aaron Hernandez." *Crime, Media, Culture* 16, no. 3 (2020): 392–413.

Henry and Davenport v. National Football League and NFL Properties, LLC. Civil Action No. 20-4165, 2020, https://www.classaction.org/media/henry-et-al-v-national-football-league-et-al.pdf.

Higbee, Mark, Jon Eliason, Hilary Weinberg, Jonathan Lifshitz, and Hirsch Handmaker. "Involving Police Departments in Early Awareness of Concussion Symptoms during Domestic Violence Calls." *Journal of Aggression, Maltreatment & Trauma* 28, no. 7 (2019): 826–37.

Hine, Christine. "Strategies for Reflexive Ethnography in the Smart Home: Autoethnography of Silence and Emotion." *Sociology* 54, no. 1 (2000): 22–36.

Hoge, Charles W., Dennis McGurk, Jeffrey L. Thomas, Anthony L. Cox, Charles C. Engel, and Carl A. Castro. "Mild Traumatic Brain Injury in U.S. Soldiers Returning from Iraq." *New England Journal of Medicine* 358, no. 5, (2008): 453–63.

Hokowhitu, Brendan. "Māori Rugby and Subversion: Creativity, Domestication, Oppression and Decolonization." *International Journal of the History of Sport* 26, no. 16 (2009): 2314–34.

Hokowhitu, Brendan S., John Sullivan, and Les R. Tumoana Williams. "Rugby Culture, Ethnicity, and Concussion." *MAI Review* 1, no. 1 (2008): 1–9.

Holmes, Dave, Stuart J. Murray, Amélie Perron, and Geneviève Rail. "Deconstructing the Evidence-Based Discourse in Health Sciences: Truth, Power and Fascism." *International Journal of Evidence-Based Health Care* 4, no. 3 (2006): 180–86.

Holt, Nicholas L., Bethan C. Kingsley, Lisa N. Tink, and Jay Scherer. "Benefits and Challenges Associated with Sport Participation by Children and Parents from Low-Income Families." *Psychology of Sport and Exercise* 12, no. 5 (2011): 490–99.

Honorato, Bronwyn, Nerina Caltabiano, and Alan R. Clough. "From Trauma to Incarceration: Exploring the Trajectory in a Qualitative Study in Male Prison Inmates from North Queensland, Australia." *Health & Justice* 4, no. 3 (2016): 1–10.

Hootman, Jennifer M., Randall Dick, and Julie Agel. "Epidemiology of Collegiate Injuries for 15 Sports: Summary and Recommendations for Injury Prevention Initiatives." *Journal of Athletic Training* 42, no. 2 (2007): 311–19.

"H.R.9532—Warfighter Brain Health Act of 2022." Congress.Gov. Last modified December 14, 2022. https://www.congress.gov/bill/117th-congress/house-bill/9532.

Hunnicutt, Gwen, Kristine Lundgren, Christine Murray, and Loreen Olson. "The Intersection of Intimate Partner Violence and Traumatic Brain Injury: A Call for Interdisciplinary Research." *Journal of Family Violence* 32 (2017): 471–80.

Ibolja, Cernak, and Farid A. Ahmed. "A Comparative Analysis of Blast-Induced Neurotrauma and Blunt Traumatic Brain Injury Reveals Significant Differences in Injury Mechanisms." *Medical Data* 2, no. 4 (2010): 297–304.

Iliadis, Mary, Bridget Harris, Zarina Vakhitova, Delanie Woodlock, Asher Flynn, and Danielle Tyson. "How Police Body-Worn Cameras Can Facilitate Misidentification in Domestic and family Violence Responses." *Trends & Issues in Crime and Criminal Justice* 684 (2024), Canberra: Australian Institute of Criminology, doi: https://doi.org/10.52922 /ti77277.

Iverson, Grant L., Andrew J. Gardner, Sandy R. Shultz, et al. "Chronic Traumatic Encephalopathy Neuropathology Might Not Be Inexorably Progressive or Unique to Repetitive Neurotrauma." *Brain* 142, no, 12 (2019): 3672–93.

Iverson, Grant L., Dirk C. Keene, George Perry, and Rudolph Castellani. "The Need to Separate Chronic Traumatic Encephalopathy Neuropathology from Clinical Features." *Journal of Alzheimer's Disease* 61, no. 1 (2018): 17–28.

Iverson, Grant L., Teemu M. Luoto, Pekka J. Karhunen, and Rudolph J. Castellani. "Mild Chronic Traumatic Encephalopathy Neuropathology in People with No Known Participation in Contact Sports or History of Repetitive Neurotrauma." *Journal of Neuropathology and Experimental Neurology* 78, no. 7 (2019): 615–25.

Jackson, John L. "Lights, Camera, Police Action!" *Public Culture* 28, no. 1 (2016): 3–8.

Jackson, Nate. *Slow Getting Up: A Story of NFL Survival from the Bottom of the Pile.* HarperCollins, 2014.

Jain, S. Lochlann. *Malignant: How Cancer Becomes Us.* University of California Press, 2013.

Jannace, Kalyn C., Lisa Pompeii, David Gimeno Ruiz de Porras, et al. "Lifetime Traumatic Brain Injury and Risk of Post-Concussive Symptoms in the Millennium Cohort Study." *Journal of Neurotrauma* 41, no. 5–6 (2024): 613–22.

Jette, Shannon, Krishna Bhagat, and David L. Andrews. "Governing the Child-Citizen: 'Let's Move!' as a National Biopedagogy." *Sport, Education and Society* 21, no. 8 (2016): 1109–26.

Johnson Thornton, Davi. *Brain Culture: Neuroscience and Popular Media.* Rutgers University Press, 2011.

Jones, Edgar, Nicola T. Fear, and Simon Wessely. "Shell Shock and Mild Traumatic Brain Injury: A Historical Review." *American Journal of Psychiatry* 164, no. 11 (2007): 1641–45.

Kalman-Lamb, Nathan. *Game Misconduct: Injury, Fandom, and the Business of Sport.* Fernwood, 2018.

Kamins, Joshua, and Christopher C. Giza. "Concussion—Mild TBI: Recoverable Injury with Potential for Serious Sequelae." *Neurosurgery Clinics of North America* 27, no. 4 (2016): 441–52.

Karton, Clara, and T. Blaine Hoshizaki. "Concussive and Subconcussive Brain Trauma: The Complexity of Impact Biomechanics and Injury Risk in Contact Sport." In *Handbook of Clinical Neurology*, edited by Brian Hainline and Robert A. Stern. Vol. 158. Elsevier, 2018.

Kazemi, Sona. "Disabling Power of Class and Ideology: Analyzing War Injury through the Transnational Disability Theory and Praxis." *Disability Studies Quarterly* 39, no. 3 (2019). doi: https://doi.org/10.18061/dsq.v39i3.6496.

Kazemi, Sona. "Whose Disability (Studies)? Defetishizing Disablement of the Iranian Survivors of the Iran-Iraq War by (Re)Telling their Resilient Narratives of Survival." *Canadian Journal of Disability Studies* 8, no. 4 (2019): 195–226.

Keeling, June, and Coleen Fisher. "Health Professionals' Responses to Women's Disclosure of Domestic Violence." *Journal of Interpersonal Violence* 30, no. 13 (2015): 2363–78.

Kelley, Mireille E., Jillian E. Urban, Derek A. Jones, et al. "Analysis of Longitudinal Head Impact Exposure and White Matter Integrity in Returning Youth Football Players." *Journal of Neurosurgery: Pediatrics* 28, no. 2 (2021): 196–205.

Kelly, Judy C., Efland H. Amerson, and Jeffrey T. Barth. "Mild Traumatic Brain Injury: Lessons Learned from Clinical, Sports, and Combat Concussions." *Rehabilitation Research and Practice* (2012): 371970.

Kemm, John. "The Limitations of 'Evidence-Based' Public Health." *Journal of Evaluation in Clinical Practice* 12, no. 3 (2006): 319–24.

Kendall, Marshall, Anna Oeur, Susan E. Brien, et al. "Accident Reconstructions of Falls, Collisions, and Punches in Sports." *Journal of Concussion* 4 (2020): doi: https://doi.org/10.1177/2059700220936957.

Kerr, Zachary Y., Jason P. Mihalik, Kevin M. Guskiewicz, Wayne D. Rosamond, Kelly R. Evenson, and Stephen W. Marshall. "Agreement Between Athlete-Recalled and Clinically Documented Concussion Histories in Former Collegiate Athletes." *American Journal of Sports Medicine* 43, no. 3 (2015): 606–13.

Kerr, Zachary Y., Sara L. Dalton, Karen G. Roos, Aristarque Djoko, Jennifer Phelps, and Thomas P. Dompier. "Comparison of Indiana High School Football Injury Rates by Inclusion of the USA Football 'Heads Up Football' Player Safety Coach." *Orthopedic Journal of Sports Medicine* 4, no. 5 (2016): doi: https://doi.org/10.1177/2325967116648441.

Kerrison, Erin M., Jennifer Cobbina, and Kimberly Bender. "Stop-Gaps, Lip Service, and the Perceived Futility of Body-Worn Police Officer Cameras in Baltimore City." *Journal of Ethnic & Cultural Diversity in Social Work* 27, no. 3 (2018): 271–88.

Kim, Mimi. "The Carceral Creep: Gender-based Violence, Race, and the Expansion of the Punitive State, 1973–1983." *Social Problems* 67, no. 2 (2020): 251–69.

King, Samantha. "Offensive Lines: Sport-State Synergy in an Era of Perpetual War." *Cultural Studies ⇌ Critical Methodologies* 8, no. 4 (2008): 527–39.

Klein, Sebra L., Londa Schiebinger, Marcia L. Stefanick, et al. "Sex Inclusion in Basic Research Drives Discovery." *Proceedings of the National Academy of Sciences of the United States of America* 112, no. 17 (2015): 5257–58.

Kontos, Anthony P., Russ S. Kotwal, R. J. Elbin, et al. "Residual Effects of Combat-Related Mild Traumatic Brain Injury." *Journal of Neurotrauma* 30, no. 8 (2013): doi: https://doi.org/10.1089/neu.2012.2506.

Krane, Vikki. "We Can be Athletic and Feminine, But Do We Want to? Challenging Hegemonic Femininity in Women's Sport." *Quest* 53, no. 1 (2001): 115–33.

Kraus, Michael W., Brittany Torrez, and LaStarr Hollie. "How Narratives of Racial Progress Create Barriers to Diversity, Equity, and Inclusion in Organizations." *Current Opinion in Psychology*, 43 (2022): 108–13.

Kroshus, Emily, Aly J. Sonnen, Sara P. D. Chrisman, and Frederick P. Rivara. "Association between Community Socioeconomic Characteristics and Access to Youth Flag Football." *Injury Prevention* 25, no. 4 (2019): 278–82.

Kroshus, Emily, Christine M. Baugh, Cynthia J. Stein, S. Bryn Austin, and Jerel P. Calzo. "Concussion Reporting, Sex, and Conformity to Traditional Gender Norms in Young Adults." *Journal of Adolescence*, 54 (2017): 110–19.

Kuhn, Andrew W., Aaron M. Yengo-Kahn, Zachary Y. Kerr, and Scott L. Zuckerman. "Sports Concussion Research, Chronic Traumatic Encephalopathy and the Media: Repairing the Disconnect." *British Journal of Sports Medicine* 51, no. 24 (2017): 1732–33.

Kulig, Teresa C. and Francis T. Cullen. "Where is Latisha's Law? Black Invisibility in the Social Construction of Victimhood." *Justice Quarterly* 34, no. 6 (2017): 978–1013.

Kusz, Kyle W. "Trumpism, Tom Brady, and the Reassertion of White Supremacy in Militarized Post-9/11 America." In *Sport and Militarism: Contemporary Global Perspectives*, edited by Michael L. Butterworth, 229–44. Routledge, 2017.

Lakisa, David, Daryl Adair, and Tracy Taylor. "Pasifika Diaspora and the Changing Face of Australian Rugby League." *Contemporary Pacific* 26, no. 2 (2014): 347–67.

Lam, Anita. "Decoding the Crime Scene Photograph: Seeing and Narrating the Death of a Gangster." *International Journal for the Semiotics of Law* 34, no. 1 (2021): 173–90.

Langton, Marcia, and Kristen Smith. "The Role of Brain Injury in Family Violence for Aboriginal and Torres Strait Islander Peoples" (paper presented at the Brain Injury Australia Conference, Sydney, NSW), June 30, 2022.

Lattimore, Pamela K., Nicholas J. Richardson, Pamela L. Ferguson, and E. Elisabeth Pickelsimer. "The Association of Traumatic Brain Injury, Post-Traumatic Stress Disorder, and Criminal Recidivism, *Health & Justice* 10, no. 7 (2022): 1–7.

Laurendeau, Jason, and Dan Konecny. "Where is Childhood? In Conversation with Messner and Musto." *Sociology of Sport Journal* 32, no. 3 (2015): 332–44.

Leat, Sarah R., Kristen Ravi, Abha Rai, Caterina Obenauf, and Sean Bryant. "Do I Belong Here? Experiences of Transgender Survivors of Intimate Partner Violence in Domestic Violence Shelters." *Families in Society* (2023): doi: https://doi.org/10.1177/1044389423 1196929.

Lee, Bandy X. "Causes and Cures VII: Structural Violence." *Aggression and Violent Behavior* 28 (2016): 109–14.

Lee, Edward B., Kevin Kinch, Victoria E. Johnson, John Q. Trojanowski, Douglas H. Smith, and William Stewart. "Chronic Traumatic Encephalopathy is a Common Co-Morbidity, But Less Frequent Primary Dementia in Former Soccer and Rugby Players." *Acta Neuropathologica* 138, no. 3 (2019): 389–99.

Lefebvre, Helene, Genevieve Cloutier, and Marie Josée Levert. "Perspectives of Survivors of Traumatic Brain Injury and Their Caregivers on Long-Term Social Integration." *Brain Injury* 22, nos. 7–8 (2008): 535–43.

Lehrner, Amy, and Nicole E. Allen. "Still a Movement After All These Years? Current Tensions in the Domestic Violence Movement." *Violence Against Women* 15, no. 6 (2009): 656–77.

Lempke, Landon B., Samuel R. Walton, Benjamin L. Brett, et al. "Relating American Football Age of First Exposure to Patient-Reported Outcomes and Medical Diagnoses Among Former National Football League Players: An NFL-LONG study." *Sports Medicine* 53 (2023): 1073–84.

Leonard, David J. *Playing while White: Privilege and Power on and off the Field*. University of Washington Press, 2017.

Levin, Harvey S., Nancy R. Temkin, Jason Barber, et al. "Association of Sex and Age with Mild Traumatic Brain Injury-Related Symptoms: A TRACK-TBI Study." *JAMA Network Open* 4, no. 4 (2021): e213046.

Light, Richard, and David Kirk. "High School Rugby, the Body, and the Reproduction of Hegemonic Masculinity." *Sport, Education and Society* 5, no. 2 (2000): 163–76.

Lincoln, Andrew E., Shane V. Caswell, Jon L. Almquist, Reginald E. Dunn, Joseph B. Norris, and Richard Y. Hinton. "Trends in Concussion Incidence in High School Sports: A Prospective 11-Year Study." *American Journal of Sports Medicine* 39, no. 5 (2011): 958–63.

Logan, Kelsey, Steven Cuff, Cynthia R. LaBella, et al. "Organized Sports for Children, Preadolescents, and Adolescents." *Pediatrics* 143, no. 6 (2019): e20190997.

Loignon, Alexandra, Marie-Christine Ouellet, and Geneviève Belleville. "A Systematic Review and Meta-analysis on PTSD Following TBI Among Military/Veteran and Civilian Populations." *Journal of Head Trauma Rehabilitation* 35, no. 1 (2020): E21–35.

Lorenz, Stacy L., and Geraint B. Osborne. "'Nothing More Than the Usual Injury': Debating Hockey Violence During the Manslaughter Trials of Allan Loney (1905) and Charles Masson (1907)." *Journal of Historical Sociology* 30, no. 4 (2017): 698–723.

Lovell, Mark, Micky Collins, and Jamie E. Pardini. "Management of Cerebral Concussion in Military Personnel: Lessons Learned from Sports Medicine." *Operative Techniques in Sports Medicine* 13, no. 4 (2005): 212–21.

Lutz, Catherine, and Andreas Mazzarino, eds. *War and Health: The Medical Consequences of the Wars in Iraq and Afghanistan*. New York University Press, 2019.

Macaulay, Stewart. "Presidential Address: Images of Law in Everyday Life: The Lessons of School, Entertainment, and Spectator Sports." *Law & Society Review* 21, no. 2 (1987): 185–218.

MacDonald James, and Gregory D. Myer. "'Don't Let Kids Play Football': A Killer Idea." *British Journal of Sports Medicine* 51, no. 20 (2017): 1448–49.

Mackay, Daniel F., Emma R. Russell, Katy Stewart, John A. MacLean, Jill P. Pell, and William Stewart. "Neurodegenerative Disease Mortality among Former Professional Soccer Players." *New England Journal of Medicine* 381, no. 19 (2019): 1801–08.

MacLeish, Ken. "Churn: Mobilization–Demobilization and the Fungibility of American Military Life." *Security Dialogue* 51, no. 2–3 (2020): 194–210.

Macy, Jonathan T., Kyle Kercher, Jesse A. Steinfeldt, and Keisuke Kawata. "Fewer U.S. Adolescents Playing Football and Public Health: A Review of Measures to Improve Safety and an Analysis of Gaps in the Literature." *Public Health Reports* 136, no. 5 (2021): 562–74.

Mah, Katie, Brenda Gladstone, Deb Cameron, and Nick Reed. "Re-Producing the Pediatric Concussion Discourse in Clinical Rehabilitation Practice." *Disability and Rehabilitation* 44, no. 24 (2022): 7464–74.

Maker, John. "Hand Grenades and Hockey Sticks: The Positive Influence of the Military on Physical Education and Sport in Canada, 1900–1945." *Physical & Health Education Journal* 75, no. 1 (2009): 16–19.

Malcolm, Dominic. "Soccer, CTE, and the Cultural Representation of Dementia." *Sociology of Sport Journal* 38, no. 1 (2020): 1–10.

Malcolm, Dominic. *The Concussion Crisis in Sport*. Routledge, 2020.

Manly, Jennifer J. "Advantages and Disadvantages of Separate Norms for African Americans." *Clinical Neuropsychologist* 19, no. 2 (2005): 270–75.

Mannix, Rebekah, William P. Meehan III, and Alvaro Pascual-Leone. "Sports-Related Concussions—Media, Science and Policy." *Nature Reviews Neurology* 12, no. 8 (2016): 486–90.

Manzanero, Silvia, Lisa J. Elkington, Stephan F. Praet, Greg Lovell, Gordon Waddington, and David C. Hughes. "Post-Concussion Recovery in Children and Adolescents: A Narrative Review." *Journal of Concussion* 1 (2017): doi: https://doi.org/10.1177/2059700217726874.

Marcus, George. "Ethnography in/of the World System: The Emergence of Multi-Sited Ethnography." *Annual Review of Anthropology* 24 (1995): 95–117.

Marcus, George E., and Erkan Saka. "Assemblage." *Theory, Culture & Society* 23, no. 2–3 (2006): 101–06.

Mariani, Megan, Michael L. Alosco, Jesse Mez, and Robert A. Stern. "Clinical Presentation of Chronic Traumatic Encephalopathy." *Seminars in Neurology* 40, no. 4 (2020): 370–83.

Marmot, Michael, Sharon Friel, Ruth R. Bell, Tanya A. J. Houweling, and Sebastian Taylor. "Closing the Gap in a Generation: Health Equity Through Action on the Social Determinants of Health." *Lancet* 372, no. 9650 (2008): 1661–69.

Martin, Aryn, and Alasdair McMillan. "Concussion Killjoys: CTE, Violence, and the Brain's Becoming." *BioSocieties* 17, no. 2 (2022): 229–50.

Masic, Izet, Mila Miokovic, and Belma Muhamedagic. "Evidence Based Medicine—New Approaches and Challenges." *Acta Inform Medica* 16, no. 4 (2008): 219–25.

Mason, Jan. "Child Protection Policy and the Construction of Childhood." In *Children Taken Seriously: In Theory, Policy and Practice*, edited by Jan Mason and Toby Fattore, 91–97. Jessica Kinsley, 2005.

Master, Christina L., Barry P. Katz, Kristy B. Arbogast, et al. "Differences in Sport-Related Concussion for Female and Male Athletes in Comparable Collegiate Sports: A Study from the NCAA-DoD Concussion Assessment, Research and Education (CARE) Consortium." *British Journal of Sports Medicine* 55, no. 24 (2021): 1387–94.

Matthews, Christopher, and Alex Channon. "'It's Only Sport'—The Symbolic Neutralization of 'Violence.'" *Symbolic Interaction* 39, no. 4 (2016): 557–76.

Matthews, Christopher, and Alex Channon. "Understanding Sports Violence: Revisiting Foundational Explorations." *Sport in Society* 20, no. 7 (2017): 751–67.

McAlister, Merran, and Samantha Bricknell. *Deaths in Custody in Australia 2021–22*. Statistical Report no. 41. Australian Institute of Criminology, 2022. https://www.aic.gov.au/publications/sr/sr41.

McDermott, Lisa. "A Governmental Analysis of Children 'At Risk' in a World of Physical Inactivity and Obesity Epidemics." *Sociology of Sport Journal* 24, no. 3 (2007): 302–24.

McDonald, Brent, and Lena Rodriguez. "'It's Our Meal Ticket': Pacific Bodies, Labor, and Mobility in Australia." *Asia Pacific Journal of Sport and Social Science* 3, no. 3 (2014): 236–49.

McDonald, Mary G. "Mapping Whiteness and Sport: An Introduction." *Sociology of Sport Journal* 22, no. 3 (2005): 245–55.

McDonald, Mary G. "Queering Whiteness: The Peculiar Case of the Women's National Basketball Association." *Sociological Perspectives* 45, no. 4 (2002): 379–96.

McGannon, Kerry R., Sarah M. Cunningham, and Robert J. Schinke. "Understanding Concussion in Socio-Cultural Context: A Media Analysis of a National Hockey League Star's Concussion." *Psychology of Sport and Exercise* 14 (2013): 891–99.

McKee, Ann C., and Meghan E. Robinson. "Military-Related Traumatic Brain Injury and Neurodegeneration." *Alzheimer's & Dementia* 10, no. 35 (2014): S242–53.

McKee, Ann C., Jesse Mez, Bobak Abdolmohammadi, et al. "Neuropathologic and Clinical Findings in Young Contact Sport Athletes Exposed to Repetitive Head Impacts." *JAMA Neurology* 80, no. 10 (2023): 1037–50.

McKee, Ann C., Thor D. Stein, John F. Crary, Kevin F. Bieniek, Robert C. Cantu, and Gabor G. Kovacs. "Practical Considerations in the Diagnosis of Mild Chronic Traumatic Encephalopathy and Distinction from Age-Related Tau Astrogliopathy." *Journal of Neuropathology and Experimental Neurology* 79, no. 8 (2020): 921–24.

McKee, Ann C., Thor D. Stein, Patrick T. Kiernan, and Victor E. Alvarez. "The Neuropathology of Chronic Traumatic Encephalopathy." *Brain Pathology* 25, no. 3 (2015): 350–64.

McMullen, John. "Lost Lives at Westray: Official Discourse, Public Truth and Controversial Death." *Canadian Journal of Law and Society* 22, no. 1 (2007): 21–42.

McNamee, Michael J., Bradley Partridge, and Lynley Anderson. "Concussion Ethics and Sports Medicine." *Clinics in Sports Medicine* 35, no. 2 (2016): 257–67.

McNamee, Mike, Lynley C. Anderson, Pascal Borry, et al. "Sport-Related Concussion Research Agenda beyond Medical Science: Culture, Ethics, Science, Policy." *Journal of Medical Ethics* (2023): doi: https://doi.org/10.1136/jme-2022-108812.

McParland, Patricia, Fiona Kelly, and Anthea Innes. "Dichotomizing Dementia: Is There Another Way?" *Sociology of Health & Illness* 39, no. 2 (2017): 258–69.

Meehan III, William P., Alex M. Taylor, and Mark Proctor. "The Pediatric Athlete: Younger Athletes with Sport-Related Concussion." *Clinics in Sports Medicine* 30, no. 1 (2011): 133–44.

Mehrotra, Gita R., Ericka Kimball, and Stéphanie Wehab. "The Braid That Binds Us: The Impact of Neoliberalism, Criminalization, and Professionalization on Domestic Violence Work." *Affilia* 31, no. 2 (2016): 153–63.

Mejia-Lancheros, Cilia, James Lachaud, Vicky Stergiopoulos, et al. "Effect of Housing First on Violence-Related Traumatic Brain Injury in Adults with Experiences of Homelessness and Mental Illness: Findings from the At Home/Chez Soi Randomized Trial, Toronto Site." *BMJ Open* 10 (2020): e038443.

Messner, Michael. "Sports and Male Domination: The Female Athlete as Contested Ideological Terrain." *Sociology of Sport Journal* 5, no. 3 (1988): 197–211.

Messner, Michael. *Power at Play: Sports and the Problem of Masculinity*. Beacon, 1992.

Messner, Michael, and Michela Musto. *Child's Play*. Rutgers University Press, 2016.

Messner, Michael A., and Michela Musto. "Where Are the Kids?" *Sociology of Sport Journal* 31, no. 1 (2014): 102–22.

Mez, Jesse, Daniel H. Daneshvar, Bobak Abdolmohammadi, et al. "Duration of American Football Play and Chronic Traumatic Encephalopathy." *Annals of Neurology* 87, no. 1 (2020): 116–31.

Mez, Jesse, Michael L. Alosco, Daniel H. Daneshvar, et al. "Validity of the 2014 Traumatic Encephalopathy Syndrome Criteria for CTE Pathology." *Alzheimer's & Dementia* 17, no. 10 (2021): 1709–24.

Michaels, David. *The Triumph of Doubt: Dark Money and the Science of Deception*. Oxford University Press, 2020.

Mihalik, Jason P., Erin B. Wasserman, Elizabeth F. Teel, and Stephen W. Marshall. "Head Impact Biomechanics Differ between Girls and Boys Youth Ice Hockey Players." *Annals of Biomedical Engineering* 48, no. 1 (2020): 104–11.

Miyashita, Theresa L., Eleni Diakogeorgiou, and Christina Vander Vegt. "Gender Differences in Concussion Reporting among High School Athletes." *Sports Health* 8 (2016): 359–63.

Mol, Annemarie. *The Body Multiple: Ontology in Medical Practice*. Duke University Press, 2003.

Mollayeva, Tatyana, Shirin Mollayeva, and Angela Colantonio. "Traumatic Brain Injury: Sex, Gender, and Intersecting Vulnerabilities." *Nature Reviews Neurology* 14 (2018): 711–22.

Montenigro, Philip H., Christine M. Baugh, et al. "Clinical Subtypes of Chronic Traumatic Encephalopathy: Literature Review and Proposed Research Diagnostic Criteria for Traumatic Encephalopathy Syndrome." *Alzheimer's Research & Therapy* 6, no. 5 (2014): 1–17.

Montenigro, Philip H., Daniel T. Corp, Thor D. Stein, Robert C. Cantu, and Robert A. Stern. "Chronic Traumatic Encephalopathy: Historical Origins and Current Perspective." *Annual Review of Clinical Psychology* 11, no. 1 (2015): 309–30.

Moore, Dawn and Rashmee Singh. "Seeing Crime, Feeling Crime: Visual Evidence, Emotions and the Persecution of Domestic Violence." *Theoretical Criminology* 22, no. 1 (2018): 116–32.

Moore, R. Davis, Jacob J. Kay, and Dave Ellemberg. "The Long-Term Outcomes of Sport-Related Concussion in Pediatric Populations." *International Journal of Psychophysiology* 132, part A (2018): 14–24.

Morrison, Daniel M. and Monica J. Casper. "Gender, Violence, and Brain Injury in and out of the NFL: What Counts as Harm?" In *Football, Culture, and Power*, edited by David J. Leonard, Kimberly B. George, and Wade Davis, 165–75. Routledge.

Murphy, Michelle. *Sick Building Syndrome and the Problem of Uncertainty: Environmental Politics, Technoscience, and Women Workers*. Duke University Press, 2006.

Narcotta-Welp, Eileen. "A Black Fly in White Milk: The 1999 Women's World Cup, Briana Scurry, and the Politics of Inclusion." *Journal of Sport History* 42, no. 3 (2015): 382–93.

National Network to End Domestic Violence. *Funding Challenges for Domestic Violence Programs: The Impact on Victims*. July 2019. Accessed December 5, 2023. https://nnedv.org/resources-library/library_public_policy_fundingchallenges/.

Nead, Lynda. "Stilling the Punch: Boxing, Violence, and the Photographic Image." *Journal of Visual Culture* 10, no. 3 (2011): 305–23.

Nixon, Howard L. "A Social Network Analysis of Influences on Athletes to Play with Pain and Injuries." *Journal of Sport & Social Issues* 16, no. 2 (1992): 127–35.

Nixon, Howard L. "Explaining Pain and Injury Attitudes and Experiences in Sport in Terms of Gender, Race, and Sport Status." *Journal of Sport & Social Issues* 20, no. 2 (1996): 33–44.

Nnawulezi, Nkiru A., and Cris M. Sullivan. "Oppression Within Safe Spaces: Exploring Racial Microaggressions Within Domestic Violence Shelters." *Journal of Black Psychology* 40, no. 6 (2024): 563–91.

Noble Tesh, Sylvia. *Uncertain Hazards: Environmental Activists and Scientific Proof.* Cornell University Press, 2018.

Nowinski, Christopher J., Samantha C. Bureau, Michael E. Buckland, et al. "Applying the Bradford Hill Criteria for Causation to Repetitive Head Impacts and Chronic Traumatic Encephalopathy." *Frontiers in Neurology* 13 (2022): doi: https://doi.org/10.3389/fneur.2022.938163.

Nowinski, Christopher J., Samantha C. Bureau, Michael E. Buckland, et al. "Applying the Bradford Hill Criteria for Causation to Repetitive Head Impacts and Chronic Traumatic Encephalopathy." *Frontiers in Neurology* 13 (2022): 938163.

Nowinski, Christopher J., Hye Chang Rhim, Ann C. McKee, et al. "'Subconcussive' Is a Dangerous Misnomer: Hits of Greater Magnitude than Concussive Impacts May Not Cause Symptoms." *British Journal of Sports Medicine* (2024): doi: https://doi.org/10.1136/bjsports-2023-107413.

Omar, Samira, Stephanie Nixon, and Angela Colantonio. "Integrated Care Pathways for Black Persons with Traumatic Brain Injury: A Critical Transdisciplinary Scoping Review of the Clinic Care Journey." *Trauma, Violence, & Abuse* (2021): doi: https://doi.org/10.1177/15248380211062221.

Oreskes, Naomi, and Erik M. Conway. *Merchants of Doubt: How a Handful of Scientists Obscured the Truth on Issues from Tobacco Smoke to Climate Change.* Bloomsbury Press, 2011.

Ozonoff, David. "Legal Causation and Responsibility for Causing Harm." *American Journal of Public Health* 95, no. S1 (2005): S35–38.

Parker, William L. and James Trifunov. "The Sport of Amateur Boxing—Good or Evil?" *Canadian Medical Association Journal* 83, no. 9 (1960): 432–35.

Parry, Keith, Adam J. White, Jamie Cleland, et al. "Masculinities, Media and the Rugby Mind: An Analysis of Stakeholder Views on the Relationship between Rugby Union, the Media, Masculine-Influenced Views on Injury, and Concussion." *Communication & Sport* 10, no. 3 (2022): 564–86.

Parsons, Joanne L., Stephanie E. Coen, and Sheree Bekker. "Anterior Cruciate Ligament Injury: Towards a Gendered Environment Approach." *British Journal of Sports Medicine* 55 (2021): 984–90.

Patricios, Jon S., Kathryn J. Schneider, Jiri Dvorak, et al. "Consensus Statement on Concussion in Sport: The 6th International Conference on Concussion in Sport—Amsterdam, October 2022." *British Journal of Sports Medicine* 57, no. 11 (2023): 695–711.

Pearce, Warren, and Sujatha Raman. "The New Randomized Controlled Trials Movement in Public Policy: Challenges of Epistemic Governance." *Policy Science* 47 (2014): 387–402.

Peitzmeier, Sarah M., Mannat Malik, Shanna K. Kattari, et al. "Intimate Partner Violence in Transgender Populations: Systematic Review and Meta-analysis of Prevalence and Correlates." *American Journal of Public Health* 110 (2020): e1–14.

Pierre, Kevin, Kyle Dyson, Abeer Dagra, Eric Williams, Ken Porche, and Brandon Lucke-Wold. "Chronic Traumatic Encephalopathy: Update on Current Clinical Diagnosis and Management." *Biomedicines* 9, no. 4 (2021): 415.

Pierre, Kevin, Vanessa Molina, Shil Shukla, et al. "Chronic Traumatic Encephalopathy: Diagnostic Updates and Advances." *AIMS Neuroscience* 9, no. 4 (2022): 519–35.

Pietrzak, Robert H., Douglas C. Johnson, Marc B. Goldstein, James C. Malley, and Steven M. Southwick. "Posttraumatic Stress Disorder Mediates the Relationship Between Mild traumatic Brain Injury and Health and Psychosocial Functioning in Veterans of Operations Enduring Freedom and Iraqi Freedom." *Journal of Nervous and Mental Disease* 197, no. 10 (2009): 748–53.

Pitts-Taylor, Victoria. *The Brain's Body: Neuroscience and Corporeal Politics*. Duke University Press, 2016.

Pitts-Taylor, Victoria. "Neurobiologically Poor? Brain Phenotypes, Inequality, and Biosocial Determinism." *Science, Technology, & Human Values* 44, no. 4 (2019): 660–85.

Pope, Steve W. "An Army of Athletes: Playing Fields, Battlefields, and the American Military Sporting Experience, 1890–1920." *Journal of Military History* 59, no. 3 (1995): 435–56.

Puar, Jasbir. *The Right to Maim: Debility, Capacity, Disability*. Duke University Press, 2017.

Puar, Jasbir K. *Terrorist Assemblages: Homonationalism in Queer Times*. Duke University Press, 2007.

Quarrie, Kenneth Lincoln, John H. M. Brooks, Nicholas Burger, Patria A Hume, and Steve Jackson. "Facts and Values: On the Acceptability of Risks in Children's Sport Using the Example of Rugby—A Narrative Review." *British Journal of Sports Medicine* 51, no. 15 (2017): 1134–39.

Rabadi, Meheroz H., and Barry D. Jordan. "The Cumulative Effect of Repetitive Concussion in Sports." *Clinical Journal of Sport Medicine* 11, no. 3 (2001): 194–98.

Ray, Bradley, and Nicholas J. Richardson. "Traumatic Brain Injury and Recidivism Among Returning Inmates." *Criminal Justice and Behavior* 44, no. 3 (2017): 472–86.

Razack, Sherene H. "Timely Deaths: Medicalizing the Deaths of Aboriginal People in Police Custody." *Law, Culture and the Humanities* 9, no. 2 (2011): 352–74.

Reimann, Paul A. "The G.I. Bill and Collegiate Football Recruiting after World War II." *International Sports Journal* 8, no. 2 (2004): 126–33.

Resch, Jacob E., Amanda Rach, Samuel Walton, and Donna K. Broshek. "Sport Concussion and the Female Athlete." *Clinics in Sport Medicine* 36, no. 4 (2017): 717–39.

Richardson, Ruth. *Death, Dissection and the Destitute*. 2nd ed. University of Chicago Press, 2001.

Richardson, Sarah S., Meredith Reiches, Heather Shattuck-Heidorn, Michelle Lynne LaBonte, and Theresa Consoli. "Focus on Preclinical Sex Differences Will Not Address Women's and Men's Health Disparities." *Proceedings of the National Academy of Sciences of the United States of America* 112, no. 44 (2015): 13419–20.

Richie, Beth E. *Arrested Justice: Black Women, Violence, and America's Prison Nation*. New York University Press, 2012.

Richie, Beth. "A Black Feminist Reflection on the Anti-Violence Movement." *Signs* 25, no. 4 (2000): 1133–37.

Rivera, Echo A., Cris M. Sullivan, and April M. Zeoli. "Secondary Victimization of Abused Mothers by Family Court Mediators." *Feminist Criminology*, 7, no. 3 (2012): 234–52.

Robinson, Louise, and Karen Spilsbury. "Systematic Review of the Perceptions and Experiences of Accessing Health Services by Adult Victims of Domestic Violence." *Health and Social Care in the Community* 16, no. 1 (2008): 16–31.

Rollins, Oliver. *Conviction: The Making and Unmaking of the Violent Brain*. Stanford University Press, 2021.

Rothman, Kenneth J., and Sander Greenland. "Causation and Causal Inference in Epidemiology." *American Journal of Public Health* 95, no. S1 (2005): S144–50.

Roussell, Aaron, Lori Sexton, Paul Deppen III, Marisa Omori, and Esther Scheibler. "The Dark Footprint of State Violence: A Synthetic Approach to the American Crime Decline." *Theoretical Criminology* 26, no. 2 (2022): 326–46.

"Rowan's Law: Concussion Safety." Ontario Government. Accessed December 5, 2023. https://www.ontario.ca/page/rowans-law-concussion-safety.

Ruck, Rob. *Tropic of Football: The Long and Perilous Journey of Samoans to the NFL*. New Press, 2018.

Rugg, Adam. "America's Game: The NFL's 'Salute to Service' Campaign, the Diffused Military Presence, and Corporate Social Responsibility." *Popular Communication* 14, no. 1 (2016): 21–29.

Rugg, Adam. "Working Out Their Future: The NFL's Play 60 Campaign and the Production of Adolescent Fans and Players." *Journal of Sport and Social Issues* 43, no. 1 (2019): 69–88.

Rule, Latoya Aroha, and Larissa Behrendt. "*The Families of Indigenous People Who Die in Custody Need a Say in What Happens Next*." The Conversation. April 28, 2021. https://theconversation.com/the-families-of-indigenous-people-who-die-in-custody-need-a-say-in-what-happens-next-159127.

Russell, Emma R., Daniel F. Mackay, Katy Stewart, John A. Maclean, Jill P. Pell, and William Stewart. "Association of Field Position and Career Length with Risk of Neurodegenerative Disease in Male Former Professional Soccer Players." *JAMA Neurology* 78, no. 9 (2021): 1058–63.

Russell-Brown, Katheryn. "Body Cameras, Police Violence and Racial Credibility." *Florida Law Review Forum* 67 (2016): 207–13.

Ruston, Scott W., Jessica K. Kamrath, Alaina C. Zanin, Karlee Posteher and Steve R. Corman. "Performance Versus Safety: Understanding the Logics of Cultural Narratives Influencing Concussion Reporting Behaviors." *Communication & Sport* 7, no. 4 (2019): 529–48.

Sailofsky, Daniel, and Madeleine Orr. "One Step Forward, Two Tweets Back: Exploring Cultural Backlash and Hockey Masculinity on Twitter." *Sociology of Sport Journal* 38, no. 1 (2021): 67–77.

Sandel, Elizabeth. *Shaken Brain: The Science, Care, and Treatment of Concussion*. Harvard University Press, 2020.

Sanders, Rachel. "The Color of Fat: Racializing Obesity, Recuperating Whiteness, and Reproducing Injustice." *Politics, Groups, and Identities* 7, no. 2 (2019): 287–304.

Sanderson, Jimmy, and David Cassilo. "'I'm Glad I Played When the Country Still Had Gonads': Pop Warner's Kickoff Policy Change and the Framing of Health and Safety Initiatives in Football." *Journal of Sports Media* 14, no. 1–2 (2019): 1–22.

Scherer, Jay, and Jordan Koch. "Living with War: Sport, Citizenship, and the Cultural Politics of Post-9/11 Canadian Identity." *Sociology of Sport Journal* 27, no. 1 (2010): 1–29.

Schimmel, Kimberly S. "From 'Violence-Complacent' to 'Terrorist-Ready': Post-9/11 Framing of the U.S. Super Bowl." *Urban Studies* 48, no. 15 (2011): 3277–91.

Schimmel, Kimberly S. "Not an 'Extraordinary Event': NFL Games and Militarized Civic Ritual." *Sociology of Sport Journal* 34, no. 1 (2017): 79–89.

Shanley, Ellen, Charles Thigpen, Michael Kissenberth, et al. "Heads Up Football Training Decreases Concussion Rates in High School Football Players." *Clinical Journal of Sport Medicine* 31, no. 2 (2021): 120–26.

Sheard, Kenneth G. "'Brutal and Degrading': The Medical Profession and Boxing, 1838–1984." *The International Journal of the History of Sport* 15, no. 3 (1998): 74–102.

Shelby, Renee. "Technology, Sexual Violence, and Power-Evasive Politics: Mapping the Anti-violence Sociotechnical Imaginary." *Science, Technology, & Human Values* 48, no. 3 (2023): 552–81.

Sheth, Suril B., Dharun Anandayuvaraj, Saumil S. Patel, and Bhavin R. Sheth. "Orthopedic and Brain Injuries over Last 10 Seasons in the National Football League: Number and Effect on Missed Playing Time." *BMJ Open Sport and Exercise Medicine* 6, no. 1 (2020): 1–8.

Shew, Ashley, and Keith Johnson. "Companion Animals as Technologies in Biomedical Research." *Perspectives on Science* 26, no. 3 (2018): 400–417.

Shuting, Bote, Qi, Jin, Hongsheng Qian, and Yu Zou. "Bibliometric Analysis of Chronic Traumatic Encephalopathy Research from 1999 to 2019." *International Journal of Environmental Research and Public Health* 17, no. 15 (2020): 5411.

Sigford, Barbara, David X. Cifu, Rodney Vanderploeg, et al. "Care of War Veterans with Mild Traumatic Brain Injury." *New England Journal of Medicine* 361, no. 5 (2009): 536–38.

Siler, Kyle. "Pipelines on the Gridiron: Player Backgrounds, Opportunity Structures and Racial Stratification in American College Football." *Sociology of Sport Journal* 36, no. 1 (2019): 57–76.

Simon, Jonathan. *Governing through Crime: How the War on Crime Changed American Democracy and Created a Culture of Fear.* Oxford University Press, 2007.

Smart, Carol. *Feminism and the Power of Law.* Routledge, 1989.

Sokoloff, Natalie, and Ida Dupont. "Domestic Violence: Examining the Intersections of Race, Class, and Gender." *Violence Against Women* 11, no. 1 (2005): 3–64.

Solomon, Gary. "Chronic Traumatic Encephalopathy in Sports: A Historical and Narrative Review." *Developmental Neuropsychology* 43, no. 4 (2018): 279–311.

Sone, Je Yeong, S. Courtney-Kay Lamb, Kristina Techar, et al. "High Prevalence of Prior Contact Sports Play and Concussion among Orthopedic and Neurosurgical Department Chairs." *Journal of Neurosurgery* 22, no. 1 (2018): 1–8.

Sontag, Susan. *Regarding the Pain of Others.* Farrar, Straus, and Giroux, 2003.

St. Ivany, Amanda, Linda Bullock, Donna Schminkey, Kristen Wells, Phyllis Sharps, and Susan Kools. "Living in Fear and Prioritizing Safety: Exploring Women's Lives after Traumatic Brain Injury from Intimate Partner Violence." *Qualitative Health Research* 28, no. 11 (2018): 1708–18.

Stamm, Julie M. *The Brain on Youth Sports: The Science, the Myths, and the Future.* Rowman & Littlefield, 2021.

Steele, Linda. *Disability, Criminal Justice, and the Law: Reconsidering Court Diversion.* Routledge, 2020.

Stein, Murray B., and Thomas W. McCallister. "Exploring the Convergence of Posttraumatic Stress Disorder and Mild Traumatic Brain Injury." *American Journal of Psychiatry* 166, no. 7 (2009): 768–76.

Stern, Robert A., David O. Riley, Daniel H. Daneshvar, Christopher J. Nowinski, Robert C. Cantu, and Ann C. McKee. "Long-Term Consequences of Repetitive Brain Trauma: Chronic Traumatic Encephalopathy." *PM & R* 3, no. 10 (2011): S460–67.

Stewart, William, Kieren Allinson, Safa Al-Sarraj, et al. "Primum non nocere: A Call for Balance When Reporting on CTE." *Lancet Neurology* 18, no. 3 (2019): 231–33.

Stockman, Jamila K., Hitomi Hayashi, and Jacquelyn C. Campbell. "Intimate Partner Violence and its Health Impact on Ethnic Minority Women." *Journal of Women's Health* 24, no. 1 (2015): 62–79.

Stokes, Keith A., Duncan Locke, Simon Roberts, et al. "Does Reducing the Height of the Tackle through Law Change in Elite Men's Rugby Union (The Championship, England) Reduce the Incidence of Concussion? A Controlled Study in 126 Games." *British Journal of Sports Medicine* 55, no. 4 (2021): 220–25.

Stubbs, Jacob L., Allen E. Thornton, Jessica M. Sevick, et al. "Traumatic Brain Injury in Homeless and Marginally Housed Individuals: A Systematic Review and Meta-Analysis." *Lancet Public Health* 5, no. 1 (2020): e19–32.

Suter, Catherine M., Andrew J. Affleck, Alan J. Pearce, Reimar Junckerstorff, Maggie Lee, and Michael E. Buckland. "Chronic Traumatic Encephalopathy in a Female Ex-professional Australian Rules Footballer." *Acta Neuropathologica* 146 (2023): 547–49.

Suter, Catherine M., Andrew J. Affleck, Maggie Lee, Alan J. Pearce, Linda E. Iles, and Michael E. Buckland. "Chronic Traumatic Encephalopathy in Australia: The First Three Years of the Australian Sports Brain Bank." *Medical Journal of Australia* 216, no. 10 (2022): 530–31.

Tanielian, Terri, and Lisa H. Jaycox, eds. *Invisible Wounds of War: Psychological and Cognitive Injuries, Their Consequences, and Services to Assist Recovery* (Santa Monica: RAND Corporation, 2008).

"Tanya Day—Overview of the Coronial Inquest into Her Death." Human Rights Law Centre. Accessed June 14, 2023. https://www.hrlc.org.au/tanya-day-overview.

Tator, Charles, Jill Starkes, Gillian Dolansky, Julie Quet, Jean Michaud, and Michael Vassilyadi. "Fatal Second Impact Syndrome in Rowan Stringer, a 17-Year-Old Rugby Player." *Canadian Journal of Neurological Sciences* 46, no. 3 (2019): 351–54.

Terrio, Heidi, Lisa A. Brenner, Brian J. Ivins, et al. "Traumatic Brain Injury Screening: Preliminary Findings in a U.S. Army Brigade Combat Team." *Journal of Head Trauma Rehabilitation* 24, no. 1 (2009): 14–23.

Terry, Jennifer. *Attachments to War: Biomedical Logics and Violence in Twenty-First-Century America.* Duke University Press, 2015.

Terwilliger, Virginia K., Lincoln Pratson, Christopher G. Vaughan, and Gerard A. Gioia. "Additional Post-Concussion Impact Exposure May Affect Recovery in Adolescent Athletes." *Journal of Neurotrauma* 33, no. 8 (2016): 761–65.

Teterina, Anastasia, Suvd Zulbayar, Tatyana Mollayeva, Vincy Chan, Angela Colantonio, and Michael Escobar. "Gender Versus Sex in Predicting Outcomes of Traumatic Brain

Injury: A Cohort Study Utilizing Large Administrative Databases." *Scientific Reports* 13 (2023): 18453.

Theberge, Nancy. "Studying Gender and Injuries: A Comparative Analysis of the Literature on Women's Injuries in Sport and Work." *Ergonomics* 55, no. 2 (2012): 183–93.

Thomas, Elizabeth, Melinda Fitzgerald, and Gill Cowen. "Post-Concussion States: How Do We Improve Our Patients' Outcomes? An Australian Perspective." *Journal of Concussion* 4 (2020): doi: https://doi.org/10.1177/2059700220960313.

Townsend, Stephen. "'The Tragedy of the Punch Drunk': Reading Concussion in Australian Sporting Newspapers, 1843–1954." *Frontiers in Sports and Active Living* 3 (2021): 676463.

Trammel, Aaron. *Repairing Play: A Black Phenomenology.* Massachussetts Institute of Technology Press, 2023.

Traumatic Brain Injury Center of Excellence. "DoD Numbers for Traumatic Brain Injury—Worldwide Totals." Health.mil. Accessed February 3, 2025. https://health.mil/Military -Health-Topics/Centers-of-Excellence/Traumatic-Brain-Injury-Center-of-Excellence /DOD-TBI-Worldwide-Numbers.

Traumatic Brain Injury Center of Excellence. "Warfighter Brain Health Hub." Health.mil. Accessed February 3, 2025. https://www.health.mil/Military-Health-Topics/Warfighter -Brain-Health?type=Articles.

Trevillion, Kylee, Emma Williamson, Gursimran Thandi, Rohan Borschmann, Sian Oram, and Louise M. Howard. "A Systematic Review of Mental Disorders and Perpetration of Domestic violence among Military Populations." *Social Psychiatry and Psychiatric Epidemiology* 50 (2015): 1329–46.

Trimbur, Lucia, and Lundy Braun. "Race-ing the NFL: How Anti-Black Standards Are Built into the 2015 Concussion Settlement." Tropics of Meta, November 1, 2020, https://trop icsofmeta.com/2020/11/01/race-ing-the-nfl-how-anti-black-standards-are-built-into -the-2015-concussion-settlement//.

Tropeano, Maria Pia, Riccardo Spaggiari, Hernán Ileyassoff, et al. "A Comparison of Publication to TBI Burden Ratio of Low- and Middle-Income Countries Versus High-Income Countries: How Can We Improve Worldwide Care of TBI?" *Neurosurgical Focus* 47, no. 5 (2019): E5.

Trujillo, Nick. "Machines, Missiles, and Men: Images of the Male Body on ABC's Monday Night Football." *Sociology of Sport Journal* 12, no. 4 (1995): 403–23.

Turmel, André. *A Historical Sociology of Childhood: Developmental Thinking, Categorization and Graphic Visualization.* Cambridge University Press, 2008.

Uperesa, Fa'anofo Lisaclaire. "Fabled Futures: Migration and Mobility for Samoans in American Football." *Contemporary Pacific* 26, no. 2 (2014): 281–301.

Uperesa, Lisa. *Gridiron Capital: How Football Became a Samoan Game.* Duke University Press, 2022.

Valera, Eve, Annie-Lori C. Joseph, Katherine Snedaker, et al. "Understanding Traumatic Brain Injury in Females: A State-of-the-Art Summary and Future Directions." *Journal of Head Trauma Rehabilitation* 36, no. 1 (2021): E1–17.

Ventresca, Matt. "The Curious Case of CTE: Mediating Materialities of Traumatic Brain Injury." *Communication & Sport* 7, no. 2 (2018): 135–56.

Ventresca, Matt. "Mixed Feelings: Understanding Emotion in Media Coverage of Sport-Related Traumatic Brain Injuries." In *Head in the Game: Critical Sociocultural Analyses of Sports Concussion*, edited by Stephen Townsend, Rebecca Olive, Murray Phillips, and Gary Osmond. University of Manchester Press, forthcoming.

Ventresca, Matt. "The Tangled Multiplicities of CTE: Scientific Uncertainty and the Infrastructures of Traumatic Brain Injury." In *Sports, Society, and Technology*, edited by Jennifer J. Sterling and Mary G. McDonald, 73–98. Palgrave Macmillan, 2020.

Ventresca, Matt, and Kathryn Henne. "How Portrayals of the NFL Are Shaping Criminal Justice Reform." The Conversation. February 20, 2020. https://theconversation.com/how-portrayals-of-the-nfl-are-shaping-criminal-justice-reform-131766.

Ventresca, Matt, and Mary G. McDonald. "Forces of Impact: Critically Examining Sport's 'Concussion Crises.'" In *Sociocultural Examinations of Sports Concussions*, edited by Matt Ventresca and Mary G. McDonald, 3–20. Routledge, 2020.

Ventresca, Matt, and Samantha King. "'Anesthetized Gladiators': Painkilling and Racial Capitalism in the NFL." *Sociology of Sport Journal* 40, no. 1 (2023): 21–29.

Vertinsky, Patricia. "Exercise, Physical Capability, and the Eternally Wounded Woman in Late Nineteenth Century North America." *Journal of Sport History* 14, no. 1 (1987): 7–27.

Vismann, Cornelia. *Files: Law and Media Technology*. Translated by Geoffrey Winthrop-Young. Stanford University Press, 2008.

Wall, Kristi, Kim Gorgens, Judy Dettmer, Terri M. Davis, and Jennifer Gafford. "Violence-Related Traumatic Brain Injury in Justice-Involved Women." *Criminal Justice and Behavior* 45, no. 10 (2018): 1588–1605.

Walsh, Tamara. "Women Who Die in Custody: What Australian Coroners' Reports Tell Us." *The Howard Journal of Crime and Justice* 61, no. 4 (2022): 540–55.

Walters, Mikel L. *Invisible at Every Turn: An Examination of Lesbian Intimate Partner Violence*. Georgia State University, 2009.

Wamsley, Kevin B., and David Whitson. "Celebrating Violent Masculinities: The Boxing Death of Luther McCarty." *Journal of Sport History* 25, no. 3 (1998): 419–31.

Warner, Mariah K., and Chris Knoester. "When Kids Hitting Each Other Is Okay: Examining U.S. Adult Support for Youth Tackle Football." *Social Currents* 9, no. 3 (2022): 286–307.

Watego, Chelsea. "Racism is a Public Health Crisis—But Black Death Tolls Aren't the Answer." The Conversation. February 15, 2022. https://theconversation.com/racism-is-a-public-health-crisis-but-black-death-tolls-arent-the-answer-176453.

Watego, Chelsea, Lisa J. Whop, David Singh, et al. "Black to the Future: Making the Case for Indigenist Health Humanities." *International Journal of Environmental Research and Public Health* 18, no. 16 (2021): doi: https://doi.org/10.3390/ijerph18168704.

Weber Rawlins, Michelle L., Brian R. Johnson, Johna K. Register-Mihalik, et al. "United States Air Force Academy Cadets' Perceived Costs of Concussion Disclosure." *Military Medicine* 185, no. 1–2 (2020): e269–75.

Weinberg, Jill D. *Consensual Violence: Sex, Sports, and the Politics of Injury*. University of California Press, 2016.

White, Adam John, John Batten, Nathan E. Howarth, et al. "Imposing Compulsory Rugby Union on Schoolchildren: An Analysis of English State-Funded Secondary Schools." *Frontiers on Sports and Active Living* 4 (2022): 784103.

White, Adam John, John Batten, Stefan Robinson, et al. "Tackling in Physical Education Rugby: An Unnecessary Risk?" *Injury Prevention* 24, no. 2 (2018): 114–15.

Whittaker, Alison. "Aboriginal Woman Tanya Day Died in Custody. Now an Inquest Is Investigating if Systemic Racism Played a Role." The Conversation. August 28, 2019. https://theconversation.com/aboriginal-woman-tanya-day-died-in-custody-now-an-inquest-is-investigating-if-systemic-racism-played-a-role-122471.

Whitworth, Sandra. *Men, Militarism and UN Peacekeeping: A Gendered Analysis.* Lynne Rienner, 2004.

Williams, David R., and Selina A. Mohammed. "Discrimination and Racial Disparities in Health: Evidence and Needed Research." *Journal of Behavioral Medicine* 32, no. 1 (2009): 20–47.

Williams, Elisabeth M. P., Freja J. Petrie, Thomas N. Pennington, et al. "Sex Differences in Neck Strength and Head Impact Kinematics in University Rugby Union Players." *European Journal of Sport Science* 22, no. 11 (2021): 1649–58.

Wolfensohn, Sarah, and P. Honess. "Laboratory Animal, Pet Animal, Farm Animal, Wild Animal: Which Gets the Best Deal?" *Animal Welfare* 16, no. S1 (2007): 117–23.

Wood, Jennifer K. "In Whose Name? Crime Victim Policy and the Punishing Power of Protection." *National Women's Studies Association Journal* 17, no. 3 (2005): 1–17.

Woodward, Kath. *Boxing, Masculinity, and Identity: The "I" of the Tiger.* Routledge, 2007.

Woolgar, Steve, and Dorothy Pawluch. "Ontological Gerrymandering: The Anatomy of Social Problems Explanations." *Social Problems* 32, no. 3 (1985): 214–27.

Wunderle, Kathryn, Kathleen M. Hoeger, Erin Wasserman, and Jeffrey J. Bazarian. "Menstrual Phase as Predictor of Outcome after Mild Traumatic Brain Injury in Women." *Journal of Head Trauma Rehabilitation* 29, no. 5 (2014): e1–8.

Yearby, Ruqaiijah. "Structural Racism and Health Disparities: Reconfiguring the Social Determinants of Health Framework to Include the Root Cause." *Journal of Law, Medicine & Ethics* 48, no. 3 (2020): 518–26.

Young, Iris Marion. *Justice and the Politics of Difference.* Princeton University Press, 1990.

Young, Kevin. *Sport, Violence and Society.* Routledge, 2013.

Younis, Rafif, Mustafa Younis, Samer Hamidi, Mohamed Musmar, and Anthony R. Mawson. "Causes of Traumatic Brain Injury in Patients Admitted to Rafidia, Al-Ittihad and the Specialized Arab Hospitals, Palestine, 2006–2007." *Brain Injury* 25, no. 3 (2011): 282–91.

Yudell, Michael, Dorothy Roberts, Rob Desalle, and Sarah Tishkoff. "NFL Must Confront the Use of Race in Science." *Science* 369, no. 6509 (2020): 1313–14.

Zuckerman, Scott L. "Benefits of Team Sport Participation versus Concerns of Chronic Traumatic Encephalopathy: Prioritizing the Health of Our Youth." *Future Medicine* 5, no. 2 (2020): doi: https://doi.org/10.2217/cnc-2020-0006.

Zuckerman, Scott L., Aaron M. Yengo-Kahn, Benjamin L. Brett, et al. "Benefits of Team Sport Participation Versus Concerns of Chronic Traumatic Encephalopathy: Prioritizing the Health of Our Youth." *Concussion* 5, no. 2 (2020): CNC75.

Zuckerman, Scott L., Benjamin L. Brett, Aaron S. Jeckell, Aaron M. Yengo-Kahn, and Gary S. Solomon. "Prognostic Factors in Pediatric Sport-Related Concussion." *Current Neurology and Neuroscience Reports* 18, no. 104 (2018): 1–8.

Founded in 1893,
UNIVERSITY OF CALIFORNIA PRESS
publishes bold, progressive books and journals
on topics in the arts, humanities, social sciences,
and natural sciences—with a focus on social
justice issues—that inspire thought and action
among readers worldwide.

The UC PRESS FOUNDATION
raises funds to uphold the press's vital role
as an independent, nonprofit publisher, and
receives philanthropic support from a wide
range of individuals and institutions—and from
committed readers like you. To learn more, visit
ucpress.edu/supportus.

www.ingramcontent.com/pod-product-compliance
Ingram Content Group UK Ltd.
Pitfield, Milton Keynes, MK11 3LW, UK
UKHW041922080725
460575UK00002B/7